The Rock Climber's Guide
to **MONTANA**

edited by
Randall Green

with additional contributions by
**Brad Hutcheson, Matthew Taylor, Rafael Grana,
Dwight Bishop, Ron Brunckhorst, Brian Hatfield
and Jason Taylor**

FALCON™

Falcon Press® Publishing Co., Inc.
Helena, Montana

Falcon Press is continually expanding its list of recreational guidebooks using the same general format as this book. All books include detailed descriptions, accurate maps, and all the information necessary for enjoyable trips. You can order extra copies of this book and get information and prices for other Falcon guidebooks by writing Falcon Press, P.O. Box 1718, Helena, MT 59624. Also, please ask for a free copy of our current catalog listing all Falcon Press books.

© 1995 by Falcon Press Publishing Co., Inc.,
Helena and Billings, Montana.

Printed in the United States of America.

Cover photo: Susan Zazzali on *This Ain' Nuthin* , by Randall Green.
Back cover photo: Ted Steiner on *Heart of Stone,* by Quinn Sande.

Library of Congress Cataloging–in–Publication Data

The rock climber's guide to Montana / edited by Randall Green : with
    additional contributions by Brad Hutcheson ... [et al.].
        p. cm.
    "A Falcon guide"—P. [4] of cover.
    Includes bibliographical references and index.
    ISBN 1-56044-335-9
    1. Rock climbing—Montana—Guidebooks. 2. Montana—Guidebooks.
I. Green, Randall. II. Hutcheson, Brad.
GV199.42.M9R63 1995   95-17822
796.5'223'09786—dc20   CIP

CAUTION

Outdoor recreation activities are by their very nature potentially hazardous. All participants in such activities must assume the responsibility for their own actions and safety. The information contained in this guidebook cannot replace sound judgment and good decision-making skills, which help reduce risk exposure, nor does the scope of this book allow for disclosure of all the potential hazards and risks involved in such activities.

Learn as much as possible about the outdoor recreation activities you participate in, prepare for the unexpected, and be safe and cautious. The reward will be a safer and more enjoyable experience.

CONTENTS

ACKNOWLEDGMENTS

In the process of compiling the information for this book I made many new friends (and no doubt, some enemies) and learned a tremendous amount about Montana climbing. This book was not written by one person; it was written by Montana climbers. Without the help of dozens of folks who provided first-hand information and photos, shared previously published materials, and painstakingly reviewed drafts of the manuscript, this guide would not have been possible.

A special thanks to: Chris Alke, John Alke, Van Alke, Greg Allen, Kyle Austin, Dwight Bishop, Donnie and Penny Black, Ron Brunckhorst, Bill Bucher, Jerry Buck, Keith Calhoun, Pat Callis, Chad Chadwick, Hunter Coleman, Jandy Cox, Bill Dockins, Kristen Drumheller, Jim Durkin, Jim Emerson, Dan Fox, Rafael Grana, Theresa DeLorenzo Green, Will Harmon, Adam Hudson, Brad Hutcheson, Jaime Johnson, Tobin Kelley, Aaron LeFohn, Phyllis LeFohn, Tom Lund, Scott Payne, Mark Pearson, Shawn Perretto, Gary Phoenix, Richard Plummer, Ivan Pyatt, Darrin Schreder, Jim Semmelroth, Gary Skaar, Chris Stamper, Ted Steiner, Greg Stenger, Sonny Stewart, Jack Tackle, Jason Taylor, Matt Taylor, Gray Thompson, Jim Wilson, Jeff Wincapaw, David Vaughan, and Susan Zazzali.

For all who participated, especially those of you who helped above and beyond the call of duty, I'm truly indebted.

—*Randall Green*

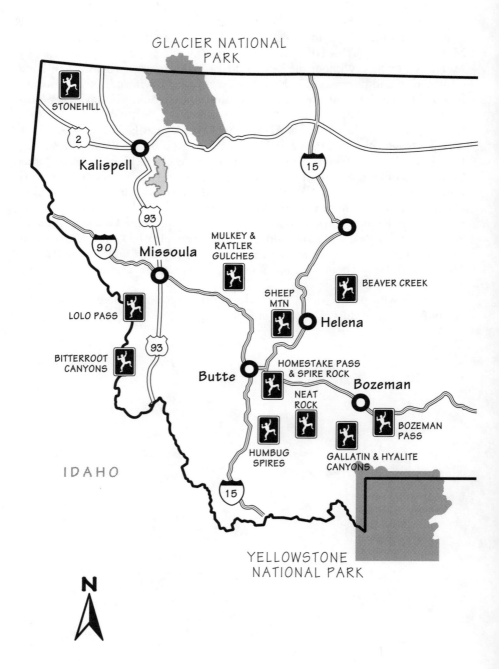

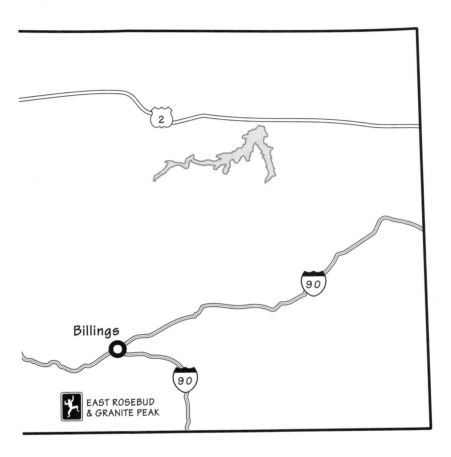

CANADA

WYOMING

MONTANA'S ROCK
CLIMBING AREAS

MAP LEGEND

 Trail

 Interstate

 Paved Road

 Gravel Road

 Unimproved Road

 State Line

 Waterway

 Lake/Reservoir

 Building

 Camping

 Town

 City

 Climbing Area

 Mountain Peak

 Trailhead

 Parking

 Mile Marker

 Interstate

 U.S. Highway

State Highway

Forest Road

Gate

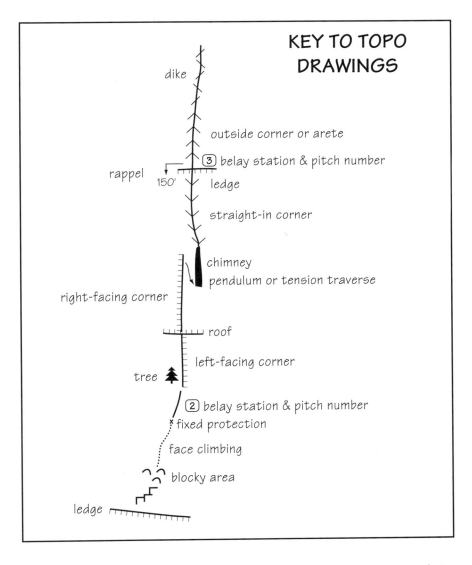

KEY TO TOPO
DRAWINGS

dike

outside corner or arete

③ belay station & pitch number

rappel

150'   ledge

straight-in corner

chimney
pendulum or tension traverse

right-facing corner

roof

left-facing corner

tree

② belay station & pitch number

fixed protection

face climbing

blocky area

ledge

lb	lieback	thin	thin crack (to 1 ½")
chim.	chimney	3rd	class 3
OW	off-width	4th	class 4
HD, RP	very small chocks	KB	knife blade
TCU	small cramming devices	LA	lost arrow

Photo by Ted Steiner.

INTRODUCTION

Montana is a vast and varied state, offering a lifetime of adventure and challenge for rock climbers. Tucked away in the mountain ranges that give the state its name are climbing areas as different as the topography. Sweeping expanses of granite and gneiss, craggy limestone fins and faces, and steep quartzite cliffs are but samplers of the main entrees on Montana's climbing menu.

Most of the good rock climbing in Montana is on outcrops of superb, compact rock hidden away in often idyllic settings. For example, the granite batholiths exposed in the forested hillsides of Lolo and Homestake passes and much of the metamorphosed granite in the glacier-carved eastern drainages of the Bitterroot Range is excellent; in its own unique and sometimes peculiar ways the Madison limestone near Drummond, Helena, and Bozeman is superb; and the gneiss in Gallatin Canyon and the quartzite along Lake Koocanusa are equally fine. But note the exclusion in this sampling of the big peaks of Glacier National Park and the Swan and Mission ranges. Although the grandeur of these peaks is awe-inspiring, the rock is less so. Many of the technical climbing routes on these peaks often go unrepeated because the rock is dangerously loose, making hand and foot holds portable and anchors unreliable. However, the Absaroka and Beartooth mountains in the south-central portion of the state offer better rock for those interested in bagging a peak via a good technical route in a wilderness setting.

Populated by more livestock than people, this state has plenty of climbing areas to go with its big sky. Climbing in Montana is relatively unknown outside local circles and has a reputation of being obscure and idiosyncratic. Locals will be the first to admit Montana climbing has some unique qualities, which in some ways have helped perpetuate the image of obscurity. Among other things, the lack of publicized information, tight-lipped locals, fickle weather, a short climbing season, some rock that often can require weird combinations of movement and protection placements, and blood-sucking ticks and biting flies can deter all but the most persistent practitioners. Also, Montana doesn't offer much in the way of long continuous crack lines in granite like those found in Yosemite or the sport climbing "scene" of Smith Rocks. But the climbing in the Big Sky State has its own endearing qualities. Obscurity can mean few people at the crags, the chance encounter with a mountain goat or bear, and the sense of adventure that comes from doing a route with less than the "max beta." Routes here are often a mixture of face holds and cracks, requiring a variety of techniques and equipment. The granites can be flaky and granular with discontinuous cracks and flaring seams; the limestone can be prickly and sharp or smooth, slick, and devoid of good holds; and the horde of touring "hotshots" that frequent some of the sport climbing areas around the country usually go elsewhere. During weekdays it is unlikely you will meet another party at most crags. And even on weekends few if any other parties will be vying for the same route. While access to some climbing areas is a sport climber's dream (with routes so close to the parking areas that it's possible to belay from your vehicle), other areas are miles from any road or town, requiring arduous approach marches and providing the backcountry experience that many equate to Montana. This book describes routes at most of the popular technical climbing areas in the state, but there are many other obscure areas, indeed.

A few of the areas are on private land, but most are on land managed by the USDA Forest Service or the Bureau of Land Management. Montana climbing with all its obscurity is not immune to the scrutiny of land managers and the non-climbing public, however. While you are having the time of your life be responsible for your own actions and act as a representative role model for the sport.

GEOLOGY

Much of the rock exposed in northwestern Montana is Precambrian sedimentary formations that are between 1,500 and 800 million years old. These rocks are arguilites and quartzite. Younger limestone cliffs exposed near Drummond, Helena, and Bozeman are part of the Madison formation. Although the granites southwest of Missoula, surrounding Butte, and south of Helena formed at about the same time, they are from two different batholiths. Batholiths form when molten magma cools below the surface. The domes on Lolo Pass are part of the 50-million-year-old Lolo batholith, and the rocks exposed on Sheep Mountain near Helena and those on Homestake Pass near Butte are part of the 80-million-year-old Boulder batholith. Many factors such as mineral composition, hardness, and erosion helped shape the rock that is visible today.

The layered gneiss exposed in Gallatin Canyon is metamorphosed rocks that were subjected to tremendous pressure and heat, which made the rocks pliable like modeling clay. Similarly, some of the granite south of Lolo Pass in the Bitterroot mountains also was metamorphosed.

The quartzite cliffs of Stone Hill are Precambrian sedimentary rock. Dense and fine grained, the rock tends to be blocky fand ractured along the horizontal layering.

MAKE IT A SAFE TRIP

Be forewarned that rock climbing is dangerous. Mistakes and the hazards associated with the sport can result in serious injury and death. But if you are interested in learning about a sport that can kill you, then read on.

Entire books have been written on safety and the hazards of backcountry activities. Climbing in particular by its very nature is potentially hazardous. Participating in this sport in remote settings compounds the equation. The scope and content of this book cannot replace sound judgment and good decision-making skills, which help reduce risk exposure. Nor does this book intend to disclose all potential hazards and risks one might encounter. Instead, the following information will give you some general guidelines to help you prepare for a safe and enjoyable experience. For more specific information on safety and climbing skill preparations see *Wild Country Companion*, by Will Harmon (Falcon Press) and *Mountaineering: The Freedom of the Hills*, by the Mountaineers. For "hands-on" experience contract a guide or take a climbing course offered by qualified professionals. Guides and shops that offer instruction are listed for many areas. Look in the "Trip Planning Information" sections of this guidebook for the area in which you intend to climb or see Appendix C for specific listings where available.

A Beaver Creek black bear pauses from dining on the remains of a climber that didn't back-up an anchor—just kidding. *Photo by Phyllis Lefohn.*

WEATHER

Since most of the climbing areas described in this book are in or near the mountains, expect changeable weather. Many places in Montana have recorded snowfall every month of the year. It may not snow in August at one of the lower elevation crags, but it is possible for it to be 90-plus degrees one minute and below freezing the next. Along with sudden drops or increases in temperature come torrential downpours and hailstorms replete with high winds. So go prepared. Take extra clothing and protective rain gear, even for an afternoon at the sport crags.

Cold- and heat-related injuries and illnesses are dangerous. Temperatures need not be below freezing for hypothermia to be a threat; most cases occur at temperatures between 40 and 50 degrees Fahrenheit. The best treatment is prevention. Wear layers of clothes as dictated by the weather and level of exertion. Exposure to hot air temperatures, when combined with too much sun and/or strenuous exercise, will lead to an elevated body temperature. Heat stress, heat exhaustion, and even heat stroke can result. Be sure to bring along plenty of water and drink often and stay out of the sun. Sunburn also can be debilitating and ruin a climbing vacation. Wear protective clothing and use sunscreens for sensitive skin.

Lightning causes about 300 deaths each year in the United States. And since climbers are drawn to the same targets as lightning, it is important to be aware of changing weather conditions that may bring on lightning strikes. Fortunately, most of these accidents can be avoided.

- Watch the weather. Spring and summer are the busiest seasons for lightning. Storms are usually preceded by wind and the approach of dark, towering clouds. Lightning may travel far ahead of the storm. Seek shelter before lightning is imminent.

- Avoid exposed ridges, tall trees, and moist areas. Stay away from overhangs, caves, and crevices.

- If unable to get to shelter during a lightning storm assume a crouch position. Sit on a coiled rope or sleeping bag pad for insulation.

- Avoid rappelling during lightning storms.

EQUIPMENT

Wear a **helmet** when climbing and belaying. Although wearing a helmet hasn't become "fashionable" in many cragging areas, it can reduce the risk of injury that may ruin your future health or your weekend.

Many areas in Montana still have loose rock strewn about on ledges and on cliff faces near popular climbing routes. The movement of a climber or the rope may dislodge a rock. Be especially careful when retrieving rappel ropes.

Hunter Coleman enjoys some fine limestone climbing at Beaver Creek.
Photo by Randall Green.

And even wearing a helmet while crag climbing has its merits. In 1994 a climber took a short fall on a bolted sport route near Helena that resulted in a pendulum—his scalp and ear were nearly torn off as his head skidded across the cliff face. Needless to say it is more fun to climb than to sit in an emergency room at a hospital. Luckily for the victim nothing more than stitches was required to patch up his head. But it ruined his and his partner's day. Expect the unexpected. Wear a helmet.

Make sure ropes, harnesses, and webbing are in good condition. Use only UIAA (an international independent organization that tests climbing equipment) approved equipment. Follow recommendations by the manufacturer for use and maintenance of your equipment. For many climbing areas in Montana, a 45-meter (150-foot) rope is not long enough. Ropes of 50 meters or longer are recommended. Also it may be noted in the route descriptions that some climbs require two ropes for descents. View all climb length estimates in this book with skepticism. It is hoped that when in doubt, the authors overestimated the distances. But that is not guaranteed. Make sure to have an extra rope along just in case.

Protective hardware and anchors should always be backed up when possible. Never rappel or toprope from a single anchor point. Most areas require a standard gear rack for lead climbing or placing toprope anchors. Each area description has a section to discuss special gear recommendations. Be wary of all anchors.

When possible use "non-invasive" protection hardware (removable nuts, chocks, cams, and slings) for running belays and anchors. See individual areas for discussions on fixed anchors. All climbers must accept responsibility for the level of risk assumed when participating in this sport. Remember, emergency services are a long way from most climbing areas. Make sure you and your climbing companions know first aid, mountain rescue, self rescue, and life-saving techniques.

Avoid dislodging rocks or purposefully tumbling them over a precipice (a practice known as trundling) no matter how enticing it may be. Someone may be below you. A climber recently was killed on Granite Peak because another party higher on the mountain caused a rock slide.

INSECTS AND THEIR KIN

Don't let insects bug you. They are unavoidable but not unbeatable in the backcountry, especially in June and July at higher elevations. Mosquitos, biting flies, and ticks are the most common nuisances. Carry a good insect repellent.

Ticks are fairly common throughout wooded, brushy, and grassy areas of Montana, which means nearly all climbing areas. These blood-sucking critters are most active from March until early summer. All ticks are potential carriers of Rocky Mountain spotted fever. The western black-legged tick, only 1/8-inch long, is responsible for transmitting Lyme Disease, a bacterial infection named for the Connecticut town where it was first recognized. These diseases are transmitted to humans and other mammals by the bite of an infected tick.

The best defense against hosting a tick is to avoid areas infested with ticks (or take along your dog or a friend as tick bait). Of course the urge to climb may be too great to keep you from these tick havens in the spring. So wear clothing with a snug fit around the waist, wrists, and ankles. And since ticks do not always bite right away (they often crawl around on a potential host for several hours before deciding where to feed), a strong insect repellent can also be an effective deterrent against tick bites.

Carefully check your clothing and your partner's clothing (making sure not to get blamed for sexual harassment) for ticks at the crag and before getting back into your vehicle. And don't forget to check your gear and your pack.

SELECT LISTING OF ROUTES

Not every Montana crag or climb is included in this book. And because everyone has different interests and climbing styles, it is improbable that every climber will enjoy every climb included in this book (we recommend those dissatisfied with Montana climbing go to North Dakota). Some routes have received so few ascents that no consensus has developed whether the climbs should be "recommended" or not. What may be one person's commendation may be another person's curse. But the majority of the routes listed in this guide were recommended by climbers in each respective area, offering an unprecedented variety of technical rock climbs of varying length and difficulty for most regions of the state. In addition, a more comprehensive listing is included for some areas lacking previously published information. Because of this, some route descriptions may offer an extra word of caution or warning (i.e., loose, dirty, vegetated, not recommended, etc.) regarding the nature of the climb. If the terminology used in the descriptions is unclear, refer to the glossary (or try to get a local to explain it—good luck!).

WILDERNESS ROUTES NOT INCLUDED

For the sake of preserving the spirit of adventure (and the health of those writing this guide due to threats of bodily injury if information on "secret" areas were publicized), we chose to leave out many routes hidden in Montana's vast wilderness areas. Montanans have enjoyed uncrowded recreation opportunities for years and justifiably fear that publicity will destroy the wilderness experience that now exists in some locales. For more than 30 years Montanans generally have adhered to a non-publication ethic in hopes of preserving those special places. That attitude prevails in some areas today, especially in the Beartooths and the Absarokas. To honor that ethic and "gentleman's agreement" within the state's climbing community, most of the routes in wilderness areas purposefully have been left out of this guide (Granite Peak, the highest peak in the state, is the only exception).

Information for specific wilderness routes may be obtained by inquiring at local climbing shops or clubs around the state. See Appendix C for a list of clubs and shops in the state.

HOW TO USE THIS GUIDE

The Rock Climber's Guide to Montana offers information for more than 500 routes. A locator map at the front of the book shows the general locations of the main climbing areas. The areas are organized geographically—Northwest, West Central, Southwest, and South Central. Each area write-up includes: an overview, which may include a brief summary of the climbing history and ethics; trip planning information, which includes condensed summaries of specific information on each area; directions and maps to find the areas; and specific climbing route descriptions, which in many cases are accompanied by photos with overlays and maps identifying routes and showing the locations.

The **area overviews** describe the setting, the type of rock and climbing. Also included are recommendations for climbing equipment as well as some discussions of the local climbing history and ethics.

Trip Planning Information includes a brief synopsis of the following categories.

• **Area description:** A brief summary of the area.

• **General location:** Reference to largest nearby towns and major roads, etc.

• **Camping:** Information on developed campgrounds and suggestions for camping in undeveloped locations.

• **Climbing season:** Description of when is the best time of year to visit an area.

• **Restrictions and access issues:** Important issues to be aware of such as private land, parking, safety, land use, etc.

• **Guidebooks:** Published sources of information for that area.

• **Nearby retail mountain shops, guide services, and gyms:** Listings include names, addresses, and phone numbers.

Area write-ups include:

• **Finding the area:** Description and "how-to-get-there map" with descriptions starting at nearest major road and town.

• **The cliff name:** Detailed discussion of location, special information pertaining to equipment, approaches, and descents.

• **Route descriptions:** Routes are listed numerically (for those climbers who can count beyond the number of their remaining fingers and toes), showing name and rating followed by a brief discussion of the location and nature of the climb, special equipment recommendations, length, and descent information. An overview map of each climbing area and photos—showing cliffs and route locations—accompanies the descriptions. Some of the more intricate and difficult routes on the big faces have route topo maps, detailing the climb.

The road map legend and key to topo map symbols are located at the front of the book on page viii.

Appendices offer further reading (**Appendix A**), rating comparison charts (**Appendix B**), a listing of climbing equipment retail shops and clubs (**Appendix C**), and a glossary of terms (**Appendix D**).

An index in the back of the book lists all proper names (names of areas, people, and climbs) alphabetically.

RATING SYSTEM

The ratings in this guide are based on the decimal system (commonly known as the Yosemite Decimal System or YDS, even though it originated at Tahquitz Rock), which is used throughout most U.S. climbing areas to gauge the technical difficulty of a route. But climb ratings are highly subjective and may vary from area to area. Also, the rocks Montanans climb on vary as much as the rating systems between areas. For instance it is difficult to compare the ratings of climbs on granite to those on limestone.

One suggestion to develop consensus on ratings is to only compare like kinds of climbs on like kinds of rock to one another (i.e., face climbs characterized by edging or friction, crack climbs by size of crack, etc.). But even some of the same types of rock vary so much from area to area, such as the limestones on Bozeman Pass or Gallatin Canyon versus those near Helena or Drummond, that sometimes a comparison of this nature is difficult. To compound the equation, many climbs in Montana are "hybrids," meaning they can require several types of face climbing and crack climbing techniques. Moreover, many crag areas in Montana have climbs that were toprope rehearsed before being led. This practice tends to repress the ratings, giving the sense of "sandbagging." Climbers argue that an on-sight lead with no prior knowledge of the route is the best way to rate a climb. Unfortunately, that isn't always reflected in the grades published in this guide. Typically the first ascent party names and rates a climb. But the climbers who rate a route may have very little experience outside their local area or have the tendency to underestimate or overestimate the difficulty. Physical strength or flexibility also may not be considered in the technical rating.

Those who contributed information for this guide gave a fair estimation of the route difficulties, but some ratings may be off (high or low) a half grade or more. So to put all this in perspective, use discretion and common sense when visiting a new area. There is an old saying that there are bold climbers and there are old climbers, but there are not any/many old bold climbers. With that advice, warm up on a few routes that may be well below your limit; get used to the rock and the area's rating system before pushing the limits of your ability.

Mountain travel is typically classified as follows:

Class 1—Trail hiking.

Class 2—Hiking over rough ground such as scree and talus; may include the use of hands for stability.

Class 3—Scrambling that requires the use of hands and careful foot placement.

Class 4—Scrambling over steep and exposed terrain; a rope may be used for safety on exposed areas.

Class 5—Technical "free" climbing where terrain is steep and exposed, requiring the use of ropes, protection hardware, and related techniques.

The decimal rating system fails to follow mathematical logic. It is an open ended scale where the 5 denotes the class, and the difficulty rating is tacked on behind the decimal point, with 5.0 being the easiest and 5.14 (read five-fourteen) being the hardest (to date). When a route has had too few ascents for a consensus or the estimated difficulty rating is unclear, a plus (+) or minus (-) subgrade may be employed (5.8- or 5.9+ or 5.11- or 5.12+ for example). Where there is a consensus of opinion, additional subgrades of a, b, c, and d are used on climbs rated 5.10 and harder. To further complicate the matter, where the subgrade is uncertain, two letters may be used such as 5.11a/b. These subgrades represent a finer comparison of technical difficulty than the more general plus and minus signs. A climb rated 5.10a is considered to be harder than 5.9+ but easier than 5.10d, which is approaching the 5.11- standard. Thoroughly confused now?

More often than not, routes are rated according to the most difficult move. Some climbs may be continuously difficult, seeming more difficult than other routes rated the same but with only one or two hard moves. In some instances, routes will be described as "sustained" or "pumpy" to give an indication of the continuous nature of the climbing. Also, differences in strength and reach as well as distance between protection points may be factors contributing to rating variations. Where these factors seem significant, they may be pointed out in the written descriptions.

Aid climbing—using artificial means to progress up the rock—has a different set of ratings.

Class 6—Aid climbing; climbing equipment is used for balance, rest, or progress; denoted with a capital letter A followed by numbers progressing from 0.

A0—Equipment may have been placed to rest on or to pull on for upward progress.

A1—Solid equipment placements that can hold a fall; aid slings (etriers) are used.

A2—Placements are more difficult to position, and they support less weight than an A1 placement.

A3—Progressively weaker placements; may not hold a short fall.

A4—Placements can support body weight only; long falls can occur (this grade and the next one [A5] are only practiced by individuals not afraid of flying).

A5—Enough A4 placements to risk falls of 50 feet or longer.

A pitch or rope-length of technical climbing may have a combination "free" and aid rating such as 5.9/A3, meaning the free climbing difficulties are up to 5.9 with an aid section of A3 difficulty. On the route "topo" drawings or marked photos in this guide, the crux (most difficult section) often is marked with the difficulty rating.

An additional "overall seriousness" grade, referring to the level of commitment, overall technical difficulty, ease of escape, and length of route has been given to some of the longer routes. A Roman numeral from I to V may appear in front of the free/aid rating. Grade I typically is represented by Class 4 scrambles and easy Class 5 climbs that take only a few hours to complete. At the upper end of the scale, a Grade VI climb may take several days with a great deal of commitment in regard to technical difficulties, weather, and other objective hazards such as rockfall or avalanche danger. In this guide, the seriousness grades are only included on routes of Grade IV or more. For example, routes on Parking Lot Wall in Blodgett are one- to two-pitch routes with relatively easy access and descents such as *Leisure Suite Larry* (5.10c); but routes on the larger Flathead Buttress are more serious, thus the added Roman numeral grade: *South Face Route* (IV 5.10+).

An additional "danger" rating may be tacked on to some climbs. Where the protection may not hold and a fall could result in injury or death, an R or X may be added. A route rated 5.9 R may mean that the protection is sparse or "runout" or that some placements may not hold a fall. X-rated (read skull and crossbones) routes have a fall potential that can be fatal, unless one has the confidence and ability to solo a route safely with absolutely no protection and without falling.

Injuries sustained from falls are always possible, even on routes that can be well protected. This guide does not give a protection rating nor does it provide detailed information on how, when, or where to place protective hardware. Suggested "standard" gear racks are described in the overview for each area, and some recommendations are made on types and sizes of protection that may be useful on some climbs. But safety and the level of risk assumed are the responsibility of the climber.

See Appendix B for a table comparing the American or Yosemite Decimal System (YDS) to the British, French, and Australian systems.

ETHICS

By definition an ethic is a group of moral principles or set of values—a standard of behavior. This subject has been discussed and argued, in some cases at great length, by most climbers. Typically, these discussions focus on style of ascent and tactics employed to get up a stretch of rock. Much of the argument is **egocentric** with little consideration for how the environment or the future of the sport may be affected by a person's actions. With few people participating in the sport early on there was little impact on climbing areas. But now with more and more people venturing onto the cliffs and into the mountains, a new awareness is necessary to preserve the resources and the outdoor activities we cherish.

More now than ever before, climbers must go beyond petty egocentric arguments about style and change behavior that does not favorably reflect upon the sport. All climbers must develop an "ethos" or spirit that motivates ideas, customs, and practices. The issue goes beyond argument over whether a particular style of ascent is better than another or whether bolting should be done on lead or from rappel. The issue is about how we behave and how that behavior affects others and the environment.

Unfortunately many climbers today don't know any better or worse yet, don't care. More and more people are entering the sport without spending time under the tutelage of a more experienced partner or mentor. And the sensationalized "been-there, done-that, got-to be-extreme" attitude fostered by the media has not helped depict a true picture of what climbing is really about. Ignorance, arrogance, and disrespect generally are not considered to be favorable traits. Yet some climbers today exhibit such behavior without a second thought. As a result, the non-climbing public and land management agencies are developing a jaded attitude toward the sport and rock climbers in general, which may result in future restrictions.

New route development should be well thought out if it involves the placement of fixed anchors. The use of fixed anchors should be minimized. If fixed anchors are absolutely necessary, they should be camouflaged to match the color of the rock. Also, we must responsibly manage disposal of human waste and litter and help reduce human-caused erosion. Please consider the following guidelines (and get your papers in order in case the rock police come around).

- Defecate or urinate at least 200 feet from climbing routes, approach trails, camping areas, and water sources. Use a stick or trowel to bury feces 6 to 8 inches deep. If burying waste is not feasible, use a **"poop tube"** to carry it out. This is handy for long climbs or those involving a bivouac. Build a poop tube with a length of 4-inch diameter plastic PVC pipe capped at one end and threaded for a screw-on lid on the other end. Simply scoop waste from the ground into a small paper bag, sprinkle a little kitty litter or powdered chlorinated lime in the bag after each deposit to control odors. Then roll up the bag, slide it into the tube, and screw on the lid. Dispose of the contents at a waste disposal dump site. Some campgrounds and many service stations now have suitable dump stations used by RVs. Do not dump human waste in trash cans or dumpsters (unless, of course, they belong to that neighbor with the "yappy" dog that always craps in your yard—just kidding).

- Do not alter the rock by chiseling, drilling, manufacturing, or gluing on holds. If a climb is too difficult to ascend without resorting to these debasing tactics, leave it for future generations to try.
- Never add fixed anchors to established climbs without consulting the first ascent party or other active climbers in the area.
- Treat other people, including non-climbers, with respect.
  - Treat the land with respect and reverence; leave gates as you find them; pick up your trash and that left by others.
- Stay on established trails to reduce erosion. Get involved with volunteer groups to improve and repair trails and unsafe fixed anchors.
- Go lightly on the land and learn as much as possible about the environment and how to preserve it.
- HAVE FUN! and contribute to future editions of this guide by letting us know your thoughts on using this book. Please send corrections for any errors or additional information for omissions (of which undoubtedly there will be some): Guidebook Editor, Falcon Press, P.O. Box 1718, Helena, MT 59624.

—Randall Green

Gene Klein on *Screwdge McDuck* at Stone Hill. *Photo by Randall Green.*

NorthWest

REGION

LAKE KOOCANUSAAREA

STONE HILL
(Lake Koocanusa)

OVERVIEW

Stone Hill is a sport and practice climbing area located in the sparsely populated northwestern corner of the state near the Canadian border. Since the late 1970s, climbers have been drawn to these steep quartzite cliffs. Stone Hill has all the ingredients necessary for a premier sport climbing area—quality rock, easy access, and the ambiance of an open ponderosa pine forest with Lake Koocanusa's waters lapping against the lower cliffs. Although Stone Hill has its share of climbs rated 5.12 and harder, it offers a myriad of easy and moderate climbs. Most routes can be toproped, but an ample supply of bolts supplement the unfractured sections of cliff to offer well-protected leads.

If the popular Hold Up Bluffs are too close to the road and too much of a social scene, then wander toward one of the seldom-visited crags above or below the road; you likely will have the area all to yourself.

The rock at Stone Hill generally takes and holds gear well (if properly placed), including small wired stoppers. **Use care and discretion when placing natural gear. Always back up natural-gear anchors and placements when possible.** Bolts (3/8") have been placed to protect leads on many routes and for anchors at the tops of cliffs. **But never trust a single bolt for an anchor.** Take extra slings for setting belay or toprope anchors.

Climbing history: It was in the summer of 1977 while on a motorcycle ride around Lake Koocanusa that Greg Allen first went by Stone Hill and realized the great climbing potential. After too much exposure to rotten limestone in the Rockies, Allen liked the looks of the reasonably solid quartzite. In the spring and summer of 1978, Allen ventured down to Hold Up Bluffs with Kelly Grismer, the only other person he knew in the Fernie, British Columbia, area who had nuts and pins that weren't for eating and sewing. In that historic year of 1978

▲ –

Ted Steiner, Greg Allen, Jandy Cox, Gary Phoenix, Kyle Austin, and Adam Hudson provided information for this section. Allen, with contributions from Cox, Steiner, and Phoenix, wrote the climbing history section.

STONEHILL

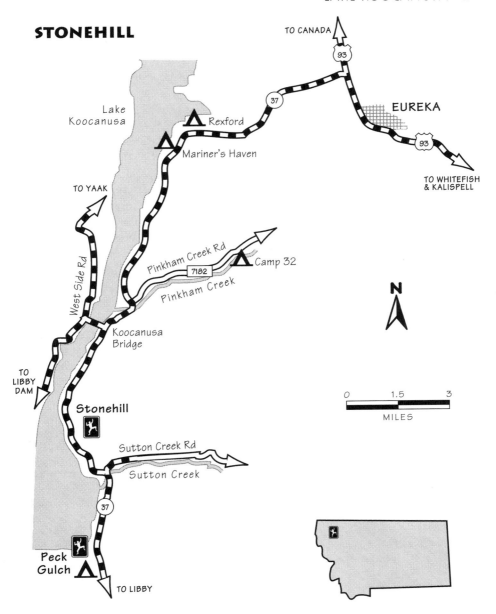

B.E. (before EBs), they were content to scramble up and down loose, dirty fifth-class gullies and toprope some 5.5s and 5.6s in Vibram-soled hiking boots.

Over the next few years a small group of Canadian pioneers made regular trips across the line. Ron Clark, Rod Geddis, Bruce Jamieson, Barb Clemes, and others entertained the passing motorists on weekends. They proceeded to discover EBs, chalk, Friends, and 5.8s, but 5.9s and 5.10s were still pretty desperate. They did, however, set standards in the consumption of beer, before, during, and after climbs. Some routes were belayed in fine style—sitting in the passenger seat, with seat belt on, beer in one hand, rope in the other, and the B-52s cranked on the stereo.

Perhaps the most insidious environmental hazard they encountered was the wood tick. From early to late spring, the hills are teeming with the tiny terrors. Post-climb activities involved going to the closest bar in Eureka for beer, pizza, and tick races on the tables.

In the year 1980 A.C. (after chalk), Americans finally made their presence known at Stone Hill. Paul Clark was teaching in Eureka at the time, and over the next few years set the standards at Stone Hill by putting up most of the first ascents in the 5.7 to 5.10 range. He also met, but failed to exceed, the Canadian standards for consumption of beer. Allen was disappointed to see a reference to one of Paul's climbs was not spelled correctly in an early magazine article. Solid Courage should be *Solid Coorage*, obviously reflecting the major influence of the climb. Paul put together the first guidebook of sorts for the area and also instituted the annual spring International Climbing Festival at Stone Hill (which predated the Koocanusa Crank by one climbing generation).

The late 1980s saw the gradual demise of the Canadian contingent and an increase in locals on the rocks. Standards continued to rise as more people began to discover Stone Hill. Area activists such as Gary Phoenix, Mike Ander-

Photo by Randall Green.

son, and others from Libby, Whitefish, Kalispell, and elsewhere developed many excellent 5.10 and 5.11 lines on the cliffs. Greg Stenger firmly established the 5.12 grade with several test pieces; and Stenger produced another guide. New route development continued with energy from the prolific Phoenix, Ted Steiner, Jandy Cox, and others. More recently, Kyle Austin and Adam Hudson have added several new hard routes; one of Austin's climbs is thought to be 5.13 and to date has not seen a second redpoint ascent.

The Koocanusa Crank annual climbing festival, which used to be hosted in early August by Rocky Mountain Outfitter of Kalispell, has since lost favor with the Forest Service due to liability and user-impact concerns and is no longer happening. It ran from 1988 through 1993. Dozens of topropes were set up, prizes were given away, food and drink was available, and generally a good time was had by all.

Ethics: Although many of the easier natural lines were done on sight from the ground up, most of the modern routes have been toproped with fixed anchors being placed prior to lead ascents.

High-grade concrete expansion bolts (3/8" by 2 to 2 1/2" or longer) have become the fixed anchors of choice; for rappel stations use 2 bolts with heavy duty or high-tensile chains. The quartzite is quite hard and the climate relatively dry, so well-placed bolts last a long time. Use care and discretion when placing fixed anchors. Because of growing concerns over visual pollution, all fixed-anchor systems should be camouflage painted to match the color of the rock.

Chipping, manufacturing, or gluing on holds is not tolerated. If a climb is too difficult to ascend without resorting to these debasing tactics leave it for future generations to try.

Do not add fixed anchors to any existing climb unless there is general consensus from the local climbing community.

Trip Planning Information

Area description: Roadside/lakeside crags of quartzite offering steep face and crack climbing along Montana Highway 37; bolted sport routes and natural crack lines.

General location: About 15 miles southwest of Eureka and 50 miles northeast of Libby; 65 miles northwest of Kalispell; and 65 miles southwest of Fernie, British Columbia.

Camping: Camp 32 is a free USDA Forest Service campground 8 miles north of Stone Hill on Pinkham Creek Road. Peck Gulch Forest Service campground and boat launch is 5 miles south of Stone Hill on Lake Koocanusa; fee required. Mariner's Haven, a private campground on MT 37 about five miles west of Eureka, has a convenience store, gas, and showers.

Climbing season: Late February through late October.

Restrictions and/or access issues: Human waste management continues to be a problem. The outhouse at Hold Up Bluffs is a health hazard due to lack of care and disposal of waste. Use no-trace techniques (dig a 6-inch-deep cat hole and bury waste well away from water sources, trails, and climbing areas) when the urge arises. Litter is a growing problem, too. Please pick up any refuse, whether it is yours or not.

Other guidebooks: *Stone Hill Climbs*, by Greg Stenger. "Rock & Ice Guide to Stone Hill," by Ted Steiner, Rock & Ice Magazine May/June 1993.

Nearby mountain shops, guide services, and gyms: Rocky Mountain Outfitter, Kalispell.

Finding the area: From Kalispell, the shortest route is via U.S. Highway 93 to Eureka. Continue north on US 93 about 2 miles north of Eureka and turn left at the junction with MT 37. The Lake Koocanusa Bridge is at about 12 miles. For the main cliffs and Hold Up Bluffs continue on MT 37 for another 3 miles. Peck Gulch is another 4 miles south of the main cliffs on MT 37.

HOLD UP BLUFFS

OVERVIEW

The Hold Up Bluffs are the main crag of tan-gray quartzite cliffs that lie on the east side of MT 37, 3 miles south of the Koocanusa Bridge. These bluffs received the first recorded technical ascents at Stone Hill. The cliffs average about 50' high and are set back from the highway just far enough to provide convenient parking. The western aspect of the bluffs offers early- and late-season climbing, but often it can be too hot on summer afternoons. The bluffs are split by a prominent gully and divided into a north and south section; most routes have fixed anchors at the top and can be easily toproped.

Descents: Unless bolts are rigged with slings or chains for rappels, it is possible to walk or scramble off the backside of the bluffs; North section—walk off north end; South section—walk north and downclimb prominent gully between south and north cliff sections.

HOLD UP BLUFFS NORTH

1. **Disco Man** (5.11-) Left-most route on north end of bluff; 4 bolts; 40'; 2 bolts on top.

2. **Phoenix-Bailey** (5.11a) Thin crack to face line that skirts two small roofs; 2 bolts, gear to 1"; 40'; 2 bolts on top.

3. **Solid Coorage** (5.10c) From left side of block, line follows thin crack to roof and around left side; 2 bolts, gear to 1" (take small wires for thin crack at bottom) 45'; 2 bolts on top.

4. **Power Bulge** (5.11+) Direct start to 'COORAGE and goes through roof; 3 bolts, gear to #2.5 Friend; 45'; use same anchor as for 'COORAGE on top.

LAKE KOOCANUSA
STONE HILL

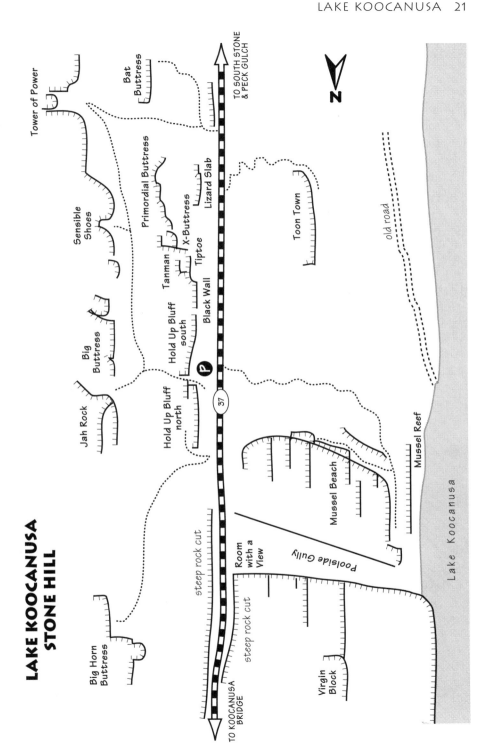

5. **Relentless** (5.10b) Next obvious line right of POWER BULGE roof system; 3 bolts, gear to 1.5" plus wired nuts and extra slings for top; 50'; 1 bolt and cracks/blocks on top.

6. **Full Sail Direct** (5.10a) Face climb to obvious crack system left of tree; 1 bolt, gear to 2" and extra slings for top; 50'; 1 bolt and cracks/blocks on top.

7. **Full Sail** (5.8) Line follows obvious crack behind trees and moves left at mid-height to join 'SAIL DIRECT; gear to 2" and extra slings; 50'; 1 bolt and cracks/blocks on top.

8. **Fade to Black** (5.11b) Scramble to block right of tree and follow finger crack to face; 3 bolts, gear to 1" (TCUs, small Tri-Cam helpful); 40'; 2 bolts on top.

9. **Clark's Nutcracker** (5.9) Crack line right of FADE' (crux is passing bolt); 1 bolt, gear to 2.5" (extra slings); 40'; 1 bolt and cracks/blocks on top.

10. **Block Dance** (5.7) Start at layback crack and follow left facing flakes and blocks; 65'; gear to #3 Friend (stoppers and extra slings useful); 1 bolt and cracks/blocks on top.

10a. **Direct Dance** (5.10b) Variant starts at layback crack and assaults first block then wanders past 2 bolts on thin edges then exit up slab to right.

Photo by Ted Steiner.

10b. **Friend Cracker** (5.8) Variant shares same start and traverses right at first roof and goes up a 5.8 seam to top; gear (wires, TCUs, and Friends up to #2.5 useful); 60'; 2-bolt anchor on top.

11. **Wish for Dish** (5.12b/c) Difficult direct start to FRIEND CRACKER finish; 2 bolts, gear to # 2.5 Friend; 60'; 2 bolts on top.

12. **Fantasy Land** (5.8) Cracks past rock spike to roof; move right from ledge; 2 bolts, gear to #2.5 Friend; 60'; 2 bolts on top.

13. **Why Think** (5.11a R) Vertical crack to horizontal break/crack and face; 1 bolt, gear to 3" (#1.5 Friend, TCUs, RPs, and extra slings useful); 60'; 1 bolt close to edge and 1 bolt 10' back on top.

14. **Another Thought** (5.11d) Dynamic face climbing right of WHY THINK; 5 bolts, gear for horizontal to #2.5 Friend; 2 bolts on top.

15. **Fear and Smear** (5.9) On south side of block at end of north Hold Up Bluff—face to horizontal crack; hand traverse left and climb up through small roof on good holds; gear (wires, TCUs, small Friends useful); 30'; 2 bolts on top.

16. **Beer and Smear** (5.8) Shares same start as FEAR'; at horizontal break continue up on easy ground; gear (see 'FEAR); 30'; 2 bolts on top of FEAR'.

Photo by Ted Steiner.

Photo by Ted Steiner.

DUCK FACE

This face actually is a higher portion of the North Hold Up Bluff. The south end of the bluff is taller and steps back over the shoulder above the lower main cliff. Duck Face adds about another 50' of climbing to the lower cliff. Either *Ducky Doo* or *Screwdge McDuck* makes a nice second pitch after climbing something on the main Hold Up Bluffs.

Cripple Crack and *Seaweed Patch* are further to the right of Duck Face and longer routes than those found on the main North Hold Up Bluff.

17. **Ducky Doo** (5.10-) Face climb that goes through horizontal breaks left of SCREWDGE McDUCK on upper tier at south end and slightly above lower north bluff; 2 bolts, gear to 2" and extra slings; 50'; no fixed anchors on top, use tree back from edge. **Descent:** Walk off to the north.

18. **Screwdge McDuck** (5.10-) Steep face climb right of DUCKY'; 2 bolts, gear (wired stoppers/TCUs and extra slings useful); 50'; no fixed anchors on top, use tree back from edge. **Descent:** Walk off to the north.

19. **Cripple Crack** (5.7) Obvious crack right of chimney corner where taller, upper tier connects to south end of north bluff; gear to 3"; 75'; **Descent:** Rappel; chain anchors on top.

20. **Seaweed Patch** (5.10d) Face line right of CRIPPLE CRACK; 4 bolts, gear to 3.5" for roof; 75'; **Descent:** Rappel; chain anchors on top.

Photo by Ted Steiner.

Photo by Ted Steiner.

HOLD UP BLUFFS SOUTH

This section of the Hold Up Bluffs continues south along the east side of the highway but is separated from the northern section by a gully. The routes are longer on this portion of cliff.

21. **Psycho Killer** (5.11d) Face of pillar right of access gully; 5 bolts; 80'; 2 bolts on top.

22. **Great Escape** (5.8) Climb slab with crack past a fixed pin to steeper crack/corner and "escape" up and left past another pin to easier ground; gear to 2"; 80'; 2 bolts on top.

23. **Night Flyer** (5.10b) Crack and face line right of dark stain; climb to obvious crack and go right at top of crack to ledge and face above; 1 bolt, gear up to #3 Friend; 80'; no fixed anchors on top.

24. **Widow Maker** (5.12a/b) Crack line right of 'FLYER; thin to horizontal break/pod (crux); gear to #2.5 Friend (extra finger-sized gear); 80'; 2 bolts on top.

THE BLACK WALL

Black Wall is the tallest of the east-side buttresses adjacent to and at the same level as the highway. It is the next one south of the South Hold Up Bluff. A large black chimney splits the right side.

Photo by Ted Steiner.

Descent: Walk off north to a prominent gully; or rappel (double rope) from chains at top of *Black Bat Crack* (toprope climb between *Heart of Stone* and *Lightning Bolt Crack*); or walk south to chains at Tanman Area then rappel to chains on *Loose Goose* and once more to ground.

25. **Heart of Stone** (5.11b) Traverse right along ledge to base of route, which ascends line in middle of face; 7 bolts, gear up to #3 Friend; 140 '; 2 bolts on top.

26. **Lightning Bolt Crack** (5.12b) Ascend fractured face to prominent roof right of chimney. Turn roof and face climb past thin cracks to top. One bolt, TCUs, small and medium nuts and cams to #3 Friend; 120'; chain anchors on top.

TIPTOE AREA

Several routes are on the wall south and east of *Lightning Bolt Crack* and north of X Buttress. All routes are equipped with bolts on top. Rappel chain anchors are on *Cop a Feel* and *Loose Goose*.

27. **Tiptoe** II (5.9) Crack and face route (mostly 5.7/.8) that starts in a wide crack; 12 bolts; 120'; easier finish variant is to traverse right to ledge at 9th bolt to avoid crux finish; 2 bolts on top.

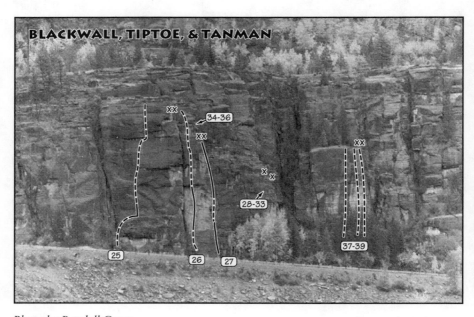

Photo by Randall Green.

Photo by Ted Steiner.

28. **Cop a Feel** (5.12b/c) Excellent bolted sport route right of TIPTOE'. Bouldery start behind grove of aspen trees; 5 bolts; chain anchor on top.

29. **Bum's Rush** (5.8) A bolted direct start to crack system on arete; 2 bolts and gear to 2"; 75'; chain anchor on top.

30. **Squeeze Play** (5.9) Left side of right-leaning parallel crack system; climb crack past small roof then onto face; 3 bolts, gear at bottom; 70'; shares same anchor with BUM'S.

31. **Loose Goose** (5.6) Right side of parallel crack system; easy steps and wide crack; big cams to 4"; 70'; chain anchor above LEFT SLICE.

32. **Left Slice** (5.8) Face climb up and over left side of roof then keep right to avoid loose area; 7 bolts; 70'; chain anchor same as for LOOSE GOOSE.

33. **Right Hook** (5.9) Face climb through weakness at right side of roof then up face above; 6 bolts; 65'; 2 bolts on top.

TANMAN AREA

Small south-facing cliff above and east of TIPTOE.

34. **Transfer** (5.8) Crack and face climb on left side of blocky face; 2 bolts and gear (small cams and TCUs useful); 50'; chain anchors on top. (connect from easy finish of TIPTOE for a nice second pitch).

35. **Torso** (5.8) Face climb up center of wall right of TRANSFER; 2 bolts, gear (small TCU or Tri-Cam useful); 30'; 2 bolts on top.

36. **Trio** (5.8) Farthest right of routes on this face; 3 bolts; 30'; 2 bolts on top.

X BUTTRESS

This buttress is the next cliff south of Black Wall along the highway. **Descent:** Rappel off bolts or walk down gully on the south side.

37. **Sailin' the Seas of Cheese** (5.12a/b) Thin face line that ascends left side of a clean tan swath that extends to the top; 5 bolts; 80'; 2 bolts on top.

38. **X Marks the Rock** (5.8+) Great line that wanders up arete right of SAILIN'; 6 bolts, gear to 2"; 80'; chain anchor on top.

39. **Flake Free** (5.9+) Excellent, sustained face climb right of X'; 5 bolts, gear to 1.5" (#0.5, #1, #1.5 Tri-Cams useful in horizontal cracks); 75'; use anchors at top of X'.

LIZARD SLABS

These slabs are named after the northern alligator lizard that frequents the area. These low-angled cliffs are just south of X Buttress and slightly uphill from the highway. The routes here are all moderate with abundant toprope anchors. **Descent:** Walk off either end of the slab.

40. **Scotty's Delight** (5.6) Crack line on left side of slab; gear; 50'; chain anchor on top.

41. **Alley Oop** (5.7) Start in corner, pass small roof, and continue up face; 3 bolts (easy between bolts); 60'; shares chains on top of SCOTTY'S.

42. **Thin Ice** (5.8) Face and crack climb. Bolt protects bulge at start then follow crack to top; 1 bolt, gear to 1.5" (small cams and nuts useful); 60'; 2-bolt anchor on top.

43. **Thin Pudding** (5.8) Line immediately right of THIN ICE. Share same start as THIN ICE then stay right on thin features; gear; 60'; shares anchor with PLUM PUDDING.

44. **Plum Pudding** (5.8) Face climb slab past tree and follow finger and hand cracks to top; gear to 3"; 60'; chains on top (take long slings for toprope anchors).

45. **Lizard Follies** (5.8) Face/crack up middle of slab; gear; 60'; no anchors on top.

46. **Terrordactyl** (5.8) Easy slabs lead up to steeper face; 2 bolts; 60'; need slings on top.

Photo by Ted Steiner.

PRIMORDIAL BUTTRESS

Located directly above Lizard Slabs and characterized by a large roof on the north side with broken cliffs on the south, which are not frequented because of hazardous loose rock. **Descent:** Walk off toward the south side or rappel from bolts at top of climbs.

47. **Prince of Thieves** (5.10c) Face line right of corner system that leads to prominent roof; 5 bolts; 65'; 2-bolt rappel anchor below top.

BAT BUTTRESS

This area is named after the small brown bat sometimes seen here. It is just north of the obvious white wall at far south end of main bluffs. To get there ascend the trail just north of short cliff near road and once on top go south and up through easy rock steps to the base of the cliff. Cairns mark the way. **Descent:** Rappel routes.

48. **G & G** (5.10d) On the far left/north side is an easy face with crack leads to bolted face; 2 bolts; 55'; chain anchor on top.

49. **Bat's Belfry** (5.9+) Discontinuous crack line with a roof up left side of cliff right of G&G; gear to 3"; 65'; chain anchor on top.

50. **Escher's Staircase** (5.8) The original route up cliff that takes a right-leaning line of least resistance; follow right-facing corner and continue traversing

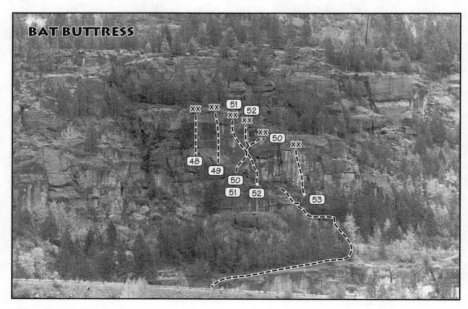

Photo by Randall Green.

right over slab past bolt and around right edge of roof; 1 bolt, gear to 2";
70'; 2 bolts on top.

51. **Sinister Exit** (5.10b/c) Shares same start as ESCHER'S but step left after
first bolt and ascend steep corner past bolts and discontinuous cracks; 4
bolts, gear to 2.5"; 65'; chain anchor on top.

52. **Belvedere** (5.10+) Starts in corner capped with a roof right of ESCHER'S;
continue past bolt and across ESCHER'S line past bolts on upper left side
of right-slanting roof to top; 4 bolts, gear to 2.5"; 75'; 2 bolts on top.

Bighorn Buttress

Named after the bighorn sheep that roam the Stone Hill area, this buttress is
at the north end of the next tier of cliffs above North Hold Up Bluff. Approach
via the trail at the north end of the North Hold Up Bluff. **Descent:** Walk off
toward the southeast and down the gully at the south side of the buttress.

53. **Double Clutching** (5.10b) Bolted face north of big cave and overhang, which
is down and north of Bighorn area; 5 bolts; 50'; anchors on top.

54. **Super Crack** (5.10b) Obvious finger and hand crack that splits the west
face; 1 bolt, gear to #4 Friend and extra slings; 80'; no fixed anchors on
top.

55. **Bighorn Roof Direct** (5.12) Line starts right of SUPER CRACK and left of
two large roofs on southwest corner of buttress; climb shallow corner to

Photo by Randall Green.

first roof, traverse right to crack line through final roof; direct finish is crux (which can be avoided by a 5.11c finger traverse right and up); 2 bolts, gear to #3 Friend (TCUs useful—use two ropes to avoid rope drag); 85'; belay from block on top.

JAH ROCK

Separated from Bighorn Buttress by a gully, Jah Rock is part of the same tier and is directly above the North Hold Up Bluff. Approach via the same trail to Bighorn Buttress. **Descent:** Rappel off bolts or walk off gullies to the north toward Bighorn or south toward Big Buttress/Sensible Shoes area, then rappel off chains on Anaerobic Avenue to access climbs to south.

56. **Permagrin** (5.11a/b) Steep face left of IN SEARCH FOR JAH; 3 bolts, gear (wired stopper at bottom); 40'; chain anchor on top.

57. **In Search for Jah** (5.11a) Second bolted face from left end of rock; 4 bolts; 40'; 2 bolts on top.

58. **Up in Smoke** (5.12b) Follows incipient crack (seam) and skirts small roof to right; 5 bolts; 50'; 2 chain anchors (two links each) on top.

59. **Burnin'** (5.11c/d) Left-arching line that joins 'SMOKE near the top; 5 bolts; 50; same anchors as 'SMOKE.

60. **Crank'n Stein** (5.10a) Vertical, pumpy jug haul; 4 bolts; 35'; 2 bolts on top.

Photo by Ted Steiner.

Big Buttress/Sensible Shoes

Big Buttress is on the same tier as Jah Rock and Bighorn Buttress but farther south and directly above the South Hold Up Bluff. The south end has a steep face with several roofs. A small pillar sits back up hill from the overhanging south face. *Anaerobic Avenue* is on the pillar. *Sensible Shoes* is farther south on the next buttress. Approach via the gully between the Hold Up Bluffs or from the trails to Bighorn and Jah. **Descent:** Walk off north or rappel from anchors at top of *Anaerobic Avenue*.

61. **Anaerobic Avenue** (5.10a) South end of Big Buttress on face of pillar; slightly overhanging face of positive edges; 5 bolts; 70'; chain anchors on top.

62. **Sensible Shoes** (5.11a) South of Big Buttress toward Tower of Power. This classic Stone Hill face route ascends large buttress below steep yellow face; 5 bolts; 70'; 2 bolts on top (bring webbing).

Tower of Power

The Tower is located on the second tier but farther uphill and south. **Descent:** Rappel off anchors at tops of routes on Tower pillar.

63. **Four-Play** (5.9) Located on the second tier above Primordial Buttress just below and north of the Tower. Bolts protect face that leads to steep crack;

TOWER OF POWER

Photo by Ted Steiner.

2 bolts; 50'; no anchors on top; **Descent:** scramble and downclimb gully to right/south that leads to base of Tower routes.

64. **Stranger Than Friction** (5.10b) Line of steep jugs and thin cracks on north side of tower; 5 bolts, gear to 1.5"; 70'; chain anchors on top.

65. **Forearm Infarction** (5.11b) Follows arete on left side of Tower pillar; 8 bolts; 80'; chain anchors.

66. **Prescribed Burning** (5.11b/c) Take natural crack line up face in middle of pillar; 4 bolts, gear to #3 Friend; 80'; chain anchors.

UPPER POOLSIDE GULLY/ROOM WITH A VIEW

Room With a View refers to two climbs located on the south end of the cliff road that cuts through across the highway from the north end of Hold Up Bluffs. The two routes ascend the south-facing blocky overhang. **Descent:** Rappel off or walk off to the north and downclimb the roadcut.

67. **Room With a View** (5.8+) Climb steep, blocky face through overhang on south side of rock; 5 bolts; 60'; bolt on top.

68. **Room With a View Direct** (5.9) Starts left and shares last bolt with original route; 5 bolts; 60'.

69. **No Rest for the Wicked** (5.12b) Thin sustained face; rappel into gully from ledge below ROOM WITH A VIEW to approach base; 6 bolts; 60'; 2 bolts on top.

LOWER POOLSIDE GULLY

The routes are on the south-facing walls above the gully directly below Room With a View and opposite Mussel Beach. See overview photo and map for more precise location. **Descent:** Rappel off bolts or walk off.

Virgin Block

70. **Klingon** (5.11a) Reachy face climb right of 'BLONDES; 4 bolts; 40'; 2 bolts on top.

71. **Virgin Blondes** (5.11a) Left-most bolted face line on south side of block; 5 bolts; 50'; 2 bolts on top.

72. **The Flight of Amadeus** (5.12d/.13a) Overhanging shallow dihedral on west side of block; scramble to base can be problematic. Easiest to rappel down route to base or scramble left from start of 'BLONDES; 5 bolts; 60'; 2 bolts on top.

UPPER
POOLSIDE
GULLY

5.8+

5.9

68

67

69

Poolside Gully

Photo by Ted Steiner.

VIRGIN BLOCK
LOWER POOLSIDE GULLY

5.12+

70

71

72

Photo by Ted Steiner.

Photo by Ted Steiner.

MUSSEL BEACH/POOLSIDE CRAGS/MUSSEL REEF

This area is characterized by a series of cliffs that descend toward the lake in blocky steps below the highway. The approach trail descends the highway embankment directly across from the middle of the north section of Hold Up Bluffs. Follow cairns and a rough trail about 0.25 mile to the main cliffs. Most of the routes face south, with some facing west. Routes are no longer than 80' with anchor bolts at the top of nearly every one. See overview photo and map for more precise locations. **Descent:** (Mussel Beach) Rappel routes or downclimb easy chimney east of *Culdesac*; (Poolside Crags/Mussel Reef) rappel from bolts at top of cliff or walk off.

Mussel Beach

Second tier that faces west above water line. Several tall ponderosa pines inhabit the 50'-wide shelf at the base of the cliff.

73. **Poison Winter** (5.11c) Route on extreme left side of main Mussel Beach face; may be more difficult for those with a low ape index; 2 bolts, gear (up to #2 Friend useful); 70'; chain anchor on top.

74. **Forbidden Colours** (5.11d/.12a) Next route right/south of POISON' on main Mussel Beach face; 4 bolts, gear (small wires and med. Friends useful); 65'; chain anchor on top.

Photo by Ted Steiner.

75. **Silhouette** (5.10c) Located in middle of main face; starts on top of block; 5 bolts, gear to 1.5"; 65'; 2 bolts on top.

76. **Legacy** (5.11d) Thin crack and face that angles right; starts in middle of face at broken out pod area; ascend left-angling crack to small roof then traverse right 10' and go straight up; 2 bolts, gear to 2.5"; 65'; chain anchor.

77. **Eat Your Spinach** (5.10d) Face route on right side of main face that assaults roof at bottom; 1 bolt, gear to 2.5"; 70'; 2 bolts on top.

78. **Culdesac** (5.9+) Crack and face line that follows a shallow dihedral on south corner of main face; 1 bolt, gear to #3 Friend (cams useful); 80'; chain anchor on top.

79. **Submission** (5.11a) Left line on low-angled face that faces west right of CULDESAC; skirts left of roof in middle of slab; 4 bolts, gear (TCUs, small wire, #2 Friend useful if extra protection is needed); 45'; chain anchor on top.

80. **Magically Delicious** (5.9) Clean face line that skirts right side of the roof in middle of slab. To avoid unprotected move, start on SUBMISSION and traverse right; 4 bolts, gear (TCUs, #1.5-#2 Friends useful if extra protection is needed); 45'; chain anchor on top.

81. **Anchors Away** (5.8) Southern arete right of MAGICALLY'; 4 bolts, gear to 2"; 65'; chain anchor on top.

82. **Sesame Street** (5.6) Face-crack line right of ANCHORS'; gear to 3"; 60'; no fixed anchors.

83. **Great White** (5.8) Crack and steep face line on next south-facing step up the gully from SESAME ST.; 4 bolts, gear (wired stoppers); 50'; bolted rings on top.

Poolside Crags/Mussel Reef

First tier above the water line and lowest of the Poolside Gully areas. Bases of routes may be inaccessible during summer months when reservoir is full.

84. **Black Grail** (5.11c) Left-most route on face; 5 bolts, gear to #2.5 Friend; 110'; no fixed anchors on top—belay from tree.

85. **Brain Fart** (5.10d) Crack-face line right of 'GRAIL; turning roof is crux; gear to #2.5 Friend (extra small cams useful); 90'; 2 bolts on top.

86. **Noel! Noel!** (5.11c) Route right of chimney; 4 bolts; 60'; no anchors on top.

87. **Pat Wings** (5.10b/c) Face right of NOEL' that skirts roof to left and angles back up right; 5 bolts; 55'; 2 bolts on top.

Photo by Randall Green.

Photo by Ted Steiner.

Toon Town

This delightful area is located below the road south of Mussel Beach directly beneath X and Primordial buttresses. To get there descend the embankment below the highway just south of Black Wall. Walk along the guardrail to the cairn marking the rough approach trail to the top of the cliff. Go north around the end of the cliff to its base.

88. **Quickdraw McGraw** (5.11b/c) Face climb in middle of gray wall right of chimney; 4 bolts; 60'; 2 bolts on top.

89. **Popeye** (5.11b/c) Next line right of QUICKDRAW'. Follow thin left-leaning seam; 5 bolts; 60'; 2 bolts on top.

90. **Yosemite Sam** (5.9) Face to wide crack on right third of face; gear to 3.5"; 60'; 2 bolts on top.

91. **Wyle E. Coyote** (5.10b) Right-most face route on wall, follows tan swath; 4 bolts; 50'; 2 bolts on top.

SOUTH STONE

Only a few of the developed routes are mentioned here. Most have seen few ascents and may be dirty or loose. But the two listed here are worth doing to escape the popularity of the main area and for those looking for adventure in a peaceful setting. Continue past Hold Up Bluffs about 0.5 mile on MT 37. The cliffs are on the east side, a short hike uphill from the highway. **Descent:** walk off toward the south.

SOUTH STONE

Photo by Ted Steiner.

92. **Moose's Tooth** (5.10a) Obvious hand crack through a roof on the left side of main wall; gear to #4 Friend; 80'; no fixed anchors on top.

93. **Animal Tea** (5.10b R) Line ascends face left of wide crack, passing horizontal breaks; offers thin face holds and overhanging jugs; gear (extra thin wires, TCUs useful); 80'; no fixed anchors on top.

PECK GULCH AREA

The climbing at Peck Gulch is actually in a gully that descends from the road about 0.5 mile north of the Peck Gulch Campground road. To find the rocks go south past the Hold Up Bluffs about 4 miles to where the road cuts through the rocky hillside and a large block stands alone on the west side of the highway. Park on the north side of the block, hop the guardrail, and follow cairns along a rough trail down the steep embankment of talus. Walk down into the gully that descends toward the reservoir. The gully walls and climbs are described as you approach them from the top. Refer to photos and maps for more precise locations. **Descents:** It is possible to walk off or scramble down the sides or backsides of most cliffs here; bolts have been placed at the tops of most climbs.

PECK GULCH UPPER GULLY SOUTH WALL

94. **Private Dancer** (5.8) Face on left side of wall; 3 bolts, gear (cams to 2.5" useful); 50'; 2 bolts on top.

95. **Voo Doo Child** (5.11a) Face on right side; 4 bolts; 50'; 2 bolts on top.

PECK GULCH

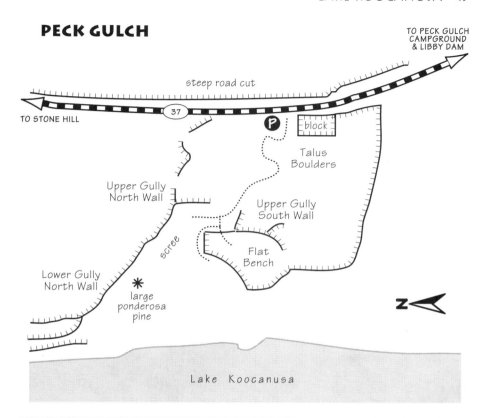

Photo by Randall Green.

UPPER GULLY
NORTH WALL

Photo by Ted Steiner.

96. **Genesis** (5.7-.9) Crack line; grade can be a sandbag unless you find the critical hold by roof (direct boulder start is 5.9); gear to 2"; 50'; 2 bolts on top.

LOWER GULLY SOUTH WALL

97. **Blessing in Disguise** (5.9) Face line through bulge and go left to hand crack at top; gear to #2.5 Friend; 65'; no fixed anchors on top.

UPPER GULLY NORTH WALL

98. **Happy Hooker** (5.11b) Crack to bulge/roof and face above; 2 bolts, gear to 1"; 30'; 2 bolts on top.
99. **Pisa Cake** (5.8) Pumpy face climb on pillar left of 'HOOKER; 4 bolts; 40'; 1 bolt on top.
100. **Dreamin'** (5.11a) Face and crack left of PISA CAKE; 2 bolts, gear to #2.5 Friend; 40'; 2 bolts on top.

LOWER GULLY NORTH WALL

101. **Rosy the Riveter** (5.11b) Right-most route on wall. Lighter gray swath marks route; 5 bolts; 75'; cold shuts at ledge.
102. **Minotaur** (5.10c) Next face climb left of ROSY' behind large ponderosa pine; 8 bolts; 80'; 2 bolts just below top.
103. **Crackin'** (5.8) Obvious crack left of MINOTAUR; steep start; gear to 3.5" (cams useful); 70'; 2 bolts on top.
104. **Zeus** (5.10b) Face line left of CRACKIN' on flaky face; 10 bolts; 75'; 2 bolts on top.
105. **Medusa** (5.10b) Face line left of ZEUS; 10 bolts; 80'; 2 bolts on top.

LOWER
NORTH
GULLY

101

102

103

104

105

Photo by Ted Steiner.

West Central

WC

REGION

Brad Hutcheson on the second ascent of a new route (*Dr. Delta*)-Crystal Theater. *Photo by Katrina Ruhmland.*

MISSOULAAREA

LOLO PASS

OVERVIEW

Scattered throughout the Lolo Pass area about 40 miles southwest of Missoula are coarse-textured granitic rock domes from 40 feet to 300 feet tall. Mostly concentrated on the north side of U.S. Highway 12 near the top of the pass, the routes here offer friction climbing with an ample share of edges, pockets, and cracks thrown in for variety. The well-weathered cracks tend to be flaring in nature so camming units are especially useful here. Although the routes are often gear dependent with bolts interspersed as needed, there also are some true sport climbs in the area.

A **standard gear rack** for Lolo should include Tri-Cams (#.5 through #1.5), which are considered essential for protecting the many holes and pockets found on the climbs, in addition to a good selection of wired stoppers, TCUs, nuts, cams, slings, and quick draws.

The Lolo Hot Springs resort is nearby for soaking tired muscles after a long day of climbing. The climbing season at the domes generally lasts from late March to November.

Unless there is a reasonable way to walk or scramble off the rock, anchors for rappels are fixed chain or the old hanger and sling system.

Ethics: Chipping, manufacturing, or gluing on holds is not tolerated. If a climb is too difficult to ascend without resorting to these debasing tactics leave it for future generations to try.

High-grade concrete expansion bolts (3/8" by 2 to 2 1/2" or longer) have become the fixed anchors of choice; for rappel stations use 2 long bolts with heavy duty or high-tensile chains. Use care and discretion when placing fixed anchors. Because of growing concerns over visual pollution caused by fixed anchors, all new anchor systems should be camouflage painted to match the color of the rock.

▲ —

Brad Hutcheson, author of *The Climber's Guide to Lolo Pass*, provided the text, maps, and photos for this section

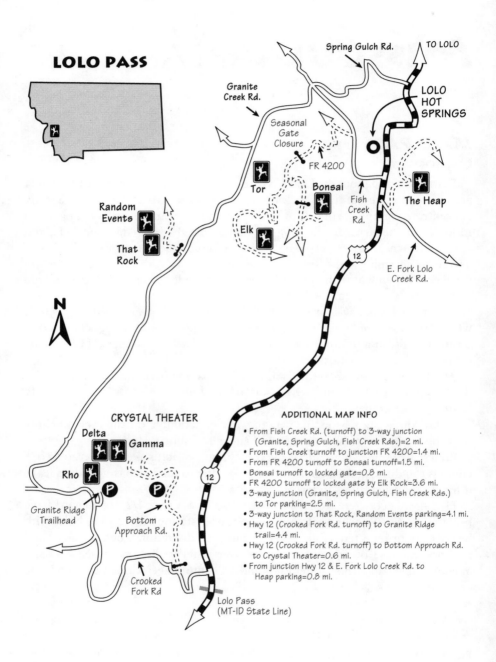

LOLO PASS

Spring Gulch Rd.

TO LOLO

Granite Creek Rd.

LOLO HOT SPRINGS

Seasonal Gate Closure

FR 4200

Tor

Bonsai

The Heap

Fish Creek Rd.

Random Events

Elk

12

That Rock

E. Fork Lolo Creek Rd.

N

CRYSTAL THEATER

ADDITIONAL MAP INFO

Delta

Gamma

Rho

P

P

12

Granite Ridge Trailhead

Bottom Approach Rd.

Crooked Fork Rd

Lolo Pass (MT-ID State Line)

- From Fish Creek Rd. (turnoff) to 3-way junction (Granite, Spring Gulch, Fish Creek Rds.)=2 mi.
- From Fish Creek turnoff to junction FR 4200=1.4 mi.
- From FR 4200 turnoff to Bonsai turnoff=1.5 mi.
- Bonsai turnoff to locked gate=0.8 mi.
- FR 4200 turnoff to locked gate by Elk Rock=3.6 mi.
- 3-way junction (Granite, Spring Gulch, Fish Creek Rds.) to Tor parking=2.5 mi.
- 3-way junction to That Rock, Random Events parking=4.1 mi.
- Hwy 12 (Crooked Fork Rd. turnoff) to Granite Ridge trail=4.4 mi.
- Hwy 12 (Crooked Fork Rd. turnoff) to Bottom Approach Rd. to Crystal Theater=0.6 mi.
- From junction Hwy 12 & E. Fork Lolo Creek Rd. to Heap parking=0.8 mi.

Trip Planning Information

Area description: Single- and multi-pitch routes on coarse granitic domes in a forested mountain setting.

General location: The Lolo domes are in the Bitterroot Mountains about 34 miles southwest of Missoula near Lolo Pass, the Lolo Hot Springs resort, and the Idaho border.

Camping: An overnight lodge, recreation vehicle camping, and some services (bar, restaurant, hot pool) are available at Lolo Hot Springs resort. Car camping is possible along Fish Creek Road. Lee Creek Campground is a Forest Service fee ($6/night) facility with 22 units and water 1.4 miles west of Lolo Hot Springs on US 12.

Climbing season: Generally from late March to November, depending on snowfall and temperatures.

Restrictions and access: Most of the domes are on private land. Please respect all restrictions, road closures, and locked gates. So far the land owners allow climbing, but it is important to continue treating the area with respect; some roads may be closed to vehicular travel, and gates may be locked. Parking is not usually a problem except at Bonsai Rock (see Bonsai section for details). **Do not park in front of any gates** and block access for the landowners.

Guidebooks: *The Climber's Guide to Lolo Pass* by Brad Hutcheson and *Bitterroot Guidebook* by Rick Torre.

Nearby mountain shops, guide services, and climbing gyms: Canyon Critters, Hamilton; Pipestone Mountaineering (retail, rental, and instruction), Missoula; The Trailhead (retail and rental), Missoula; Hold-On (climbing gym, retail, instruction, and rental), Missoula; University of Montana indoor climbing wall, Missoula.

THE HEAP

The Heap is one of the newest developed areas in Lolo. It has eight routes from 5.6 to 5.11 and is the best place for beginners in the area. Six of the routes are 5.9 and under, offering classic Lolo style climbing. There are the mandatory friction slabs, edges, dikes, and some cracks to test the full range of skills. The longest routes are only about 100' and many require some gear to supplement the bolts.

The Heap, with its easy approach and west-by-north aspect, is great for an afternoon outing.

Climbing history: The first route was established in 1992 by Mac Johnson and Chay Donnelly. During that summer, Donnelly established the test piece *Sinister Footwear* (5.11b), which sees very few on-sight ascents today. Johnson teamed up with Zack Spannagel and Brad Hutcheson later in the fall and together they produced several classic lines on the left end of The Heap. The spring of 1993 brought Hutcheson back to the rock. With various partners, he established many easy lines.

The Heap can be a busy place because of moderate routes and easy access. Climbing classes are often found here during the weekends. Because of its smaller nature and the impact from large groups of climbers please be aware of the trail erosion that is becoming a problem. Do not create new trails and don't hesitate to spend some time doing erosion control maintainence if the desire strikes.

Finding the rock: From Missoula take US 93 south to the town of Lolo. Turn right on US 12 and go toward Lolo Pass; Lolo Hot Springs is about 34 miles from Missoula. Take US 12 about 0.5 mile beyond Lolo Hot Springs Resort and turn left onto the graveled East Fork Lolo Creek Road (this is the first left after passing Lolo Hot Springs). Cross the bridge and make another left onto an unmarked road. Follow this road, and after about 0.8 mile from US 12 there should be a small pullout on the right at a large gully. Park here. A trail heads up this wash. Follow it for the 5minute approach to The Heap. All the routes described here are on the aspect facing the approach.

1. **Sinister Footwear** (5.11b) The right-most climb on the rock. Scramble up onto a small ledge to begin. The opening moves are the crux on this interesting face route; 75'; bolts, gear (#1 Camalot or equivalent is useful to protect top of seam after second bolt; large cams and nuts useful for belay). **Descent:** Scramble and walk off toward left/east side of rock.

2. **Temperature's Rising** (5.9) Shares same start as DIKE'S EDGE; first route approached from parking area and left of SINISTER'. Ascend vertical dike; after 3rd bolt step right and continue up friction slab past more bolts to 2-bolt anchor at top; 100'; 8 bolts. **Descent:** Scramble and walk off left.

3. **Dike's Edge** (5.6) Ascends vertical dike and face above. Step left across gully after 3rd bolt; 100'; 10 bolts; 2-bolt anchor. **Descent:** Scramble and walk off left.

4. **Heart Throb** (5.8) Starts about 40' left of DIKE'S EDGE. Face climb past 2 bolts to short crack (hard to protect—TCUs useful); continue up rolling friction slab past bolts to a diagonal crack; follow crack and step right to seam when feasible then exit past large pocket above; 5 bolts, gear to 3"; 2-bolt anchor. **Descent:** Scramble and walk off left.

5. **Yahtzee** (5.9 R) Left of HEART THROB. Line follows rolling face to hand crack below dike-like horns (crux); Tri-Cams or TCUs help prevent runout to top; belay at top, using gear (to 2") in cracks (do not use small tree for an anchor). **Descent:** Scramble and walk off left.

6. **Push It Along** (5.9) This and the remaining routes are all located farther left around the rock from YAHTZEE. Start at left side of pleasant alcove by a large pine tree near left end of rock; ascend good edges; 70'; 5 bolts, gear

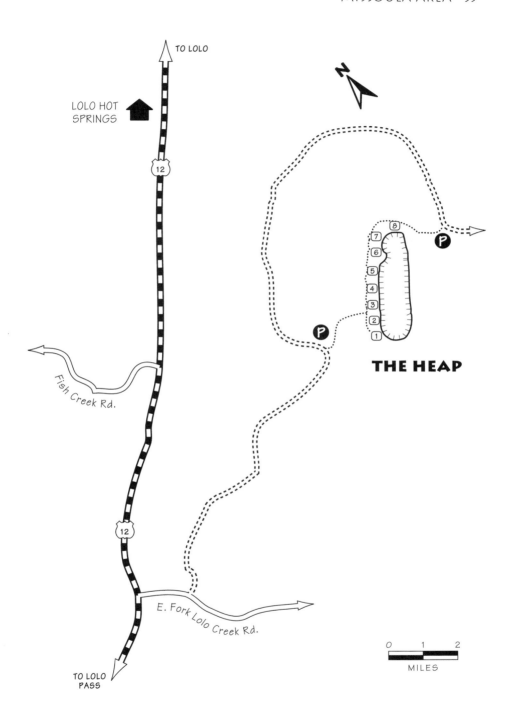

TO LOLO

LOLO HOT
SPRINGS

12

Fish Creek Rd.

12

E. Fork Lolo Creek Rd.

TO LOLO
PASS

N

8
7
6
5
4
3
2
1

THE HEAP

0   1   2
MILES

(#1 Camalot or equivalent useful). **Descent:** Single-rope rappel from chain anchor.

7. **Conjunction Junction** (5.10c) Next route left of PUSH IT ALONG. Ascend finger crack and seam to steep face and bulge (hard-to-see bolt over roof); 70'; 2 bolts, gear (TCUs to 1" and larger cams useful). **Descent:** Single-rope rappel from chain anchor.

8. **Shift and Adjust** (5.8) The left-most climb on rock. Start down and left of CONJUNCTION' in short crack; ascend crack to friction slab and roof; 70'; bolts, gear (TCUs and larger cams to 2" useful). **Descent:** Single-rope rappel from chain anchor.

BONSAI ROCK

Bonsai is a rather steep and compact rock with large boulders scattered around its base. Its tallest aspect is about 90'. The climbing is vertical, mostly with cracks and pockets used for protection. Of the six recommended climbs rated 5.8 to 5.12, there are two face routes protected by natural gear and bolts. The other four are mostly crack climbs. It is easy to walk off the north end of Bonsai where it merges with the hillside.

During the hot months of summer, the Main Face, which faces west, is a good place to climb early before it gets the sun. It can be hot in the afternoon. The other routes are better later in the day, since they are out of direct sun then.

Climbing history: Bonsai Rock was named by Tobin Kelley because of the small pine tree growing on its summit that resembles a bonsai planting. Kelley first established *Youth at Risk* and *High Plains Drifter* in 1985. The next two years saw other activists (Gray Thompson, Steve Horton, Rick Torre, Michael Scott, Ivan Pyatt, and Jim Durkin) involved with new routes to various degrees. Of notable merit were Scott's and Horton's attempts and Horton's ultimate redpoint of *Euthanasia* in 1987.

By the end of 1988, Bonsai had seen many of the best local hardmen trying its lines and contributing in one form or another. As far as recent history, Bonsai seems to be somewhat forgotten and left behind in the push for modern high-end climbs. However, Bonsai still offers some of the best natural lines and hardest cracks to be found in the Lolo area.

Seasonal road closure notice: Forest Road 4200 is closed to vehicles 1 mile past Fish Creek Road from October 15 to May 15.

Finding the rock: From US 12 about 0.25 mile past Lolo Hot Springs turn right/west onto Fish Creek Road and follow it about 1.4 miles. On the left is a turn off that should be marked FR 4200 (The turn is just before Fish Creek Road crosses the bridge over Granite Creek.). Follow FR 4200, staying left for 1.5 miles where another road drops down off to your left. Take this road; it will switchback (park here) and climb until it comes to a locked gate in 0.8 mile.

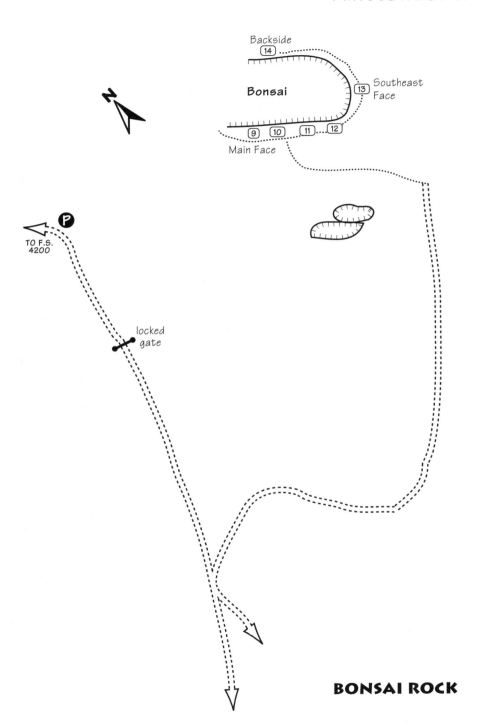

Backside
14

Bonsai

Southeast
13 Face

9 10 11 12

Main Face

P

TO F.S.
4200

locked
gate

N

BONSAI ROCK

walk-off

5.8

5.10c

5.10a

9

10

5.8

5.10d

5.10

11

12

5.10

BONSAI ROCK
MAIN FACE

Photo by Brad Hutcheson.

Do not park at the gate. There is no place to turn around here. Park 0.2 mile back up the road from the gate or leave your vehicle at the switchback.

Walk or bike up the road, staying left at the first fork (soon after the gate) and go left again at the three-way junction farther up. From the approach trail, Bonsai will be visible above and on your left.

MAIN FACE

The southwest face is the aspect first approached when walking from the road. It is about 80' high and the largest side of the rock. **Descents:** All routes can be descended by walking off to the left, which is the north side.

9. **Youth on Probation** (5.10a) Left-most route on rock. Scramble up to a small ledge to begin; sustained 5.9 with harder move past first bolt; 3 bolts, gear (TCUs and medium wires with cams to 3" useful at belay). **Descent:** Walk off.

10. **High Plains Drifter** (5.8) This route climbs crack to right of off-width, then traverses right on prominent dike to next crack; follow crack to top; gear (standard rack). **Descent:** Walk off.

11. **Youth With Anxiety** (5.10c) Located to right of HIGH PLAINS'. Start on boulder; pull through horizontal cracks and face holds to prominent dike; climb to bolt-protected face above (reaching first bolt involves 5.10 moves out above your last piece of gear); 2 bolts, gear to 4". **Descent:** Walk off. **Variant:** (5.8) Link YOUTH WITH ANXIETY with HIGH PLAINS' by traversing left on dike to finish on upper crack of HIGH PLAINS.

12. **Restless Natives** (5.10d) Next route right of YOUTH WITH ANXIETY. Begins down low in a small overhanging corner; climb corner and hand traverse out right to a sloping ledge; gain thin seam over bulge above; climb seam and face to dike; scamper unprotected 5.6 friction slab to belay; gear to 3". **Descent:** Walk off over summit and down to left.

SOUTHEAST FACE

This face is the "nose" of the rock and is about 90' high. It is easily recognized by the large roofs on the left side.

13. **Youth at Risk** (5.10d) Classic thin-to-wide crack in the center of face. A bit awkward to gain small ledge before crack; gear. **Descent:** See RESTLESS NATIVES.

BACKSIDE

This northeast face is characterized by being overhanging for almost its entire height.

14. **Euthanasia** (5.12) Ascends obvious finger-to-hand crack right of flake/crack system; gear to 4" and forearms of steel. **Descent:** Walk off.

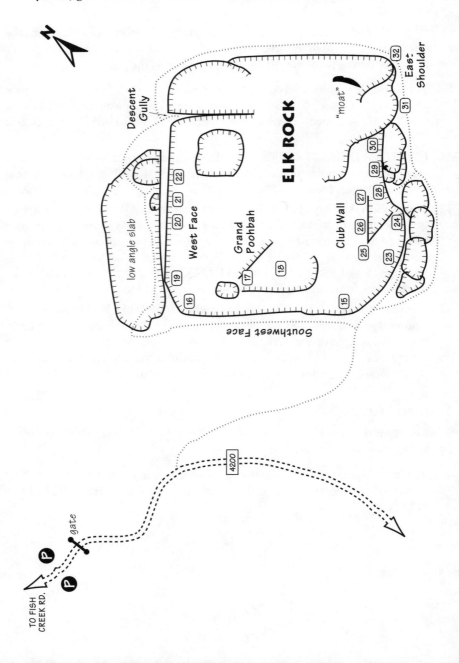

ELK ROCK

Elk Rock is multi-featured and 200' high. Although it is not visible from the roads below, it sits on a hill overlooking much of the Lolo area. It has eighteen recommended routes from 5.6 to 5.12, with many requiring knowledge of gear placement (especially Tri-Cams). There are some sport climbs, also, and some wonderful bouldering below the main rock. With its traditional gear lines and newer bolted faces, Elk Rock has something for everyone.

Elk Rock can be hot in the summer. The west and southwest faces are known for this. By climbing these faces in the morning, the heat can be avoided. However, cooler temperatures early and late in the year make these faces appealing during the sunny hours of the day. In summer, the Club Wall and the East Shoulder offer cooler climbing in the afternoon.

The main way off the summit is to scramble down the large gully that splits the northwest side of the rock. There also are chain rappel anchors set at various locations on the rock.

Climbing history: Brad Hutcheson and various other partners founded and established the first natural gear lines at Elk Rock in 1984. Its popularity was immediate because of the setting and quality of the rock. By 1986, Ivan Pyatt and Jim Durkin were putting up some of the harder 5.10s and opening up the larger faces with hand-drilled 1/4" bolts on lead. The next two years brought the 3/8" bolt into use, along with rising standards. These routes justifiably became the Lolo-area test pieces. Elk Rock had become the focal point of many of the area's better climbers.

When Kristen Drumheller flashed *Grand Poohbah's* corner and confirmed its tentative 5.11d rating, it finally gave local climbers a rating checkpoint. By 1989, Pyatt and Durkin, along with other partners, had produced the hardest sport routes at Elk Rock—ushering in 5.11+ and 5.12 standards. These routes are still the hardest on the rock.

Finding the rock: Turn right off US 12 on Fish Creek Road 0.25 mile past Lolo Hot Springs Resort (34 miles from Missoula). Follow Fish Creek Road about 1.4 miles. Take a left turn on FR 4200. If you cross the bridge over Granite Creek, you've gone too far and missed FR 4200. From the junction with FR 4200 and Fish Creek Road, it is about 3.6 miles to the locked gate; **do not block the gate; park off road on existing pullouts.** Once on FR 4200, bear left on FR 4200 at the first switchback and stay on the main road. Do not turn left at 1.5 miles, which is the turnoff to Bonsai Rock. From the locked gate walk around a corner, and Elk Rock will be visible above and on the left side of the road.

SOUTHWEST FACE

A prominent open book (*Grand Poohbah* 5.11d) is the dominant feature you will see when approaching Elk Rock from the road. There is a trail that cuts off left and up to the rock. Follow this trail to the base of the face.

ELK ROCK

GRANDMA'S PORCH & WEST FACE

Photo by Brad Hutcheson.

15. **F-104** (5.11b/c) At lower right corner of face is a well-brushed steep slab. Crank past a horizontal edge to a diagonal seam protected with a bolt above; face climb past more bolts to steep *hueco*-laced wall above; 5 bolts, gear (large Friends and TCUs useful); 75'. **Descent:** Single-rope rappel from chain anchor.

16. **Dragon's Breath** (5.10b) Follows water groove on left corner of Southwest Face. Ascend short slab to groove (5.8R); climb groove past bolts and exit left when feasible; 2 bolts, gear (#2.5-3 Friend and small Tri-Cams useful at exit; 60'. **Descent:** Single-rope rappel from chain anchor located to right on ledge.

GRANDMA'S PORCH

This is the name given to the large slabby ledge area above the Southwest Face. The large open book (*Grand Poohbah*) you see on the approach is located here. *F-104* ends here.

Reach Grandma's Porch by either climbing one of the lower routes of the Southwest Face, or via easier routes on the Club Wall (*Echo Slab* or *Lost Ethos*) and traverse left around the corner to gain the 'Porch.

17. **Grand Poohbah** (5.11d) Ascends obvious corner; gear to 3" (many small to medium wires with wide gear for belay); 70'. **Descent:** Walk northwest and downclimb a short easy slab to a large boulder wedged in main gully; downclimb and traverse left to reach ground.

18. **Dancing on Uranus** (5.11b) Face climb, which is second line to right of 'POOHBAH (right-most route on wall); gear to 3" (TCUs, wires, small Tri-Cams useful). **Descent:** See 'POOHBAH.

WEST FACE

Around to the left of the Southwest Face and Grandma's Porch is a shorter vertical wall with a low-angle slab above it. A narrow gully (3'-5' wide) separates a low-angled slab beneath this face. Scramble up on this slab to approach all climbs here. The descent gully from the summit is at the north end of the West Face and beyond the large boulders at the top.

19. **Hole-y Grail** (5.12c) Located near the lower end of the right side, this is the first climb on the face. Ascend the steep pillarlike formation; 4 bolts, gear (#3 Camalot or #4 Friend useful); 60'. **Descent:** Single-rope rappel from chain anchor.

20. **Dirty Boulevard** (5.11a) Face climb left of HOLE-Y GRAIL. Start by stepping across the gully next to the lowest large boulder; 4 bolts and #2 TCU; 60'. **Descent:** Single-rope rappel from chain anchor.

21. **Mom's Meatloaf** (5.8) Hand crack left of DIRTY BOULEVARD. Start from top of boulder and ascend crack (crux is getting into crack); continue onto slab above crack (1 bolt) to summit; standard rack; 145'. **Descent:** Scramble down gully at the northwest end of Elk Rock.

22. **Dime Store Mystery** (5.11a) Starts left of MOM'S. Climb face past bolts (5.8) and cross wide crack on left; go up steep dike past bolt (watch for hidden pocket); 4 bolts, gear to 3.5" (med. TCUs, #4 Friend for pocket); 65'. **Descent:** Single-rope rappel from chain anchor. **Variant** (5.8) Continue up wide crack after 5.8 face section; standard rack.

CLUB WALL

This is the large vertical face with a huge roof on its middle right side. Facing mostly south, it is located around to the right of the Southwest Face. It contains some of the finest edge and pocket face climbing in Lolo.

To climb *Fear From Crack*, *Club Med*, and *Moose's Lodge*, an approach pitch must be climbed. There are two options. The first is *Echo Slab* (5.8R) and the other is *Lost Echos* (5.6).

To find *Echo Slab* follow the approach trail up from the road to the right corner of the Southwest Face. Go right around the corner between some large boulders and the rock. This path will end beneath a small slab with a roof on either side and a drop on the right into a cavelike hole.

To find *Lost Echos* (and other Club Wall routes) follow the trail around to the right below the large boulders from the right side of the Southwest Face. When the trail is below the large roof (*Elk's Club Roof*) scramble up a gully and some rocks to reach the large flat ledge above. Traverse beneath the face as far left as possible until stopped by a drop into the "cave" below. *Lost Echos* ascends the diagonal crack beneath the roof to the left.

23. **Echo Slab** (5.8 R) From base of slab friction up 25' until it is possible to slot a small Tri-Cam into a pocket. Traverse right and up to turn the roof; small Tri-Cams and gear to 3". **Descent:** Continue to top and scramble down northwest gully or rappel 75' to base of southwest face from chain anchor located above F-104.

24. **Lost Echos** (5.6) See approach above. Climb the diagonal crack out left under the roof and turn it at its left corner. Belay on the ledge above; 55'; gear to 3". **Descent:** Continue to top and scramble down northwest gully or rappel 75' to base of the southwest face from chain anchor above F-104.

25. **Fear From Crack** (5.11d) The left-most climb on the Club Wall. Either climb or aid through the opening moves to 5.10 face climbing above; bolts, gear (Tri-Cams and #3 Camalot useful). **Descent:** scramble down northwest gully or rappel 150' to the base from chain anchor.

26. **Club Med** (5.10b) Located right of FEAR FROM CRACK on a light-colored swath. Start up and move left then straight up the face. Protection a bit tricky in middle. At top of face move right to belay on top of corner; 5 bolts, gear to 3"; 130'. **Descent:** Scramble down northwest gully.

27. **Moose's Lodge** (5.9+) Starts to right of upper Club Wall ledge. This face climb heads toward and passes left of large pocket with black water streak below it; 4 bolts, gear to 3" (small TCUs useful under the flake forming the "eyebrow" of the large pocket). **Descent:** Scramble down the northwest gully.

28. **Face to Face** (5.11c) Starts on clean gray face just left of where ledge is gained. Ascend face to large crack, crossing it and continuing to top; bolts, gear (small Tri-Cams, #3.5/#4 Friend; mid-sized cams useful for the belay); 150'. **Descent:** Scramble down the northwest gully.

29. **Chrysalis** (5.8 R) Could be considered a variation of ELK'S CLUB. CHRYSA-LIS shares same start, which begins in right-most of two thin seams beneath apex of ELK'S CLUB. Climb (no pro) to a ledge below the roof. Traverse left and join FACE TO FACE to wide crack. Step left and face climb toward crack again higher up. Follow crack system to top; gear; 145'. **Descent:** Scramble down northwest gully.

30. **Elk's Club** (5.10b R) Starts directly beneath apex of large roof on Club Wall. Scramble up on ledgy blocks beneath the roof; climb thin right-hand seam (no pro) to a ledge 25' up; continue straight up past a bolt and exit through roof crack (crux); follow face and crack system to top; belay at top of corner; 1 bolt, gear (4" cam useful); 145'. **Descent:** Scramble up and over top to the northwest gully.

Photo by Brad Hutcheson.

EAST SHOULDER

The East Shoulder is a good place to climb on a hot afternoon because it is shaded later in the day. This lower-angle wall starts on the east corner of Elk Rock and rounds to the left, consisting of longer routes that follow slabs and cracks.

Approach it by following the trail around to the right from the Southwest Face for several hundred yards. The bolted line that ascends the wavy gray face above a blocky dike is *Free Bird*.

31. **Free Bird** (5.10b) Begins to left of large crack and alcove (moves to first bolt are harder (5.10c/d) but can be passed by entering right from crack). Start up gray face and head for small tree; step right at tree out of gully/ crack and climb hidden hand crack up to roof; turn roof; climb dike; and belay at moat (moat is a large crevasselike feature hidden from ground); 6 bolts, gear to 3.5" (long runners for horns useful). **Descent:** either exit left and continue up ANNIE'S LAMENT (5.6) for 1 pitch or exit right and scramble off, keeping right down slabs and gullies.

32. **Annie's Lament** (5.6) 2-pitch route that begins in large low-angle layback crack on East Shoulder of rock. **Pitch 1**—Climb crack and traverse left around roof above; belay at sloping ledge by moat. **Pitch 2**—Move left, layback corner, and turn bulges staying left; exit on summit slabs and belay anywhere that is convenient; gear to 4". **Descent:** Scramble down the northwest gully that is up and left.

TOR ROCK

Tor Rock offers a dozen recommended routes from 5.9 to 5.12+, most of which are face climbs. But several good crack lines exist here, too. From the approach, Tor's Short Wall seems unimpressive because it's a bit "blobby" looking. First impressions may change when you stand on the slabby rock below the Main Face, viewing the steep, high-quality, 70' to 80' routes here. With a pleasant view of the meadow and stream below, this face is mostly in the sun and is great on cooler days. Three routes on the Backside are enjoyable afternoon climbs on hot days when the shade comes around.

Due to Tor Rock's easy access, beautiful setting, and hard sport routes, it probably is the most popular rock in the Lolo Pass area.

Climbing history: Tor was probably the first rock in Lolo to receive a technical ascent of modern standards. The first routes were developed in 1983 by Doug Colwell and Michael Scott. They climbed the natural crack lines *Indicator* and *Originator* on sight, cleaning the routes on lead.

The next push of new route development came in 1986 and 1987 when Ivan Pyatt, Jim Durkin, and Scott began to explore the blank faces. The test piece of the day was hand drilled while hanging off hooks on the lead by Pyatt and Scott. The style changed over the next few years with harder routes being established first on toprope. The major activists at the time, Pyatt, Durkin, Rafael Grana, and Rick Miller were constantly trying and succeeding on the harder face climbs.

Of the last three routes established in the 1990s, Pyatt redpointed *Accelerator* (5.12+) in 1991; *Ganjanator* (.11d/.12a) and *Eliminator* (.11c/d) were freed in 1992.

Finding the rock: From Missoula take US 93 south to the town of Lolo. Turn right on US 12 and go toward Lolo Pass; Lolo Hot Springs is about 34 miles from Missoula. At about 0.25 mile past the hot springs resort turn right on graveled Fish Creek Road (FR 343). Follow this road 2 miles until a three-way junction (Fish Creek, Granite Creek, and Spring Gulch roads) come together. Take a left turn on Granite Creek Road and go 2.5 miles to a wide turnout and parking area on the left (the top of Tor Rock is just visible before you reach this area). A well-worn path marks the 2-minute approach to the rock.

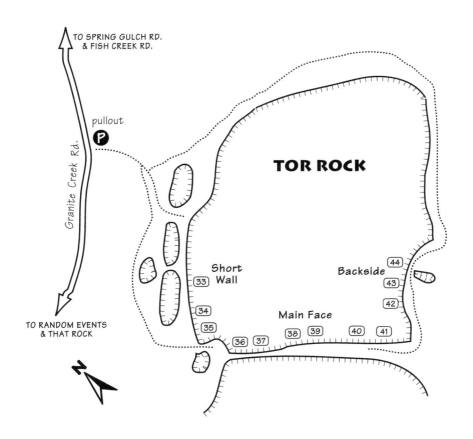

SHORT WALL

33. **Deceptor** (5.11a) Left-most route on wall. Face climb; 3 bolts and large TCUs; belay at large block or from 2.5" crack 30' behind block. **Descent:** walk off obvious left-sloping ramp that goes to ground.

34. **Aviator** (5.11c) Right of DECEPTOR; 3 bolts to same belay as DECEPTOR. **Descent:** See DECEPTOR.

35. **Animal Clinic** (5.11a) First route left of gully and right of AVIATOR; 4 bolts, gear to 2.5" for belay. **Descent:** Walk off.

MAIN/SOUTHWEST FACE

To reach the start of routes 38, 39, and 40 climb onto the slabby rock that faces the Main Face. Downclimb (easy) to the boulders and ledge to start the routes.

36. **Perculator** (5.11a/b) Starts on top of the small boulder over the entrance to the cave; reachy and thin; 4 bolts, gear to 2.5" for belay. **Descent:** Walk off left-sloping ramp that passes above top of Short Wall.

37. **Procrastinator** (5.10b R) Starts in cave below Main Face. A boulder start (crux) leads to an "up there" first bolt. Runout between second and third bolts; 3 bolts to same belay and descent as PERCULATOR.

38. **Ganjanator** (5.11d/.12a) Takes the 5-bolt line to left of INDICATOR crack system; cams to 4" useful near top; same belay and descent as PROCRASTINATOR.

39. **Indicator** (5.9) Ascend layback crack to a short traverse into a hand crack; gear for 1.5" to 4" crack; belay in large crack/flake on top at ledge. **Descent:** Scramble left and walk off.

40. **Accelerator** (5.12+) First bolted face right of INDICATOR crack; bolts. **Descent:** Single-rope rappel from chain anchor.

41. **Eliminator** (5.11c/d) Face climb that begins at the cave exit before reaching the "Backside" routes; bolts, gear (small TCUs, and wires useful). **Descent:** Single-rope rappel from chain anchor.

BACKSIDE/SOUTH FACE

To approach these routes scramble through the cave beneath the Main Face. All routes end at chain anchors. To descend rappel 80' into a corner (small open book) on a small ledge; then climb down the last 10' (easy). If you do not rappel into the corner, downclimbing the remaining section can be difficult (5.10).

42. **Originator** (5.9) Left-most route that ascends cracks and edges tending left to upper ledge; gear to 3.5"; traverse right along ledge to reach anchor.

Descent: Single-rope rappel from chain anchor. **Variant:** (5.10) Continue a second pitch above the chain anchor via an overhanging crack.

43. **Stimulator** (5.10b) Shares same start as ORIGINATOR but ascends bolt line on face above crack; bolts, gear (small wires, TCUs, and cams to 3.5" useful). Two variants are possible: a) climb small pockets straight up to ledge; b) step right and climb over horns to anchors. **Descent:** Single-rope rappel from chain anchor.

44. **Escalator** (5.10a) Route ascends steep slab and exits right at roof above. Clip "hard-to-see" bolt on slab then climb a face broken by horizontal cracks (gear to 3.5") that leads to upper bolt-protected face; bolts, gear to 3.5" (RPs useful at roof exit). **Descent:** Single-rope rappel from chain anchor.

THAT ROCK AND RANDOM EVENTS WALL

That Rock is a small 35' tower with a low-angle slab on the left side. It has a noteable sport route that ascends a steep pocketed face on its right or southeastern side. The rock is situated down in a meadow with a small stream running beneath it. Shaded by trees, it can be a nice place to escape the summer heat.

Random Events Wall is located directly behind That Rock. Random Events has three established face routes, starting at 5.10c and progressing to 5.12a. The routes are about 70' high on steep to overhanging rock with chain anchors at the tops. Most of the wall stays in the shade, making it a nice place to be in the heat.

Climbing history: Random Events Wall had been played with for several years, but nothing really was established until recently. In 1991, Jeff Swarens and Richard Plummer with Clay Morris started to work on That Rock. This was the added attraction it took to produce results on Random Events. Shawn Peretto finished his project *Lorax* (5.11+), and then Peretto and Plummer added Chris Randolph to the team and put up *Green Eggs and Ham* in 1993. Jim Durkin worked on his test piece during the same time and finally produced the wonderfully hung and pocketed *Cappuccino Cowboy* (5.12a).

Finding the rocks: Turn on Fish Creek Road (off US 12 about 0.25 mile past Lolo Hot Springs Resort). Follow Fish Creek Road for 2 miles. Take a left at the three-way fork (Fish Creek Road, Spring Gulch Road, and Granite Creek Road) onto Granite Creek Road and go about 4 miles to a turnout at a locked gate on the right (just after the 6-mile marker on Granite Creek Road).

Walk up the road until it curves hard to the right (less than 0.25 mile). A meadow will be on the left. Go along the right side of the meadow until a rock formation is reached (an abandoned road stops right before the base of the rock). This is That Rock.

Random Events Wall is behind That Rock. The best way to approach it is to walk up the gully to the right of *That Hard One* on That Rock. The gully is formed at the junction of That Rock and the large boulder on the right. After scampering up the gully between the rocks, Random Events Wall is in front of you. Finish the approach to the base by scrambling down and left.

THAT ROCK

45. **That Hard One** (5.11b) Located to left of gully that forms approach to Random Events Wall. Climb steep pocketed face; 4 bolts; 35'. **Descent:** Single-rope rappel from chain anchor.

RANDOM EVENTS WALL

46. **Green Eggs and Ham** (5.10c) First route approached from gully and right-most on wall. Climb gray face and move to crack on left; continue up and left to "wierd" pocketed orange rock; bolts, gear to 3" (small Tri-Cam useful at beginning and TCUs and small Tri-Cams useful in orange rock); 70'. **Descent:** Single-rope rappel from chain anchor.

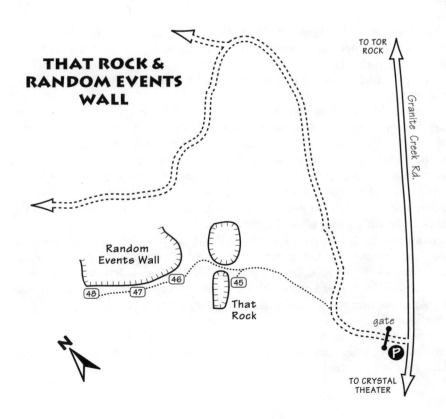

47. **Cappuccino Cowboy** (5.12a) Starts to left of GREEN EGGS. Ascend over-hanging pocketed face; bolts; 75'. **Descent:** Single-rope rappel from chain anchor.

48. **Lorax** (5.11c/d) Begins at left end of Random Events Wall. Bolt line on white rock; bolts; 70'. **Descent:** Single-rope rappel from chain anchor.

CRYSTAL THEATER (A.K.A. BABCOCK SPIRES)

This is the name given to the group of large rocks that occupy a steep, for-ested bowl near the Montana-Idaho border. These Lolo granite "towers" and "domes" range from 40' boulders to 300' monoliths. The routes here tend to be mixed, with a dependence on Tri-Cams and other camming units to supple-ment bolts. There are some sport climbs available, but mostly on the upper end of the difficulty scale.

The major formations, as seen from the bottom approach road, are named from the lower right moving upward to the left—Alpha, Beta, Gamma, Delta, and Rho. Alpha is the largest and on the lower right; Beta has twin summits; Gamma has a large corner on its south face; and Delta has a 40' visor-type roof. There are other formations, many unnamed, inside the 'Theater.

Gamma, Delta, and Rho's fourteen recommended routes, consisting of clas-sic long and short climbs from 5.6 to 5.12, are a good sampler of the area.

Climbing history: Crystal Theater was named in 1987 by Brad Hutcheson and Jim Semmelroth due to the abundance of smoky quartz crystals found in the area. A name was needed to encompass the whole area and also the indi-vidual formations. Semmelroth suggested the Greek alphabet and so the five major formations were christened with names that have endured.

A few early routes had been climbed in 1985 on the upper end of the 'Theater by Tobin Kelley, Gray Thompson, and Steve Sheriff on what they called Cherry Spire (now called Rho Rock). Other recorded ascents of the various rocks were the easy natural lines, which often had runout slab finishes. Some of these runout climbs have been retro bolted by the first-ascent party to make them enjoyable for others. Hutcheson along with various partners (notably Zack Spannagel) climbed numerous routes up to the 5.10 grade. These climbs have been estab-lished in all styles from on-sight leads to toprope rehearsed affairs with some interesting epics in between. Semmelroth along with others have also continued to input energy toward new routes in the area.

From about 1990 on, harder routes were beginning to be established. Rafael Grana and Hutcheson teamed up to produce some interesting lines, most noto-rious being the 3-pitch classic *Sundance* (5.11c) on Delta. Grana climbed the last 2 pitches on sight, with the 5.11c crux pitch being established on an eight-hour lead! Ivan Pyatt and Jim Durkin have since added their thin edged, crystal-pinching test piece on Rho Rock called *The Rogue* (5.11d).

The Theater is a fairly undeveloped area. Routes are still being established

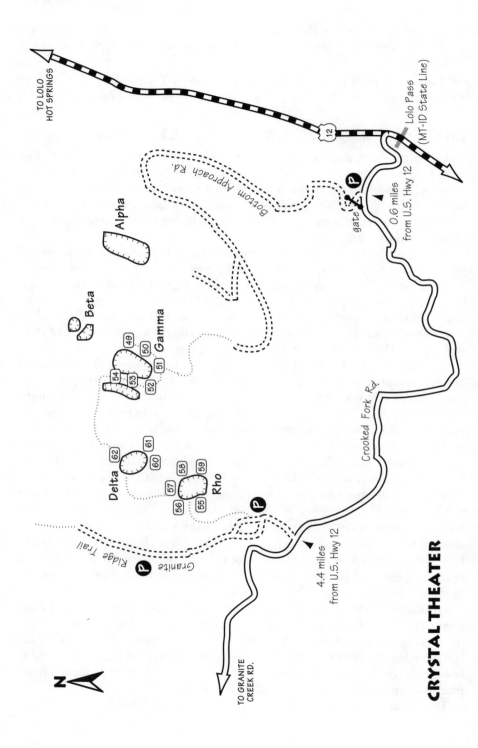

TO LOLO
HOT SPRINGS

12

Lolo Pass
(MT-ID State Line)

0.6 miles
from U.S. Hwy 12

gate

Bottom Approach Rd.

Alpha

Beta

Gamma

49
50
51
54
53
52

Delta

62
61
60

57

58
59

Rho

56
55

Crooked Fork Rd.

4.4 miles
from U.S. Hwy 12

Granite Trail

Ridge Trail

N

TO GRANITE
CREEK RD.

CRYSTAL THEATER

yearly. Currently, there are several projects underway, with Spannagel and Mac Johnson trying hard to usher in 5.12+. Crystal Theater will continue to see new route development for a long time.

Finding the rocks: Drive south from Missoula on US 93 to the town of Lolo. Turn right on US 12 and go toward Lolo Pass. Turn right on the Crooked Fork Road, which is a good graveled road less than 0.25 mile east of the visitor center at the top of Lolo Pass.

There are two approaches into Crystal Theater. The bottom approach road is the one recommended for the first-time visitor as it allows one to get a view of the Theater and a feel for the location of the rocks. The lower fork is the best approach to Alpha. The upper approach from the Granite Ridge trailhead is the easiest way to get to the upper rocks. Both are described below.

Lower approach: From US 12 continue driving up the Crooked Fork Road for about 0.6 mile. There is a hard-to-see turn off to the right on a left curve. Pull down and park by the locked gate (**do not block the gate**). Either walk or mountain bike the 3 miles into the 'Theater. There is an excellent viewpoint at the road fork in the basin. Bushwack and follow vague trails to the rock of your choice.

Upper approach: To come in from the top of Crystal Theater continue driving up the Crooked Fork Road about 4.4 miles from US 12. Turn right at a sign marking the Granite Ridge Trail. Drive about 0.25 mile or so and park before the road deteriorates and goes up a steep hill. There is an unmarked but good

Photo by Brad Hutcheson.

trail (Granite Ridge Trail) that heads off on the right through the trees. Follow this trail for about 3 to 5 minutes until it makes a hard left turn (If you go too far, you will meet up with the road again, which is part of the Granite Ridge Trail). Before the trail turns left, veer off right and contour down slightly left to the edge of the ridge. Follow a game trail or bushwack while contouring down and left into Crystal Theater. Delta with its large roof and Rho in the foreground should be visible. The approach to either of these rocks should only take about 15 to 20 minutes from your vehicle.

GAMMA

Gamma offers 1-pitch to 300' routes. The rock is one of the hardest to approach but well worth the effort. The best way for the first-time visitor is to walk or bike the lower road, staying on the upper fork at the 'Theater. When the fork ends walk uphill on old skidder trails, staying close to the ridge line. Gamma will again come into view. Cross the steep drainage when it looks good to do so and approach the rock.

The other option is to come in from the top, but there is no trail. Wander down the ridge that is a little east of Delta until Gamma is visible.

There is a small pine tree located at the north end of the summit with a permanent cable set to rappel the 60' back to the ground. Scramble around left of some large summit blocks to find the rappel station.

Photo by Brad Hutcheson.

SOUTH FACE

This the face that is visible from the lower approach road. Starting from the downhill side of the rock, it has the longest routes going to the summit. It is characterized by a steep wall at the bottom and a lower angled face above. Since all of these routes end on the summit use the 60' rappel from the tree on top to descend.

49. **Hooves and Claws** (5.10d) Two 150' pitches located on right side of wall just left of a large steep gully. Take a standard gear rack. **Pitch 1**—(5.10d) Climb past a bolt to flakes (#3 Friend useful); technical crux is passing second bolt and entering a steep layback past more bolts; when possible exit left into hand crack (#3.5 Friend useful—crack is last visible feature seen from below); mantle onto a dike and continue up and right on friction slab; 2-bolt belay near long corner system. **Pitch 2**—(5.7) Ascend the corner-crack; face moves at end lead to dirt ramp; belay from rock that juts out over face to east. **Descent:** Single-rope rappel (60') from tree at north end of summit.

50. **Friends** (5.8+) 2 pitches (165' rope mandatory, small Tri-Cams, TCUs, hand-sized cams, and #4 Friend useful to supplement bolt placements). **Pitch 1**—(5.8+) Climb vertical bolt protected dike left of HOOVES'; above dike continue face climbing to gain fist-to-hand crack and friction face to belay; 2-bolt belay at horizontal dike. **Pitch 2**—(5.8+) Continue up friction slab to top belay of HOOVES'. **Descent:** Single-rope rappel (60') from tree at north end of summit.

THE NOSE

This is the southwest foot of Gamma. This noselike, low-angled slab is located at the bottom end of the large corridor that forms the west face of Gamma. It is around to the left from the South Face.

51. **Crystal Seeker** (5.6) 2 pitches but second pitch is poorly protected and not recommended. Take a standard gear rack. Located on right side of The Nose, this climb ascends fist-to-hand crack and slab above; above crack follow bolt line to welded cold shut anchors left of steep vertical dike (belay for CELEBRATION SONG pitch 1). **Descent:** Single-rope rappel (70') from cold shuts.

52. **Celebration Song** (5.9) 2-pitch route that starts on left side of The Nose. Take quick draws, long runners, and a 1.5" nut (useful at top of vertical dike before friction slab). **Pitch 1**—(5.7) Ascend small dike past bolts to gain friction slab above and more bolts (threaded runner through pocket useful); belay from welded cold shuts left of vertical dike (top of BLACK

Photo by Brad Hutcheson.

Photo by Brad Hutcheson.

BABY). **Pitch 2**—(5.9) Climb vertical dike above belay; after steep dike continue up left on rounded arete overlooking corridor below; belay at chain anchors. **Descent:** Single-rope rappel (80') from chain anchor into The Corridor.

The Corridor

The Corridor is the wide, steep gullylike area below the west face.

53. **Black Baby** (5.8) Single-pitch line starts near lower end of The Corridor. Aptly named, it ascends large black dike to welded cold shut anchors; 3 bolts, gear (larger TCUs useful); 90'. **Descent:** Single-rope rappel from cold shuts back to Corridor.

54. **Surface Tension** (5.12) Single-pitch line starts left of BLACK BABY about midway up Corridor and ascends steep friction face; bolts, gear (small Tri-Cams and TCUs useful); 90'. **Descent:** Single-rope rappel from chain anchor back to Corridor.

RHO

From the upper (and easiest) approach, Rho is the first rock you come to (See upper approach description on Finding the rocks for details). After parking at the trailhead walk down the trail for 3 to 5 minutes. The trail will curve hard to the left. Directly before the left curve, leave the trail and angle down slope. Contour to the left/east until it is possible to look out over Crystal Theater from the ridge. Rho should be in the immediate foreground with Delta and its large roof visible behind it. Follow game trails contouring over and down to Rho.

From the lower approach enjoy climbing the steep hill to the rock from the end of the upper fork road.

North Face

From the upper/Granite Ridge approach this is the aspect first approached. It is the shortest side of the rock, about 110' to the summit. This is a great side to climb on a hot summer day as it is the cooler and shaded aspect.

55. **Rho Warrior** (5.10b) Chimney system located right of GO RHO YOUR BOAT in center of wall. This single-pitch climb is "way better" than it looks. Ascend hand, fist, then finger crack until it widens into a chimney; continue in chimney past bolts until possible to face climb waco-pocked wall to right; belay by large boulder perched on top; 110'; gear. **Descent:** Scramble up and over the boulder at belay to summit; rappel (110') from chains on northeastern corner above GO RHO YOUR BOAT anchor.

Photo by Brad Hutcheson.

56. **Go Rho Your Boat** (5.8+) First climb approached from the finger ridge leading down to Rho and the leftmost climb on face. Ascend hand-to-finger crack just right of small alcove; climb face above crack to notch and 2-bolt belay; 80'; gear. **Descent:** Single-rope rappel from bolts with runners (take extra slings to replace old rap slings if necessary).

EAST FACE

From upper approach go to the left side of the rock to gain the East Face. This can be a good place in the afternoon on a hot day because of the shade.

57. **Electric Rhoter** (5.10b R) Located about midway down the face and just uphill and right of ROGUE. Gear to 2.5" (#0.5-2 Tri-Cams, long runners supplement bolts). Protection is marginal at best on lower pocketed face with Tri-Cams (#0.5, 1, 1.5, and 2 Tri-Cams essential!) for first 45'. Head for small seam and dike below a large pocket, which has a smaller pocket inside for protection; mantle large pocket and climb to hole with white edges (first bomber pro—#1.5 Tri-Cam); continue past bolts to sloping ramp; follow ramp to large dike; an improbable 5.8 moves goes over dike onto easier ground; two belay options exist—traverse left to "hard-to-see" chain anchor set at end of ledge up high (ROGUE anchors), or continue up and traverse right to pine tree with fixed rappel cable. **Descent:** Rappel from ROGUE anchors (100') or from tree (65').

58. **The Rogue** (5.11d) Bolted face line located near left end of East Face. First 50' is sustained, difficult face climbing (edges, crystals, pockets); upper section eases to 5.9 with a 5.10 finish to chain anchors at ledge. **Descent:** Double-rope rappel (100') from chain anchor.

SOUTH FACE

The South Face is the longest aspect of Rho and is a bit convoluted.

59. **Outflow** (5.7) An unusual 2-pitch climb that is aptly named. Start in large alcove across from big flat-topped boulder and ascend large drainage gully that cleaves rock. Take a standard rack. **Pitch 1**—(5.7) Take line on white rock (left-middle side of alcove); at top of white rock and before gray pillar, friction climb past bolt and go left into chimney slot; when possible go right on steep face holds past thin vertical flakes where chimney narrows; 150'; bolts, gear; belay on flat alcove set in chimney on left above steep face. **Pitch 2**—(5.7) Climb out of alcove via short vertical section on east side to gain ramp above; follow ramp to end and exit left onto summit; belay where convenient; 70'. **Descent:** Scramble up and over large perched boulder to true summit; Rappel (110') from chains located on northeast corner.

DELTA

Located in the upper end of Crystal Theater, Delta is easily recognized by the large 40' roof on the south side of the rock. The best way to approach it is from the Granite Ridge trailhead (see "Finding the rocks" for details). From the trailhead walk 3 to 5 minutes down the trail until it takes a hard left. Just before the trail turns left wander down and contour left to the edge of the ridge. Almost immediately, Delta and Rho should be visible to the side and below. Follow game trails that contour around and down to Rho, which is in the foreground with Delta behind it. From Rho contour again to the left, crossing the small drainage up high that separates Delta from Rho. Head down the ridge to Delta.

From the bottom approach road follow the upper fork until the road ends. Head straight up to Delta.

WEST FACE

This is the face that is seen when entering Crystal Theater from the top. This 270' face is around to the left of the large roof. This is the warmest aspect of Delta and often hot in summer.

Photo by Brad Hutcheson.

60. **Sundance** (5.11c) 3-pitch route near right end of face. Take a standard rack to 3" (TCUs, #4 Friend useful) and two ropes for the descent. **Pitch 1**—(5.9) Ascend steep layback corner protected by bolts leads to lower angled slab above; 110'; 9 bolts; belay at chain anchor. **Pitch 2**—(5.11c) Follow bolt line on steep face to "dicey" traverse on small dike; gain finger-to-hand crack and belay above on sloping ledge at prominent horizontal crack (visible above the main roof); 100'. **Pitch 3**—(5.9+) Ascend groove to the right of the belay; belay from chains; 70'. **Descent:** 2 rappels; (90') from chains at top of pitch 3 to chains at top of pitch 1 and (110') to ground from top of pitch 1.

61. **Gravy Dog** (5.11b) Long single-pitch face route right of SUNDANCE just before rounding corner to south face. Ascend thin "pinchy" laybacks past small horizontal breaks to gain lower-angled face above, eventually leading to good edges on easier ground; 150'; bolts, gear (TCUs useful). **Descent:** Double-rope rappel (110') from top of SUNDANCE pitch 1.

EAST FACE

Around to the right of the large roof on Delta is the East Face. This can be a pleasant place to climb on a hot summer day as it gets shade early.

62. **White Line** (5.10a) Follows obvious crack line in white corner, which starts at blocky lower end of wall and angles right. Climb wide cracks and blocks to flat area; angle right into seam on white rock—rock quality improves after a few moves as does the pro; follow crack to its end and step right at roof to small shelf and belay; 130'; gear. **Descent:** Single-rope rappel (85') from chain anchor.

KOOTENAI CANYON

OVERVIEW

This popular Bitterroot canyon contains many fine climbs and has one of the highest concentrations of quality routes in the area. With its densely packed cliffs, beautiful creek, scenic trail, and an abundance of excellent climbs, a trip to Kootenai Canyon can be a memorable experience. However, due to these factors and its close proximity to Missoula, this area receives a great deal of traffic, by climbers and non-climbers alike. It is not uncommon for many of the popular climbs to be continuously occupied during a sunny weekend, especially when the University of Montana in Missoula is in session.

It is important to note that most of the established routes in Kootenai Canyon are on private land. The landowner has graciously allowed access and

Matthew Taylor and Rafael Grana (with help from Ivan Pyatt, Jim Durkin, Tobin Kelley, and others) provided the information for this section.

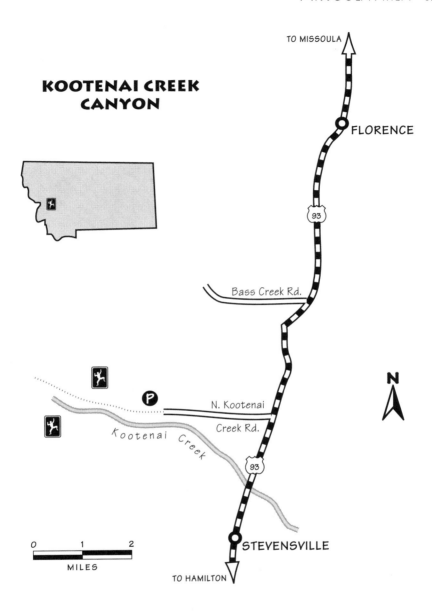

KOOTENAI CREEK CANYON

has expressed support of the local climbing community. **This access is a privilege, not a right, and we must do all we can to ensure our actions do not reverse such graciousness.** Without a doubt, we have both the ability and technology to significantly decrease our impact on the land and its users. These are the greatest resources we have as climbers to ensure the future of our sport, for ourselves and those who follow.

Matt Taylor on *11th Commandment*, First Buttress.
Photo by Randall Green.

The routes mentioned here are only a sampling of the many fine lines available. Numerous historic and scenic climbs see little traffic or are tucked away and have been excluded from this guide, left instead as little gems for the ambitious and persistent climber. The rock is metamorphic gneiss, generally of excellent quality (unless noted otherwise). However, loose rock is not uncommon on many of the less-traveled lines and often encountered in the development of new climbs. In most instances a single 165-foot rope is adequate for toproping and leading.

A typical **standard rack** for Kootenai should include about 10-12 slings/quick draws, a full set of wires, camming units up to 2.5", and small to medium Tri-Cams. Always back-up anchors when possible.

Climbing history: Kootenai Canyon has a long and colorful history that predates many other Montana climbing areas. Since the mid-1970s this area has seen numerous first ascents by some of the finest climbers in the state. The late Marvin McDonald published the first guide pamphlet to the canyon in 1980. McDonald, along with such notables as Alex Lowe, Tobin Kelley, Bill Dockins, Michael Scott, Kurt Kleiner, and many others, helped pave the way for climbers today. These early Bitterroot climbers established such classics as *Ironmonger* (5.8), *Outermost Limits* (5.8), *Pleasant Surprise* (5.8+), *Arms Race* (5.9+), *Flying Time* (5.10d), and *Wiener Pigs* (5.11a) to name a few. Many of the early routes are considered underrated by today's standards, attesting to the skill and grit of these pioneers. Some routes have been rediscovered and retrobolted. For example, the second pitch of what is now known as *The Dude* was originally free climbed by Lowe and Dockins in the early-mid 1980s with one piton and natural gear; the route now bristles with bolts.

The advent of sport climbing shifted the focus from obvious crack lines to many of the canyon's classic face routes. In 1989 the combined efforts of Ivan Pyatt and Jim Durkin established the technical route *Root Canal* (5.11 c/d). With the arrival of this and other similar climbs, it seemed a new era was dawning in the canyon. In the past two years Pyatt, Durkin, Richard Plummer, Chris Randolph, John Burbidge, and others have developed new climbs, pushing the 5.12 envelope. Pyatt established the canyon test-piece, *Venus Fly Trap* (5.12d/5.13a, first redpointed by Jason Riley in 1994). Once again it seems this canyon has made its way toward the forefront of Montana climbing.

Ethics: In light of the traffic this canyon receives and its visibility to the broader population, it is critical that climbers minimize their impact as much as possible if we are to continue having access to such a wonderful area. A great deal of effort has been put into the establishment and upkeep of trails, especially by Rick Torre and other Bitterroot locals. Cutting switchbacks to save time or creating new paths without serious forethought can lead to an unsightly and redundant web of trails and cause significant erosion. **Please respect the land and the outstanding efforts of those before you by staying on obvious trails and contributing to the healthy maintenance of these paths.**

The placement of fixed protection, whether it be bolts, pins, or sport anchors, is serious business with serious impacts, especially in an area as visible as Kootenai Canyon. The "unnecessary" placement of such equipment is a surefire way to stir controversy. Only through a sense of "minimal impact" can we ensure continued access. This includes the use of camouflaged webbing and anchors so as not to attract the attention of hikers and landowners. Furthermore, the placement of bolts should occur only when clean, safe protection is unavailable or very difficult. The solution to ethical dilemmas in climbing lies in forethought and respect, not in extreme and often scarring "improvements" on established climbs through the process of "chipping" and "chopping."

Think before you drill or hammer. Ask yourself these questions: Can this route go free? Where can the best clip be made? What is the visual impact and how can it be reduced? Are natural anchors safe and accessible? Finally, be sure to consult the first ascensionists (if possible) before altering any established climb.

One area of particular concern is the first (east) half of the Identity Wall (right of *Cube Root*, left of the obvious hump in the trail to Boardwalk Ledge) due to the presence of historic and sacred Native American pictographs. Previously established climbs in this area have been removed and it is extremely likely that any attempt to establish new climbs here, or re-bolt old ones, would result in similar actions. In order to preserve these important artifacts, **this area is off-limits to climbing and bouldering.**

The notion of respect and no-trace techniques must also extend beyond the climbs themselves: dispose of human waste properly (see Introduction for no-trace tips); be courteous to all other people who share the canyon as well as the plants and animals that live there; use established trails to minimize visual and ecological impact.

Trip Planning Information

Area description: Scenic, narrow canyon with numerous sport and traditional climbs on generally solid, high- and low-grade metamorphosed granite, with short approaches and well-marked trails.

General location: About 30 miles south of Missoula in the Bitterroot Mountains near Stevensville.

Camping: The closest public camping can be found one canyon north of Kootenai Canyon in the Charles Waters Recreation area at the mouth of Bass Creek. Campsites are free and numerous; however, a seven-day limit is imposed.

Climbing season: Due to the narrow nature of the canyon, climbing is generally three-season. But sections of the first buttress and the Boardwalk Ledge

Rafael Grana on *Elmo*, Outermost Limits Wall.
Photo by Randall Green.

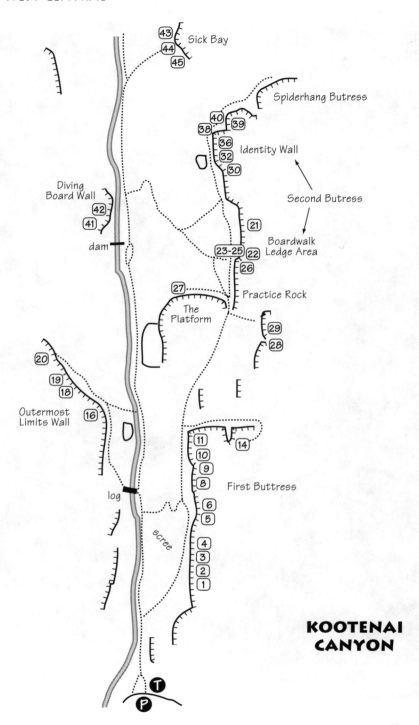

Sick Bay

Spiderhang Butress

Identity Wall

Second Butress

Diving
Board Wall

dam

Boardwalk
Ledge Area

Practice Rock

The
Platform

Outermost
Limits Wall

First Buttress

log

scree

**KOOTENAI
CANYON**

area of the second buttress receive year-round sun and can provide wonderful cold-weather climbing.

Restrictions and access issues: The trailhead, most of the climbing routes, and the surrounding land is privately owned. Open fire restrictions may apply during dry periods. Do not climb on rocks with Indian pictographs (see Ethics section above).

Other guidebooks: *Bitterroot Guidebook* by Rick Torre.

Nearby mountain shops, guide services, and climbing gyms: Canyon Critters, Hamilton; Pipestone Mountaineering (retail, rental, and instruction), Missoula; The Trailhead (retail and rental), Missoula; Hold-On (climbing gym, retail, instruction, and rental), Missoula; University of Montana indoor climbing wall, Missoula.

Finding the canyon: From Missoula drive about 30 miles south on U.S. Highway 93 until rounding a large, left bend in the road next to the Bitterroot River. On the right side of the highway there is a huge open field with an obvious line of trees at its southern end. The row of trees is where North Kootenai Road is located, just before Stevensville. Turn right onto the graveled road at the sign and continue about 2 miles to the trailhead.

First Buttress (a.k.a. Ironmonger Wall)

This is the first prominent buttress on the north (right) side of the trail located about as 5-minute walk from the trailhead. The approach for this buttress is found near the far end of the talus field next to the main trail. Follow a path to the base of wall (*11th Commandment* and *Fire Drill*). Turn right to go toward *My Favorite Hangout* and *The BRIK* (Best Route In Kootenai). To find the Town Pump area go left along the base of the wall and uphill, following the loose gully until an obvious large pine at the base of a prominent chimney.

1. **My Favorite Hangout** (5.9+ R) 2-pitch climb up obvious right-leaning crack. **Pitch 1**—(5.9+) Ascend crack to small belay alcove; 80'. **Pitch 2**—(5.9+) Climb up and right to ledge, traverse awkward ledge left to comfortable belay stance; 50'. Finish on exposed 4th-class scrambling on loose rock finishes this old-time classic. Gear to 3". **Descent:** Walk off right or left up and around TOWN PUMP.

2. **Low Fat Turkey Dog** (5.12 c/d) Begins in the same place as 'HANGOUT, but stem left across into dihedral section; continue past flakes and more stemming to awkward moves near anchor; 6 bolts; 55'. **Descent:** Rappel from 2-bolt anchor.

3. **The BRIK/Best Route In Kootenai** (5.12c) Begin 50' left of 'HANGOUT below obvious overhang. Climb easy ground then crank through well-protected, strenuous overhang; continue up sustained, steep climbing to anchor; 9 bolts; 70'. **Descent:** Rappel from 2-bolt anchor.

Several "projects" are located to the right of 'BRIK.

4. **Uncontrollable Desire** (5.11 a/b) Begin 10' left of 'BRIK. Climb up and left to fixed pin below small overhanging corner; continue past bolt (first crux), moving left around obvious roof past fixed pin; climb steep face then pull slight bulge left (second crux) and up sustained moves with bolts and natural protection to belay (gear/tree); 7 bolts, pins, and gear (small wires, TCUs useful); 150'. **Descent:** Walk off left up and around TOWN PUMP.

5. **Fire Drill** (5.11b) Begin at top of approach trail near obvious right-leaning weakness. Climb strenuous seam past 3 bolts to stance, then step left and continue face climbing to anchors; 8 bolts; 80'. **Descent:** Rappel from 2-bolt anchor.

6. **11th Commandment** (5.10a) Begin 10' left of FIRE DRILL. Climb overhanging rock past 3 bolts (crux) and continue to FIRE DRILL anchors; 7 bolts, gear (TCUs optional for traverse move after 5th bolt); 80'. **Descent:** Rappel from 2-bolt anchor.

7. **Warpig** (5.12c/d) Climb left from start of 11th and move up and left past 3 bolts (crux); continue up steep face to anchor; 9 bolts; 85'. **Descent:** Rappel from 2-bolt anchor.

8. **Look Out It's 10d** (5.10b) Begin just right of IRONMONGER. Boulder start to first bolt then continue to third bolt at roof; pull roof (crux) and continue up and right past bolts to anchor; 5 bolts, gear (TCUs optional for end); 60'. **Descent:** Rappel from 2-bolt anchor.

Photo by Matt Taylor.

9. **Ironmonger** (5.8 R) 2 pitches. Prominent left-facing corner and crack line. **Pitch 1**—(5.8 R) Climb out under roof and continue past small tree in incipient crack; move left and up through shattered rock, then right to obvious pine in corner; 150'. **Pitch 2**—(5.8) Continue up to well-protected corner, then traverse left and pull roof, continue up and right past small pine; 70'. **Descent:** Walk off left around Town Pump area.

10. **Botulism** (5.11a/b) Begin 15' left of IRONMONGER. Climb straight up through awkward overhangs protected by 3 bolts, step right and up near seam and bolts to anchor; 5 bolts; 50'. **Descent:** Rappel from 2-bolt anchor.

11. **The Corner** (5.6 R) 2 pitches; 250'. Route follows left edge of first buttress; dubious (loose) rock and creative protection; belay at ledge and continue left of orange face to top of buttress. **Descent:** Walk off left past Town Pump area.

12. **Kyle's 12** (5.12+) Start on ledge 20' left of belay tree at top of IRONMONGER pitch 1. Climb sustained, thin face moves past 5 bolts to anchor; 5 bolts; 60'. **Descent:** Two rappels; single-rope rappel from 2-bolt anchor on top to 2-bolt anchor on ledge; double-rope rappel to ground (130').

13. **Rockwork Orange** (5.11b/c) Single-pitch route up orange face near top of buttress. From ledge at two-thirds height on wall (accessible via 'CORNER or IRONMONGER) follow jug line to gain orange face (crux); 3 bolts, gear (TCUs, med wires useful); 70'. **Descent:** Walk off left past Town Pump area.

Photo by Matt Taylor..

14. **Town Pump** (5.11a) Line ascends steep wall of south-facing corner left of obvious wide chimney on west end of buttress. Face climb and pull crux bulge move to anchors; 6 bolts, pin; 70'. **Descent:** Walk off left and descend gully.

There are two enjoyable toprope cracks (5.8+??) to the right of TOWN PUMP on right wall of chimney.

15. **High Wire** (5.7) Start 10' left of TOWN PUMP. Climb steep face with good holds past 2 bolts and good wire placement to ledge; continue up corner or right-leaning crack (better) to top; 2 bolts, gear to 3"; 70'. **Descent:** Walk off left into gully.

OUTERMOST LIMITS WALL

This is the popular wall located on the south side of the creek and is the second significant climbing site located off the trail. The routes listed here offer wonderful, shaded climbing on hot summer days and have the added bonus of a refreshing walk across the stream or an interesting log crossing, depending on conditions.

To access the wall continue on the main trail past First Buttress until you can see a shaded, orange-colored cliff across the creek that faces slightly northwest up the canyon. Descend off the trail and wade the stream (**It's dangerous to ford the creek during spring runoff**), or backtrack toward the trailhead on the main trail to a log crossing; continue to a small talus field at the base of the cliff.

Photo by Matt Taylor.

The popular climb *Outermost Limits* is at the left end of cliff below the orange face and around the corner from a prominent overhang.

16. **Outermost Limits** (5.8) Pleasant and well-protected climb that begins right of prominent overhang and goes past horizontal cracks to delicate face moves on red rock; anchor in corner; 2 bolts, gear (medium wires and cams useful); 40' (second pitch not recommended). **Descent:** Rappel from anchor.

17. **Lichen to Fly** (5.10d) Located below left facing roof, 25' right of OUTERMOST LIMITS. Climb thin horizontal cracks to bolt at roof (crux) and continue up thin face to anchors; bolts, gear to 1.5" (TCUs very useful; 90'. **Descent:** Rappel from chain anchor.

18. **Elmo** (5.10b) Start 15' right of LICHEN TO FLY and up broken arete. Climb past 2 bolts and pull awkward bulge (first crux) into horizontal crack (TCU pro.); continue up arete and move right (second crux) past 2 bolts to belay on left; 4 bolts, gear (small wires, TCUs useful); 85'. **Descent:** Rappel from fixed pin-sling anchors.

19. **Sleeping Beauty** (5.9) Start right of ELMO on smooth, clean face holds past first bolt and awkward bulge (first crux) to easier climbing and several bolts; traverse up and right (medium cam optional) to slight arete; continue past 2 bolts (second crux) to anchor; 7 bolts, gear (medium cam optional); 75'. **Descent:** Rappel from 2-bolt anchor.

20. **Roofus** (5.11 c/d) Located uphill 30' from SLEEPING BEAUTY near large pine. Climb steep face past first overhang to layback moves and awkward alcove; continue up and right past sustained, strenuous roofs (crux) to anchor; 7 bolts; 80'. **Descent:** Rappel from 2-bolt anchor.

Numerous bouldering problems exist under the large overhang around the corner, and left of *Outermost Limits*

SECOND BUTTRESS (A.K.A BOARDWALK LEDGE)

The second prominent buttress located up and right on the north side of the canyon. It is visible a few minutes beyond the Outermost Limits Wall after passing under a large overhanging rock directly next to the main trail.

Approach the Second Buttress by continuing on the main trail just past a clearing and a diversion dam on the left. A well-worn path branches off the main trail to the right and ascends the hillside toward the cliffs. Continue on this trail as it switchbacks and traverses upward.

To approach the Identity Wall and *Classic Crack* area take a steep, secondary trail (departs up and left) beyond a downed tree. To gain the Boardwalk Ledge area continue up approach trail to a bench below an obvious saddle. *Pleasant Surprise*, *Venus deMilo*, and surrounding climbs are located on the large face up and left. Look for an obvious left-slanting ramp system (Board-

Photo by Matt Taylor.

walk Ledge). Scramble (5.3) 20' up shallow gully to the lower end of the ramp. This point puts you at the base of *Venus*.

21. **Pleasant Surprise** (5.8) Wonderfully exposed and well-protected climb ascends obvious dihedral. Begin near the far, left end of the main ledge/ramp area on a small arete; climb past thin, diagonal crack to good moves with 3 bolts and pull awkward move to gain horn and continue to first roof; pull exposed first roof with good pro and continue through similar second roof to top; belay from gear and tree; 3 bolts, gear to 2.5"; 80'. **Descent:** Walk off right.

22. **Ball and Chain** (5.12 c/d) Steep, sustained climb follows bolt line 30' right of PLEASANT SURPRISE. Climb up left-facing corner then left on face to second bolt and awkward bulge; climb right over slight roof and continue up and left to anchors; 6 bolts; 70'. **Descent:** Rappel from 2-bolt anchor.

23. **I Cling** (5.10c) Prominent left-facing corner with a thin crack that diagonals through a large roof system located about 35' left of VENUS FLY TRAP and just left of where the scramble approach to Boardwalk Ledge ends. Climb crack/face past old 1/4" bolt to base of roof; continue over roof with strenuous underclings past a fixed stopper and escape right on positive holds to easier climbing and gear belay; 1 bolt, 1 fixed piece, gear to 2"; 80'. **Descent:** Walk off right.

24. **Venus Fly Trap** (5.12d/5.13a) Directly left of VENUS DEMILO. Climb steep, sustained, and overhanging face; 7 bolts; 65'. **Descent:** Rappel from chain anchors.

25. **Venus deMilo** (5.11d) This popular climb ascends obvious overhanging face right of VENUS FLY TRAP. Move right and climb over roof to anchor; 6 bolts; 60'. **Descent:** Rappel from 2-bolt anchor.

26. **Flies on Shit** (5.11b) Start 30' right of VENUS DEMILO, around small outside corner. Climb arete past 3 bolts to rest stance and continue right through overhangs to anchor; 6 bolts; 50'. **Descent:** Rappel from 2-bolt anchor.

Several popular routes are located right of the Boardwalk Ledge near the prominent saddle with a ponderosa pine, which has an old rusty mailbox on it.

Practice Rock is a 35' cliff just left of the saddle, below a large obvious pine (good toprope anchor and easy to get to above the saddle). Climb any one of numerous variations to pine tree ledge (5.4-5.6).

27. **Flying Time** (5.10d) Located down and right of saddle below Boardwalk Ledge area on obvious overhanging cliff. This spectacular and strenuous overhanging climb ascends the center of the overhanging face. Begin on ledge next to large leaning pine; easy climbing leads to more difficult moves and first bolt; pull strenuous bulges with long reaches to second bolt and continue up and right with positive holds past remaining bolts to anchors under roof; 5 bolts; 65'. **Descent:** Rappel from chains or scramble left over top to saddle.

28. **Captain Ging** (5.9 depending on variation—easier variant is on right). This short, popular climb is found above the saddle at east end of Board-walk Ledge area. At tree with mailbox, scramble up and slightly left until small cliff is visible up and right. The route ascends the obvious short arete. Climb past 4 well-positioned bolts to 2-bolt anchor; 4 bolts; 40'. **Descent:** Walk off left or right.

29. **Charlie's Overhang** (5.9) Short but pleasant problem directly left of NOSE. Climb clean face past one bolt to roof with bolt (crux) and continue to gear or webbing anchors; 2 bolts; 35'. **Descent:** Walk off right or left.

IDENTITY WALL

This area contains a high concentration of excellent climbs, which generally provide challenging and interesting leads. It is also possible, although awkward and slightly dangerous, to set up toprope anchors on several of the climbs (see end of Identity Wall section).

The approach trail, described under Second Buttress, goes to the far right end of the Identity Wall proper. Follow the wall left about 100' (near large boulder). The following climbs are listed from right to left as encountered along the trail.

30. **Cube Root** (5.10c) Difficult to protect on lead. Begin with easy climbing up large crack in short left-facing corner onto face split by thin crack; awkward moves past bulges gain ledge with anchor; gear (small wires and TCUs); 50'. **Descent:** Rappel from 2-bolt anchor.

31. **Root Canal** (5.11c/d) Sustained climb with technical moves on thin, crimper holds left of CUBE'. Climb clean face to easier climbing; anchors shared with CUBE'; 4 bolts; 50'. **Descent:** Rappel.

32. **Square Root** (5.9) Ascends obvious left-leaning crack that diagonals across center of wall. Climb white face up and right through flaring crack; continue up into main diagonal crack system with bulges and difficult protection; exit right to CUBE' anchors; gear (medium cams, wires, and TCUs useful); 50'. **Descent:** Rappel.

33. **Identity Crack** (5.10c/d) Climb SQUARE ROOT as described then continue left up strenuous finger crack to anchor on small ledge below roof; gear (medium cams, wires, and TCUs useful); 65'. **Descent:** Rappel from chains.

34. **Identity Crisis** (5.11b) Climb clean face left of SQUARE ROOT past 3 bolts into IDENTITY CRACK; continue to anchor; 3 bolts, gear (wires, and TCUs mandatory); 55'. **Descent:** Rappel from chains.

35. **The Dude** (5.11b) 2 pitches. **Pitch 1**—(5.11b) Boulder start to bolt at flake; climb past discontinuous cracks (crux) to belay; 1 bolt, gear (wires, Friends, Tri Cams, and TCUs useful); 55'. **Descent:** Rappel or climb second pitch. **Pitch 2**—(5.11b) From anchors at top of first pitch follow bolt line up left-facing corner past fixed pin; step left and go over roof and continue up steep face/arete to chain anchors; 9 bolts, pin; 120'. **Descent:** Double-rope rappel to ledge from chains; single-rope rappel to ground, **or** single-rope rappel to DUDE RANCH anchors, continue second rappel to ledge, and finally, third rappel to ground.

36. **Wiener Pigs** (5.10+/.11-) Boulder start to critical 2.5" cam placement and continue up thin finger/hand crack to ledge with bush (directional) and traverse right on ledge to anchor on west-facing wall; gear to 2.5"; 55'. **Descent:** Rappel from 2-bolt anchor.

37. **Dude Ranch** (5.11a) From 2-bolt anchor on large ledge with bush (above ARMS RACE) climb bolt line out to arete and continue past overhang to anchor; 5 bolts; 60'. **Descent:** Rappel from 2-bolt anchor to anchors on ledge; rappel again to base of Identity Wall.

The following climbs are located around the corner, at the far left end of Identity Wall:

38. **Arms Race** (5.9+) Overhanging diagonal crack on west-facing wall around corner left of DUDE RANCH. Easy climbing leads to obvious crack; belay at ledge with bush; gear to 2.5"; 40'. **Descent:** Rappel from 2-bolt anchor at far right end of ledge on west face.

39. **Thing in Between** (5.8) Climb obvious left-facing corner with bulge and fun overhang with jugs; continue past small bush to easy climbing and large ledge for belay (gear/natural anchors); gear; 50'. **Descent:** Walk off left.

40. **Classic Crack** (5.7) This popular climb ascends prominent right-facing corner system next to THING IN BETWEEN. Climb crack (good protection), step right, and go up to large ledge for belay (gear/natural anchors); gear; 50'. **Descent:** Walk off left.

DIVING BOARD WALL

The Diving Board Wall is located on the south side of the creek next to the dam, which is described in the approach for the Second Buttress. Cross creek and belay at creekside.

41. **High Dive** (5.10b/c) Located on left side of wall. Ascend steep bolt line to final overhangs, gain dirty, sloping ledge with anchor; 7 bolts; 60'. **Descent:** Rappel from 2-bolt anchor.

42. **Dumpster Dive** (5.11a) Next line right of HIGH DIVE. Climb thin face with 3 bolts (close together); continue up to easier climbing, go left then right with gear to more strenuous moves past 2 bolts to anchor; gear (small-medium wires and TCUs useful); 65'. **Descent:** Rappel from 2-bolt anchor.

SICK BAY AREA

Continue on the mainKootenai Canyon Trail 300' beyond the approach trail to Second Buttress. The Sick Bay is visible up and right/north from trail. Scramble north uphill from the main trail to an obvious overhanging rock or "ceiling" formation with a large pine at its base. Climbs are listed from left to right.

43. **Doctor Dick** (5.12/A0) Lefthand bolt line with crux near anchors; 5 bolts; 45'. **Descent:** Rappel from chains.

44. **Smokin' Joe Tahoe** (5.12+) Center line of bolts. Climb straight up and out roof with crux lunge after final bolt; 6 bolts; 45'. **Descent:** Rappel from 2-bolt anchor.

45. **Clubfoot** (5.12b/c) Begin 5' right of SMOKIN' JOE. Climb up and right along horizontal jugs with crux move between 3rd and 4th bolt, continue right past roof to 2-bolt chain anchor; 7 bolts; 45'. **Descent:** Rappel from chains.

MILL CREEK CANYON

OVERVIEW

Mill Creek is a spectacular, broad glacial canyon, typical of the Bitterroot Mountain Range. The drainage is an entrance to the immense Selway Bitterroot Wilderness, and is located near the town of Hamilton. The majority of rock is found high on the north side of the drainage, with a warm, sunny southern exposure. This can make for lovely late season climbing when the sun is shining. Some of the most dramatic features in the canyon are the long, jagged aretes jutting away from broad, beautiful walls. In general, the quality of the metamorphic granite found here is good. However, due to the undeveloped nature of the canyon, only fools would venture on any new or multi-pitch route without a helmet due to loose rock.

The expanse of rock here is amazing. But a heart-pounding approach is required to reach the base of the main faces. Even the sport routes on the Pro/Gray Wall, which typically offer sustained climbing in the 5.11 range, have long, arduous approaches. In general, the approaches to any climb in Mill Creek can be somewhat confusing to the newcomer due to the intricate nature of the cliffs. These factors should be weighed when considering your plans for the day. Nonetheless, if you are comfortable leading that grade, and an aerobic hike doesn't bother you, then these climbs may provide a memorable day in a beautiful setting.

The high-quality climbs on Pro/Gray Wall, which are a testament to skill and aesthetics, were established in 1990 entirely by Jim Durkin and Ivan Pyatt.

A standard rack for Mill Creek Canyon should include a wide selection of wired stoppers from small RP/HB nuts up, TCUs, nuts/chocks, cams, slings, and quick draws. A rack of quick draws will suffice for recommended routes on the Pro/Gray Wall. Although it is possible to walk off from the tops of many multi-pitch climbs, all of the routes on Pro/Gray Wall require two 50m ropes for the descents.

Ethics: It is the responsibility of each individual climber to minimize impacts in order to preserve this canyon in its wild state. Due to the steepness of the approaches and the amount of scree and loose vegetation, it is particularly important that climbers be sensitive to erosion control when creating and using climbing trails. Furthermore, the use of natural-colored webbing at fixed anchors and escape points. It is important to note that a wilderness boundary exists not far beyond the Pro/Gray Wall area. Care must be taken to avoid raptor nesting areas. Without a doubt, it is critical that climbers, now more than ever, be conscious of their impacts if we are to continue climbing in pristine settings like the Bitterroot.

▲▲ –

Matthew Taylor and Brian Hatfield (with invaluable review comments by Ivan Pyatt and Jim Durkin) provided the text, maps, and photos for this section.

MILL CREEK & BLODGETT CREEK CANYONS

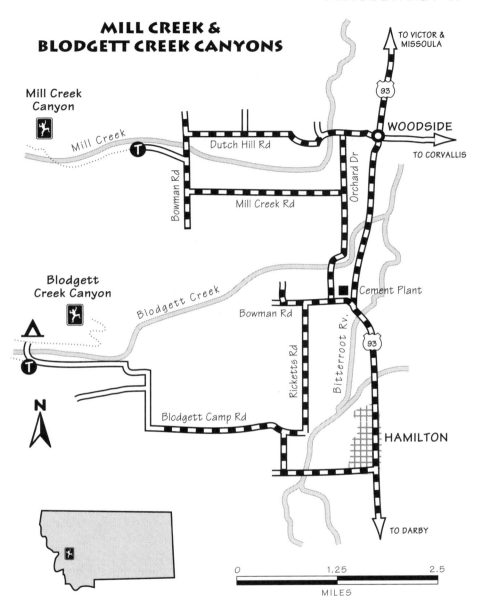

Trip Planning Information

Area description: Broad glacial valley with multi-pitch sport and traditional climbs on large, south-facing metamorphic granite walls.

General location: About 40 miles south of Missoula and 3 miles north of Hamilton, in the Bitterroot Mountains; one drainage north of Blodgett Canyon.

John Webb on *Homer the Hack Trap* in Mill Creek. *Photo by Matt Taylor.*

Camping: The closest developed campground is at the mouth of Blodgett Canyon. No services are provided except a cold outhouse. Water taken from the creek must be purified. There are six sites with fire rings and picnic tables. Camping is free with a 5-day limit; the campground is usually full on weekend nights in the summer.

Climbing season: Year-round climbing is possible since most routes are south-facing, but late spring and early fall may be the most pleasant. No Sweat Arete provides a challenging winter ascent for the aspiring alpinist; 5.7 can take on new meaning in plastic boots!

Restrictions and/or access issues: The Selway-Bitterroot Wilderness boundary is closer to the trailhead in this canyon than in many other drainages. Officially, this occurs just after the Tag Alder Lake drainage on the south side of the canyon (not far beyond the Pro/Gray Wall area). Bitterroot Wilderness restrictions presently apply to the use of mechanized equipment and human "improvements." Outside of this boundary the climbing is entirely on national forest land.

Nearby mountain shops, guide services, and gyms: Canyon Critters (retail), Hamilton; Pipestone Mountaineering (retail and group/private instruction), Missoula; The Trailhead, (retail) Missoula; Hold-On (climbing gym, retail, instruction, and rental), Missoula.

Finding the area: From Missoula drive south on U.S. Highway 93 about 40 miles (or N from Hamilton) to the Dutch Hill Road turnoff. Along US 93 there is a southbound sign for Mill Creek (the Woodside Country Store and Gas is at the intersection). Turn right/west on Dutch Hill Road and continue about 2 miles to a "T" intersection with Bowman Road. Turn left and continue 0.5 mile to the turnoff for Mill Creek Trail 64 (Forest Road 1328). Turn right and continue on FR 1328, which is a good dirt road until reaching the trailhead.

Follow the trail across the creek on a well-made hiker's bridge. Beyond this take the left fork and continue following the creek until huge cliffs are visible up and to the right. From the trail, sight the ridge line of the first major rock wall and continue up and west (left) until you see a prominent tree directly above a buttress that is roughly 700 feet high. Directly below this is the location of *Dihedrals East.*

To approach to *No Sweat Arete* and Pro/Gray Wall continue on the main trail until reaching a slight clearing that is about even with the end of the first wall and the beginning of the second. There is a lightning-scarred dead tree on the left side of trail and a steep scree/washout on the right side. At this point you have gone too far; double back about 150' to a faint climber's trail that winds through the brush on the north side of the main trail. Hiking time to this point takes about 35-45 minutes from the car, at a moderate pace. The approach trail becomes more prominent as it climbs away from the main trail and the creek. The trail leads to a point where *No Sweat Arete* looms up and right, and the Pro/Gray Wall is out of sight to the left.

1. **Dihedrals East** (III 5.10) A 5-pitch climb up main dihedral system in the Canyon. The approach is somewhat confusing but once on route the climb is relatively straightforward with good protection and pleasant exposure. In general the rock quality is good, although some sections may be dirty. Standard rack to 3.5".

   Approach: Base of Dihedrals East is located at the end of a ledge/ramp system that angles up from east side of buttress. To access the ramp hike about 0.25 mile past the pack bridge on the main trail and turn right through the brush (near where trail is close to a prominent log jam in the creek). Beginning of the ramp is about 250' above the trail. Follow this ledge/ramp system up and west to the highest ramp below the buttress; this requires some doubling back, traversing along narrow ledges, and fourth- class scrambling. At the highest and west-most point on the ledge, a prominent left-facing outside corner system becomes visible above. **Pitch 1**—(5.8) Set belay near small juniper bush; traverse out to corner (about 75') and move up and around arete into a left-facing dihedral; belay on blocky, loose ledges below and right of small roof. **Pitch 2**—(5.10) Move up and left pulling past small roof (crux) into long dihedral with thin finger crack, which opens to 4"; belay on right ledge at rope's end. **Pitch 3**—(5.9 R) Step left of rotten dihedral, climbing dirty face (very small wires useful); once under roof, traverse left to arete; continue up arete or loose, left-facing corner (5.6) until gaining large, "Sundown Ledge" below obvious corner. **Pitch 4**—(5.9)

From ledge climb obvious dihedral, pulling past small bulge until below slight roof; continue up and left, following finger crack to sloping ledge below corner system with bush; climb crack then traverse left through blocks and layback crack until gaining "Moonrise Terrace" up and right near rope's end. **Pitch 5**—(5.9+) Ascend left-facing corner (tricky start) and short off-

Photo by Matt Taylor.

DIHEDRALS EAST

III 5.10
standard gear
rack to 3.5"

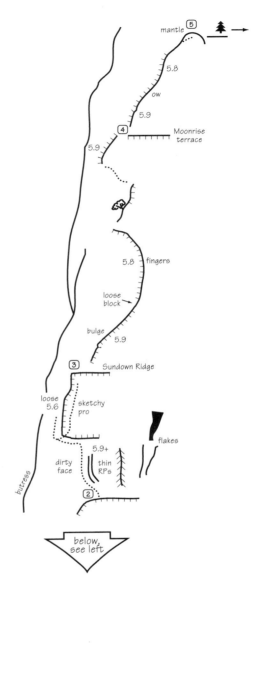

mantle ⑤

5.8

ow

5.9

④ Moonrise
terrace

5.9

5.8 fingers

loose
block

bulge 5.9

③ Sundown Ridge

loose
5.6

sketchy
pro

5.9+

flakes

dirty
face

thin
RPs

②

buttress

below,
see left

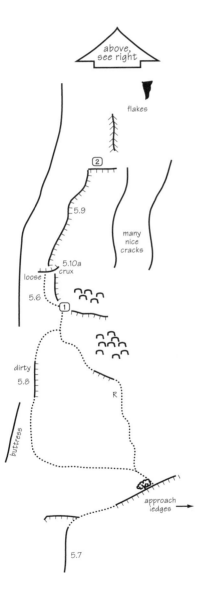

above,
see right

flakes

②

5.9

many
nice
cracks

5.10a
crux

loose

5.6

①

dirty

5.8

R

buttress

approach
ledges

5.7

width bulge (#4 Camalot useful); continue up large crack and mantle (easy) onto a car-sized block for a wonderful ending; belay at pine. **Descent:** Walk off right/east down main ramp toward the mouth of the canyon to gain valley floor.

2. **No Sweat Arete**—(III 5.7-5.9) or Lowe variation (5.10) An interesting climb, which at times has an adventuresome alpine ridge feel. Rock quality varies from marginal to surprisingly good. Due to the number of crack systems ascending the true arete and the left side of the west face, numerous route options are possible. Because of these characteristics, this climb has been the site of numerous adventures. In winter the route can be a memorable experience.

   Because of the numerous crack systems present and to maintain a spirit of adventure, only a general description is given here. The specifics of the climb will be worked out by individual experience. Wear a helmet and bring a head lamp.

   Approach: Ascend faint path that departs from the main hiking trail (see "Finding the area"). The approach trail skirts the right side of prominent scree/boulder slope that is highly prone to erosion. As the approach path becomes more obvious, it reaches two large, dead trees. Continue up, meandering to a prominent grassy ledge. At this point turn right (left trail leads to Gray Wall) and scramble up corner system past small trees until gaining talus. Continue up talus to base of Arete or scramble up and right to gain West Face.

   Climb one of the three variants (2a-2c) to the major ledge and walk off right toward the descent gully:

2a. **Arete** (5.7) 3-4 pitches, roughly following cracks along the arete to ledge where it is possible to walk-off right on ledge;

2b. **West Face** (5.9 R) until you choose to gain the true arete and ledge;

2c. **Back Side-Gully Start** (5.8) then gaining easy ground on arete to ledge;

   Once on major ledge walk off or continue up one of three variants (2d-2f):

2d. **Arete**—Lowe variation (5.10) 1-pitch obvious crack climb up golden arete, continuing up 2-3 more pitches (5.8+) to summit;

2e. **West Face** (5.7) 1-pitch crack to rotten face, then onto arete; continue 2-3 pitches (5.8+) to summit;

2f. **West Face-Right Side:** walk off ledge right to top of gully then scramble (5.5) to summit.

PRO WALL/GRAY WALL

Gray Wall is a vast, clean granite face reminiscent of Parking Lot Wall in Blodgett Canyon. The climbing is predominantly steep, thin, and delicate. Routes are mostly bolt protected with grades from 5.9 to 5.12. Although the climbs are exposed, aesthetic, and well protected, it is hard to call them typical sport routes—considering the grunt approach and alpine-like setting. Bring 2 ropes to descend. There are a few crack climbs but most routes require only quick draws (bring 16 or so). This area is a very nice place to spend a warm fall day.

Finding the wall: Find the climbers trail for Gray Wall/No Sweat Arete (see Finding the area p. 101). Ascend an approach trail to the top of a long scree slope near two huge dead pines. Continue on trail up grassy ledges, working west; eventually the trail reaches a cliff face with a 12' roof, 30' up. The 3 bolt lines above are on the Pro Wall/Gray Wall Right. About 200' west of these three routes a trail ascends to the main cliff base. This is the location of Wanna-Be Wall/Gray Wall-Left.

PRO WALL/GRAY WALL-RIGHT

3. **Shootin' Ducks**(5.12-) Line left of west-facing corner. Extremely thin face moves on micro edges (tenuous clips) then works left to gain anchors for KICKING'; bolts; 160'. **Descent:** Double-rope rappel from 2-bolt anchor.

Photo by Matt Taylor.

4. **Kicking Gravel** (5.10+) Thin friction and edging moves through middle crux sequences lead to easy 5.10 runouts; bolts, geer (TCUs useful for start and a yellow TCU useful for farther up); 160'. **Descent:** See 'DUCKS.

5. **Hooligans** (5.11) Spectacular climb, sustained and crimpy! Starts with solid 5.10 moves and goes out under roof; pull roof, continue on delicate, thin edges; bolts; 165'. **Descent:** Double-rope rappel from 2-bolt anchor.

WANNA-BE WALL/GRAY WALL-LEFT

The wall is split by a ledge 40' up the cliff. Homer the Hack Trap and Slapped by a Nun begin on the ledge. Either climb the first pitch of Chicken Hoist (5.10), a right-leaning flake (5.6) just left of Chicken Hoist, or My, What a Lovely Bunch of Coconuts to gain the ledge. Combinations of first and second pitches of various routes may make interesting link-ups .

6. **My, What a Lovely Bunch of Coconuts** (5.8) Thin seam right of NEU-TERED ROOSTER. Climb thin, runout seam to better protection, leading to belay ledge; gear (small wires, RPs, and TCUs necessary); 40'.

7. **Neutered Rooster** (5.11c) From ground (cross sloping section of ledge) climb past 2 roofs and belay under third roof; 14 bolts; 170'. **Descent:** Double-rope rappel from chain anchor (down climb or make a second rappel from ledge).

Photo by Matt Taylor.

8. **Homer the Hack Trap** (5.10d) Bolted line right of corner. Balancy, micro-edging (crux—don't get pulled too far toward crack) moves through mid-section; 11 bolts; 130'. **Descent:** Double-rope rappel from chain anchor to ledge; single-rope rappel from ledge.

9. **Slapped by a Nun** (5.11c) Bolt line in between CHICKEN' and HOMER'. Shares first bolt and anchor with second pitch of CHICKEN' ;move past third bolt and short crux section; 11 bolts; 130'. **Descent:** Double-rope rappel from chain anchor to ledge; single-rope rappel from ledge.

10. **Chicken Hoist** (5.11a) 2-pitch route near an indistinct corner system just right of SLAPPED'. **Pitch 1**-(5.10-) Climb up smooth face past bolts; passing 3rd bolt is crux; 4 bolts; 45'; chain anchor. **Pitch 2**- (5.11a) From ledge follow left-most line past bolts; unrelenting to final bolt; at last bolt traverse 12' right to anchor; 12 bolts; 140'. **Descent:** Double-rope rappel from chain anchor to ledge; single-rope rappel from ledge.

BLODGETT CREEK CANYON

Overview

Blodgett Canyon is the centerpiece among the many east-west running canyons flanking the eastern escarpment of the Bitterroot Range, which stretches from Lolo Pass south 90 miles to Nez Perce Pass. Blodgett Canyon offers many options from 1- and 2-pitch, sport-type face climbs to multi-pitched and multi-day climbs on 500- to 1,200-foot spires, walls, and buttresses. The rock in Blodgett, as in the majority of Bitterroot drainages, is a granitic gneiss. The cliffs are graced with vertical cracks, dihedrals, and exfoliation flakes. While many routes offer textured faces with sustained straight-in jamming and laybacking, most routes to some degree involve linking flared, discontinuous cracks and incipient corners.

While a rack of quick draws may suffice for some of Parking Lot Wall's routes, most routes require a well-stocked **gear rack** (meaning doubles of most sizes) of small and medium wired stoppers with various sized nuts and camming devices thrown in. For aid rack suggestions see respective route descriptions.

Since most routes are longer than 100 feet, it is advisable to take two ropes. Wear a helmet.

The climbing season extends from late March through late October. Since most of the routes in Blodgett are on predominantly south-facing cliffs, the spring and fall months offer the most comfortable temperatures. Most of the larger formations have been climbed in winter, and it is not uncommon to see die-hard locals wading through winter snow to the base of Parking Lot Wall for a day of climbing during a spell of clear weather.

Climbing history: Technical climbing in Blodgett Canyon stems back twenty-five years when Al Day and Ray Breuninger made the first ascent of the classic *South Face of Shoshone Spire* in 1970. The following year, Mark Everingham and Tom Ballard teamed up for a committing ascent of the 1,200-foot *South Face of Flathead Buttress*. This sought-after route was first free climbed in 1979 by Alex *Lowe and Ballard* (V 5.10+) and is still considered a test piece among the longer free routes in Blodgett.

Other notable early first ascents include the *Southwest Buttress of Flathead* (IV 5.10) by Marvin McDonald and Ballard in 1976 and the sweeping *Southwest Buttress of Nez Perce Spire* (IV 5.10) by Greg Lee and Tom Shrieve in 1979. The next year Tobin Kelley, Kurt Kleiner, and McDonald established *Fresh Aire* (V 5.10/A3+) on Flathead. This route proved to be the most difficult aid route in the canyon at the time, requiring three attempts to complete it.

From the mid-1980s through the early 1990s, first ascent activists concentrated their efforts on the Parking Lot Wall. With its short approach and abun-

▲ -

Rafael Grana, with help from many others, provided the text, photos, and maps for this section

BLODGETT CANYON

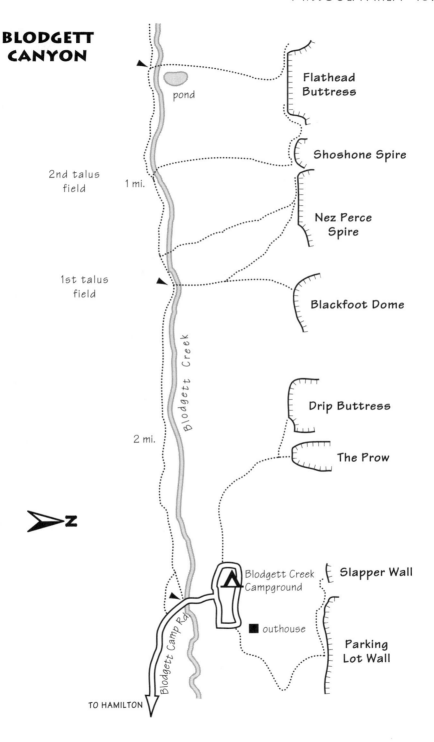

Flathead Buttress

pond

Shoshone Spire

2nd talus field

1 mi.

Nez Perce Spire

1st talus field

Blackfoot Dome

Blodgett Creek

Drip Buttress

2 mi.

The Prow

N

Blodgett Creek Campground

Slapper Wall

outhouse

Blodgett Camp Rd.

Parking Lot Wall

TO HAMILTON

Stephanie Schamb on Shoshone's South Face. *Photo by Brian Hatfield.*

dance of unclimbed rock, Parking Lot Wall offered tremendous potential for full rope length, 1- to 2-pitch routes of sustained face climbing. Here several classics were established such as *Leisure Suit Larry* (5.10c) by Jim Durkin and Ivan Pyatt in 1989; *Hairball* (5.10c) by Pyatt and Durkin in 1990; *Common Ground* (5.11a/b) by Pyatt and Rafael Grana in 1991; and the notorious first pitch of *Gray Matter* (5.11c) by Mike Scott, Andrew Sthalberj, and Pyatt, with its crux mantle move still humbling parties.

New route activity returned to the Big Walls in 1993 with Craig Kenyon, Grana, and Steve Porcella climbing *The Timebinder* (IV 5.11b). This sustained route is exemplary of Blodgett's potential for long routes with 2 pitches of 5.9+, 4 pitches of 5.10+, and a final 80-foot 5.11 finger crack crux.

In 1987 two "out-of-towners" Greg Cambron and Russ Johnson pushed Blodgett's aid standards to unprecedented heights with *Rain Dance* (V 5.9/A4); then in 1993 Bruce Anderson and Grana *established Central Aire* (V 5.10/A4). Anderson later teamed up with Kenyon for *Every Mind Is An Island* (V 5.10/A5). These routes are on the South Face of Flathead.

Finding the canyon: From Missoula drive southwest on U.S. Highway 93 about 44 miles and turn right/west onto Bowman Road at the cement plant, just before crossing the steel bridge over the Bitterroot River. Go 0.6 mile on Bowman Road and turn left/south onto Ricketts Road; stay on Ricketts Road 2 miles, taking a 90-degree turn to a four-way intersection. Continue straight on what becomes Blodgett Camp Road 4 miles to Blodgett Campground and trailhead.

Guy Pinjub on the last pitch of the *Southwest Buttress of Nez Perce. Photo by Rafael Grana.*

Trip Planning Information

Area description: Sport routes and multi-pitch, multi-day gear routes on granitic walls in the Bitterroot Mountains.

General location: Blodgett Creek Canyon is located about 50 miles southwest of Missoula and 6 miles west of Hamilton off US 93.

Camping: Forest Service campground at the end of Blodgett Camp Road; 14-day stay limit; outhouse provided. Fire pits are provided, but bring a cook stove if planning to camp. Carry drinking water or use a filter for obtaining water from Blodgett Creek; *Giardia* has been a problem.

Climbing season: Late March to late October.

Restrictions and access: The approach road into the canyon may be clogged with snow and ice ruts in early spring. A four-wheel-drive vehicle may be necessary to reach the trailheads then. But during summer and early fall, the road is passable for most passenger vehicles. Open fire restrictions may apply during dry periods.

Other guidebooks: *Bitterroot Guidebook* by Rick Torre; *The Climber's Guide to North America (Rockies)* by John Harlan III.

Nearby mountain shops, guide services, and climbing gyms: Canyon Critters, Hamilton; Pipestone Mountaineering (retail, rental, and instruction), Missoula; The Trailhead (retail and rental), Missoula; Hold-On (climbing gym, retail, instruction, and rental), Missoula; University of Montana indoor climbing wall, Missoula.

Photo by Rafael Grana.

PARKING LOT WALL

Overview

Parking Lot Wall is the first formation visible from the road about 0.5 mile after entering the canyon on Blodgett Camp Road. Perched on the north side of the canyon, its steep slab is characterized by a dominant right-angle roof on the far left side and an obvious black water streak marking the center of the wall. The rock at Parking Lot Wall is characterized by horizontal foliation, offering excellent friction, steep edging, and the requisite crux mantle move. The long 1- and 2-pitch face climbs are predominantly protected by bolts. The routes here offer an enjoyable alternative to the multi-pitch crack climbs that require a more involved approach farther up the canyon.

Finding the wall: From the campground parking lot walk east, following a faint climber's trail about 200 yards to an obvious downed log on the left side of the trail. Step left over the log and follow a faint trail up a forested talus slope. Continue climbing up and right in a long traverse below broken slabs. Then follow trail up and left on grassy ramps to the base of the wall.

Routes are described from right to left. The following six routes are on the righthand side of the wall, marked by a 40' lower angle slab. Routes 1, 2, and 3 begin atop a block on the right side of the slab.

1. **Scott-Pyatt** (5.11) Follow easy unprotected slab up and right to overhangs; crank through overhangs and face climb above; 7 bolts; 120'. **Descent:** Double-rope rappel from chain anchor.

2. **The Rack** (5.11+) Follow easy unprotected slab straight above block and up through left side of overhangs; 8 bolts; 120'. **Descent:** Double-rope rappel from chain anchor.

3. **Wally-babba** (5.11a/b) Excellent climb. Move left up slab to steep headwall; climb straight up, moving left at last bolt; 7 bolts; 140'. **Descent:** Double-rope rappel from chain anchor.

Routes 4, 5, and 6 begin on the left side of the slab.

4. **Scream Cheese** (5.10d) Climb up past 2 bolts on SWISS ROUTE, move right through overhang (pro to 3.5"), and up; 8 bolts, gear to 3.5"; 150'. **Descent:** Double-rope rappel from chain anchors.

5. **Swiss Route** (5.10b) Excellent climb. Begin 10' right of a mungy corner; climb straight up past 3 bolts; go left through overhang to steep face; 9 bolts, gear to 2"; 150'. **Descent:** Double-rope rappel from chain anchor.

6. **Route 166** (5.10c) 2-pitch route with runout sections. **Pitch 1**—(5.9+) Begin 25' left of the SWISS ROUTE on slab marked by a horizontal slot 30' off ground; climb past left-facing flake to horizontal slot (gear to 2 1/2" useful); after a long runout on progressively easier ground move right to a fixed pin; climb flake system past 2 fixed pins to lone bolt and traverse up

and right to two-bolt sling belay. **Pitch 2**—(5.10c) Climb up and right past 2 bolts to long runout to base of straight-in crack; ascend crack to face above (bolts), moving left at top of left-facing flake (crux); easier ground leads to 2-bolt sling belay. **Descent:** Two double-rope (150') rappels to base of wall.

Routes 7, 8, and 9 begin atop a 40' tower (5.7) that is left of the prominent black water streak.

7. **Leisure Suit Larry** (5.10c) Classic climb up and right past first bolt to short crack and straight up, moving left on top; 8 bolts, gear to 2"; 165'. **Descent:** Double-rope rappel from chain anchor to top of tower.

8. **Hairball** (5.10c) Excellent but runout. Clip first bolt on LEISURE SUIT' and step left then climb up; 8 bolts; 165'. **Descent:** Double-rope rappel from chain anchor.

9. **First Flight** (5.10d) Runout. Climb up and left past horizontal slots and up past 3 bolts moving left above third bolt (scary!); go up and right into corner (thin); follow corner and go back left through overhang to slab; 4 bolts, gear to 3.5" (small wired stoppers, TCUs useful); 165'. **Descent:** Double-rope rappel from chain anchors.

10. **Gray Matter** (5.11c) Excellent 2-pitch route that begins 75' left of 40' tower (approach to routes 7, 8, and 9). **Pitch 1**—(5.11c) Climb up steep slab and struggle with progressively difficult mantle moves over roof and past 3 bolts; step left into corner (thin) and climb up to 2-bolt sling belay; 3 bolts,

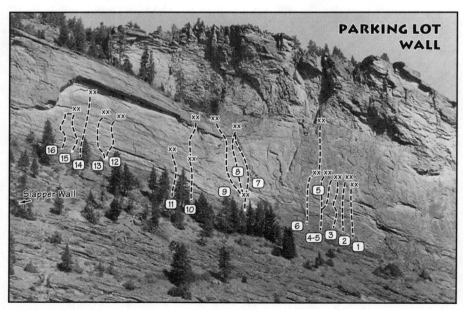

Photo by Rafael Grana.

gear to 2"; 85'. **Pitch 2**—(5.10b) Climb straight up past 6 bolts, step right and climb past 2 more bolts to short corner and 2-bolt sling belay above; 8 bolts; 165'. **Descent:** Double-rope rappel to belay ledge followed by another single-rope rappel to base of wall. **Variant:** It is possible to bypass the first pitch by climbing the 5.7 tower to LEISURE SUIT' and traversing 75' on 5.5 ground to top of GRAY MATTER pitch 1 belay.

11. **Thin for Five-Ten** (5.11) Begin 50' right of GRAY MATTER below suspect block in overhang. Climb up past block and up steep, bolt-protected slab; bolts; 120'. **Descent:** Double-rope rappel from chain anchor.

12. **Graupel Wars** (5.10d) Runout. Begin 100 yards left of GRAY MATTER at top of a grassy ramp with a small tree; climb up and right on easy face holds to first bolt; continue through overhang and go left above third bolt (crux) then straight up; 6 bolts; 130'. **Descent:** Double-rope rappel from chain anchor.

13. **Dudley Do Right** (5.10a/b) Runout. Start same as for GRAUPEL WARS; climb up and left past 2 bolts (crux); move up and left past 4 bolts stepping right on top; 6 bolts; 120'. **Descent:** Double-rope rappel from chain anchor.

Routes 14 and 15 begin on a ledge 30' right of DUDLEY'. Approach via 3rd-class scrambling.

14. **Common Ground** (5.11a/b) Excellent. Step right on belay ledge and climb up past fixed pin and small overhang to first bolt; move up and left and ascend face past more bolts with the crux coming at the last bolt; 1 fixed pin, 9? bolts, gear to 2"; 165'. **Descent:** Double-rope rappel.

15. **Bolts to Nowhere** (5.8+) Begin 10' left of COMMON GROUND; smear up past first bolt (crux), move left through an overhang and continue straight up to 2-bolt sling belay; 2 bolts, gear to 2"; 110'. **Descent:** Double-rope rappel.

16. **Virgin Dance of the Twin Chainsaws** (5.10d) Begin 20' left of BOLTS TO NOWHERE; ascend overhanging rock past a fixed pin and 2 bolts; continue through an overhang and go left past 3 bolts (crux) to easier climbing; Step right above last bolt to 'NOWHERE anchors; 1 fixed pin, 5? bolts, gear to 1.5" (TCUs useful); 110'. **Descent:** Double-rope rappel.

SLAPPER WALL

This newly developed separate and smaller crag is located left of the main Parking Lot Wall. This wall has lots of potential for new routes.

To find the Slapper Wall traverse down and right from the base of *Bolts To Nowhere* about 100 yards to the top of the cliff marked by a large ponderosa pine. **Descent:** Either rappel to the base of the wall (two ropes) or scramble down the east side to the base.

17. **Slapper** (5.11d) "Choice," strenuous route; starts at center of wall and follows right-leaning seam; 7 bolts; 70'; 2-bolt anchor.

18. **Slapped** (5.12+) Begins 20' right of SLAPPER. Crank straight up wall, sustained; 7 bolts; 70'; 2-bolt anchor.

DRIP AND PROW BUTTRESSES

The Drip and Prow buttresses are the only two larger formations up the canyon that are best approached out of the campground on the north side of Blodgett Creek.

Finding the climbs: Look for a faint trail behind the western-most campsite in the campground. Follow the path as far as possible, skirting the base of initial talus fields. After about 1 mile the trail peters out below the Prow Buttress in a small stand of trees at a big talus field.

To approach *The Timebinder* (a.k.a. South Face of the Prow), traverse up and left across the talus field and up into a broken gully directly below the Prow. At the top of the gully scramble up and left onto a large grassy ledge that has trees on the far left side. It is possible to traverse in from the right to gain the ledge and 2-bolt belay anchor at the top of the second pitch.

19. **The Timebinder/South Face of the Prow** (IV 5.11b) A fixed pin at shoulder height on the right side of the ledge marks the start of the route. Excellent, sustained route. **Pitch 1**—(5.9+/.10a) Face climb straight up past 4 bolts, moving right toward edge of slab past 2 more bolts; climb up and across

Photo by Rafael Grana.

THE PROW

The Timebinder IV
19 5.11b

19

approach

Photo by Rafael Grana.

DRIP BUTTRESS

Drip Buttress III
5.9+

20

approach

Photo by Rafael Grana.

DRIP BUTTRESS

III-IV 5.9+
TCUs, Tri-Cams,
extra small stoppers

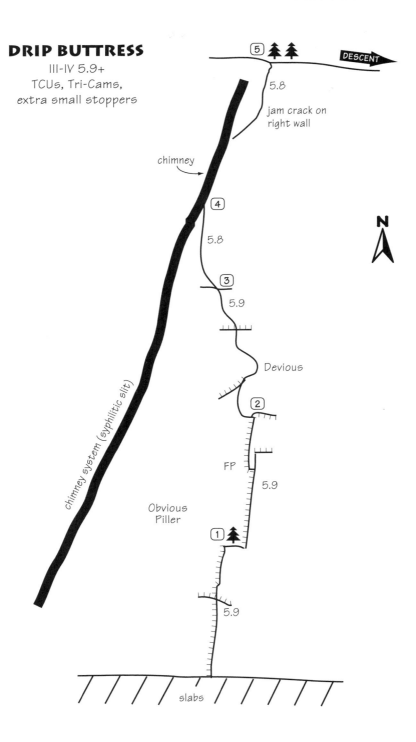

5 DESCENT

5.8

jam crack on
right wall

chimney

4

5.8

3

5.9

Devious

2

FP

5.9

Obvious
Piller

chimney system (syphilitic slit)

1

5.9

N

slabs

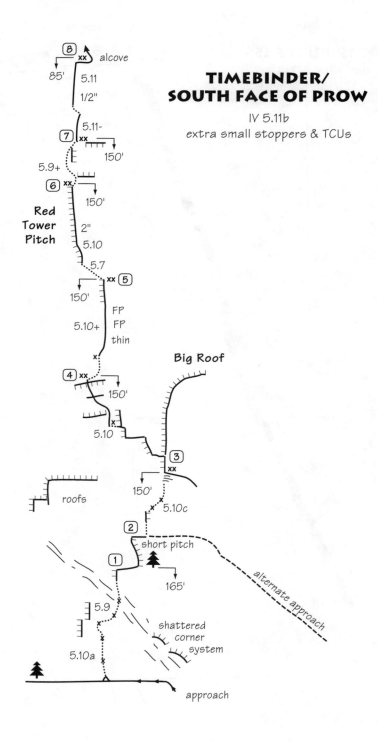

8 xx → alcove
85'   5.11
      1/2"

TIMEBINDER/
SOUTH FACE OF PROW

IV 5.11b
extra small stoppers & TCUs

      5.11-
7 xx
        ↓
        150'

5.9+
6 xx
        ↓
        150'

Red
Tower
Pitch
      2"
      5.10

      5.7
        xx 5
    ↓
   150'
        FP
5.10+   FP
        thin

Big Roof

        x
4 xx
    ↓
    150'

        x
    5.10

            3
            xx
    ↓
   150'
        x 5.10c

roofs

        2
        short pitch

        1
        ↓
        165'

    5.9

alternate approach

shattered
corner
system

5.10a

approach

left-leaning weakness into right-facing layback flakes (fixed pin) that lead right to a small belay stance just left of a prominent tree; medium cams useful for belay; 165'. **Pitch 2**—(5.6/.7) Step right and up past tree, following easy cracks to a ledge with 2-bolt sling belay; 30'. **Pitch 3**—(5.10c) Climb up and around right side of fixed pin and up right past 2 bolts (crux) to easier ground leading to bolt and fixed pin; 90'. **Pitch 4**—(5.10c) Work left off belay stance across wall, following a short corner and traverse to a bolt; step around left past bolt (not up dihedral) and go over small roof and up left past a fixed pin to Hematoma Ledge and 2-bolt sling belay; 130'. **Pitch 5**—(5.10d) Hematoma Pitch. A difficult move past a bolt leads to good holds; above this follow thin cracks up and right, finishing in a thin seam with 2 fixed pins (crux); follow easier ground to stance with a fixed nut and 2-pin sling belay; 140'. **Pitch 6**—(5.10d) Red Tower Pitch. Climb up easy slab to base of obvious right-facing dihedral; difficult layback moves start this sustained pitch (Incredible! Wow!). Belay on top of tower at 2-bolt sling belay; 120'. **Pitch 7**—(5.9+) Climb above belay via thin cracks and face holds, initially staying on face left of a small left-facing corner; eventually move right and pull through an overhang at top of corner; easier ground leads to a large ledge and 2-bolt sling belay; 100'. **Pitch 8**—(5.11b) Headwall Pitch. Ascend difficult thin crack, leading to better jams; move up left past a bolt to base of upper finger crack; crank up finger crack to a rest at fixed angle and traverse right; belay at 2-bolt sling belay in alcove just below top of buttress; (TCUs and small wires useful); 100'. **Descent:** Rappel route (8 double-rope rappels) from anchor at top of pitch 8 or continue to summit, going left through a chimney via an easy 5th-class pitch; 35'. From summit walk straight back and right into a gully to the east. Before descending all the way to the initial approach talus field, it is possible to traverse right and downclimb or rappel into the approach gully adjacent to the grassy ledge at the start of the route (it can be tricky to find the right spot to traverse into the gully).

20. **Drip Buttress/Original Route** (III 5.9+) (TCUs and Tri-Cams useful). To approach the ***Drip Buttress*** continue left across the talus field, passing the gully between the Prow and Drip buttresses (seasonally wet). Traverse left past the initial portion of the wall to the base of a long right-facing corner system that forms the right side of 500' pillar leaning against the main wall. (See overview map).

Pitch 1—(5.9+) Ascend corner and through bulge (crux) to belay stance; 120'. **Pitch 2-3**—(5.8+/.9-) Follow corner system and belay at small stance; 100'. **Pitch 4**—(5.8) Climb up and left out onto south face of pillar, belaying on highest blocky ledge; 150'. **Pitch 5**—(5.8) Move left into long chimney system that splits center of main wall (syphilitic slit) for a funky finish to this otherwise good route; belay off trees on top; 100'. **Descent:** Traverse right on 3rd- and 4th-class slabs into gully to the east (Use extreme caution in wet or icy conditions as this is a very exposed traverse). Scramble down gully to base.

BLACKFOOT DOME

Blackfoot Dome is the third major formation up the canyon and is characterized by a lower angle southeast face and a steep west face. A line of steep walls and corner systems abut its upper left side at the top of the gully/drainage between Nez Perce Spire and Blackfoot Dome. (See overview map and photo.)

Finding the climbs: Hike up the main Blodgett Canyon Trail on the south side of the creek about 2 miles to where the first major talus field encroaches on the trail from the left/south side; Blodgett Creek is immediately to the right of the trail. Cross the creek and hike up and right across a talus field between Nez Perce Spire and Blackfoot Dome. From the top of the talus field contour right (no real trail) through trees and up to the base of the dome.

21. **Southeast Face** (III 5.5/.6) A direct line that is moderate and fun. Begin at a small group of trees at the base of the southeast face. Climb up the face for about 4 pitches to top of dome. Moderately runout with tree belays. **Descent:** Walk back and right into the gully/drainages to east.

22. **The Free Lament** (III 5.9+R) Follows the obvious line up the south face.
    Pitch 1—(5.8+) In center of south face climb long pitch up slabs and thin

Photo by Rafael Grana.

corners to left end of a ledge marked by two trees; 160'. **Pitch 2**—(5.9) Ascend crack system up through overlaps, belaying near end of rope; 150'. **Pitch 3**—(5.9) Climb crack system past a bolt and belay in small alcove; 150'. **Pitch 4**—(5.9+) Move out of alcove (crux) and up crack system lead to easier ground and top of dome; 105'. **Descent:** Walk back and right into the gully/drainages to east and scramble to base.

NEZ PERCE SPIRE

Nez Perce Spire is the large wall upstream from Blackfoot Dome and is characterized by a sweeping apron on its southeast side. Its south face has three arching dihedrals, culminating on the left with an elegant southwest buttress. A large grassy ledge divides the main wall from a lower left-hand buttress. Both routes described here begin on this large ledge.

Finding the climbs: Hike up the main Blodgett Canyon Trail about 2 miles to where the first major talus field encroaches upon the trail from the left and Blodgett Creek is immediately to the right of the trail. From here two options exist: in late summer and fall, simply cross the creek and hike up the talus field between Nez Perce and Blackfoot Dome, traversing left to the base of the south face and southwest buttress; in spring and early summer, because Blodgett Creek can be a raging torrent, it may be best to continue up the trail 200-250 yards and cross ford the creek in a forested area (See overview map).

23. **A Modern Home Environment** (V 5.10/A3+) This route requires a good collection of free free climbing and aid skills. It follows a plumb line up the south face of Nez Perce Spire. Scramble up and left to a ledge with small junipers directly below the left side of the south face. The route begins just to the left of the right-most juniper bush. **Pitch 1**—(5.10) Climb up and left into a short right-facing corner; step right and go up a short face and move around right up a short right-facing corner; eventually work back left and belay on a blocky ledge 30' right of a tree; 165'. **Pitch 2-3**—(5.10b/c) Move belay left to a tree and ascend obvious right-facing weakness to a point where is possible to traverse right past a pocket (crux—#3.5 Friend useful); continue up a steep layback/jam crack and up to a small ledge with a double cold shut anchor; 150'. **Pitch 4**—(A3) Aid past 2 old 1/4" bolts and into thin seam for 30'; move right into obvious 1"to1 1/4" crack; free climb and aid up to large ledge; 120'. **Pitch 5**—(A2+) Aid past fixed pin off left side of ledge and up into thin left-facing corner; move right past fixed copperhead at top of corner to belay stance; 120'. **Pitch 6**—(A2/A3) Climb up thin right-facing corner past small overhang, moving right at key #2 Camalot pocket to a vertical knifeblade seam; nail up seam to hanging belay; 120'. **Pitch 7**—(A3) Move right through roof using hooks and continue through off-width to belay stance; 30'. **Pitch 8**—(5.9) Climb left past blocky steps

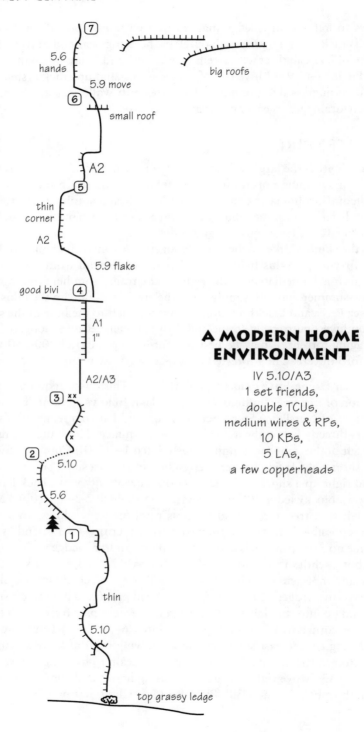

7

5.6
hands

5.9 move

big roofs

6

small roof

A2

5

thin
corner

A2

5.9 flake

good bivi 4

A1
1"

A2/A3

3 xx

x

2

5.10

5.6

1

thin

5.10

top grassy ledge

A MODERN HOME ENVIRONMENT

IV 5.10/A3
1 set friends,
double TCUs,
medium wires & RPs,
10 KBs,
5 LAs,
a few copperheads

NEZ PERCE SPIRE

Marvin's Wall

24

23

approach

Photo by Rafael Grana.

and into easier left-facing dihedral to top; 120'. **Descent:** Walk straight back and downclimb to the east or rappel to talus field/gully, which leads down between the east shoulder of Nez Perce and Blackfoot Dome.

24. **Southwest Buttress** (IV 5.10) An exposed free climb up an elegant arete. Begin 100 yards to the left of MODERN HOME' at far left side of the grassy approach ledge. **Pitch 1**—(5.6/.7) Climb a short pitch up to a blocky ledge below where buttress/arete steepens; 60'. **Pitch 2**—(5.9) Go straight up buttress via face and thin cracks to obvious belay stance; 100'. **Pitch 3**—(5.8+) Continue up buttress via face and thin cracks to highest ledge below upper buttress and belay at tree; 130'. **Pitch 4**—(5.7) Climb straight up the buttress on easier ground for half a rope length; 80'. **Pitches 5-6**—(5.10) Continue up steep corners and cracks just left of the arete for two physical and exposed pitches, finishing in a small alcove 40' below top of buttress; 150'. **Pitch 7**—(5.9+) Stem up steep right-facing corner past a fixed pin, moving right on good face holds at top; 40'. **Pitch 8**—(easy 5th) A short scramble to summit. **Descent:** Walk straight back and downclimb/rappel to the east into talus field/gully, which leads to the drainage between the east shoulder of Nez Perce Spire and Blackfoot Dome.

SHOSHONE SPIRE

Shoshone Spire is the 600' formation to the left of Nez Perce Spire and to the right of the taller Flathead Buttress. Shoshone's south face is characterized by a

Photo by Rafael Grana.

FLATHEAD BUTTRESS

NEZ PERCE

SHOSHONE

approach

Photo by Rafael Grana.

lower buttress broken by tree-covered ledges and a steep 300' upper headwall.

   Finding the climb: Hike up the main Blodgett Canyon Trail about 2.5 miles to a point where the trail crosses the second major talus field on the south side of the canyon. The gully/drainage and talus field between Nez Perce Spire and Shoshone Spire should be directly across the canyon at this point. Go down the talus and cross the creek on large boulders and downed trees. A large, standing snag on the far side of the creek helps locate this crossing. Hike straight up the talus field between Shoshone Spire and Nez Perce Spire, traversing left on indistinct paths past a seasonal waterfall (Blodgett Falls) to far left side of the lower buttress.

25. **South Face of Shoshone Spire** (III 5.8+) Probably the first multi-pitch route climbed in the canyon and still a mandatory classic. Some parties elect to bypass the initial pitches by scrambling up 3rd- and 4th-class ledge systems in the center of the lower buttress to a large open ledge below the upper headwall. **Pitch 1**—(5.8+) Begin at southwest toe of lower buttress. Climb up past short steps and into left-facing corner with a 3 1/2" to 4" crack; layback and jam up corner to good ledge; 100'. **Pitch 2-3**—(5.5-5.7) Climb straight up buttress for 2 short or 1 long pitch to large ledge below upper headwall (many variations possible). **Pitch 4**—(5.8+) Several variants possible here, too. On far left side of ledge step up chimney with thin cracks on back wall; go left through overhang (crux) and either climb right to small

SHOSHONE SPIRE

Lunch Ledge

approach

25

Photo by Rafael Grana.

belay tree or belay straight up above the overhang on the face; 80'. **Pitch 5**—(5.8) Ascend thin cracks and face holds, moving left to notch on skyline; 150'. **Pitch 6**—(5.8+/.9-) Step right onto the face (second crux) and up to second notch on skyline left of true summit; 100'. **Pitch 7**—Easy 5th-class climbing; go back on ledge and up right to summit, taking line of least resistance. **Descent:** Walk back and down drainage/gully to east, hugging the right-hand side and working back to large ledge below upper headwall. Scramble down and left to large rappel tree; one double-rope (165') rappel to base of lower buttress.

FLATHEAD BUTTRESS

Flathead Buttress is the last and tallest of the south-facing walls that extend about 3 miles in from the campground and is home to some of the longest and finest free and aid routes in western Montana. Climbing Flathead also requires the most involved approaches and descents in the canyon. Thus, an early start or bivouac at the base is standard procedure.

Finding the climbs: To approach routes on the right side of the south face follow the description for Shoshone Spire and continue traversing left across the gully between Flathead Buttress and Shoshone Spire working left on a narrowing grassy ledge to a small cairn. To approach routes on the left side of the south face and southwest buttress continue on main Blodgett Canyon Trail approximately 0.5 mile; cross the creek and follow a grassy weakness in the center of the lower slabs to the base of the wall. Traverse left above slabs on an exposed ledge and scramble up and right to the base of the southwest buttress.

26. **South Face Route/My Mom's Muscle Shirt** (IV 5.10+) This classic route begins on right side of south face and follows a long traverse left; then it ascends 5 steep crack and dihedral pitches to the summit. A couple of 3.5" to 4" are useful on the sixth (roof) pitch, while small wired stoppers (#2-6 RPs/HBs) greatly assist on the tricky second pitch. **Pitch 1**—(5.10a) Begin next to small cairn; climb broken rock moving right to steep left-facing corner; layback and jam corner to sloping ledge and chain anchor; 100'. **Pitch 2**—(5.9+) Grope up through an overhang and squeeze through a chimney to a stance on top of a flake; move up thin seam and face climb for 80' to ledge; either belay here or traverse 25' to chain anchors; 120'. **Pitch 3**—(5.4) Traverse left on ledge and downclimb chimney/flake to narrow ledge on left; 80'. **Pitch 4**—(5.10a) Step left off narrow ledge and go up left into thin finger crack; climb crack to ledge below long left-facing dihedral on the right; 90'. **Pitch 5**—(5.9) Climb dihedral (1 long or 2 short pitches) to small ledge below overhang; 165'. **Pitch 6**—(5.10c) Layback and jam out left around roof and up left-facing corner to belay stance; 100'. **Pitch 7**—(5.10c) Climb up and into left-leaning finger and hand crack (#3.5 Friend

Photo by Rafael Grana.

useful); ascend crack, moving right on top to belay stance; 100'. **Pitch 8—** (5.8+/.9-) Climb cracks and short corners to summit (variations possible); 100'. **Descent:** Scramble back and right to large tree (slings) at top of east face. Make 2-3 single-rope rappels from trees to single lone tree with rappel slings. One double-rope (165') rappel goes to a small ledge; step down and left on ledge (stay clipped to rope, very exposed here), going to lone tree on left side of ledge. Another double-rope (165') rappel from tree leads to large sloping ledge and easy scrambling down and around right side of wall to base.

Parties that need to retrieve packs at the base of the Southwest Buttress traverse left past the start of the South Face Route and rappel (85') down and left off final tree to base of the Southwest Buttress.

27. **Every Mind Is an Island** (V 5.10/A4) Route is characterized by extreme positions, crossing the big roof, then squeaking up the shield and prominent thin corners above; rationalizing your position is the theme on this insanely exposed foray into mixed free and aid. First pitches were done by Bruce Anderson and Steve Porcella in April 1994, and route was completed by Anderson and Craig Kenyon in June 1994.

Climb the first 2 pitches of South Face Route and traverse to right end of Homestake Ledge to a flake.

Rack: 1 set of Friends, double set of TCUs, medium wires, and extra RPs, 10 KBs, 5 RURPS, 25 copperheads, bird beaks.

Pitch 1—(5.10/A2+) Climb cracks and flakes up to a horizontal gray band; aid climb flake (going right) then follow shallow corner up to small stance with 1/4" bolt; 110'. **Pitch 2—**(5.9/A2) Go up 10' above belay and move right across a hollow flake; continue up cracks then right to reach large corner on right end of roof; aid climb left across roof to hanging belay below apex; many large Friends, #5, 6, 7 Metolius cams, or backclean entire traverse as leader progresses—leaving a very scary option for the second (free climbing anyone?); 145'. **Pitch 3—**(A2-) Aid climb over spectacular, sharp-edged roof to small, "stimulating" stance above the lip (committing once past the roof); 15'. **Pitch 4—**(A3) Aid climb straight up thin crack; move right several feet and follow cracks up to exposed blank face; exit right to belay with three 1/4" bolts (first ascent party enjoyed a storm with 60 mph winds here); 95'. **Pitch 5—**(5.9/A1) Traverse right to ledge and short right-facing corner; 40'; possible to bivy nearby or perhaps descend down southeast buttress route. **Pitch 6—**(5.10/A2) Climb directly up (mixed free and aid) past a tree to a belay (two 1/4" bolts) to right of left-leaning corner/overhang; 120'. **Pitch 7—**(A4 or A5 for heavyweights—pee before you start lead) Move left in flaring crack under overhang and continue (gingerly) up thin, flaring, claustrophobic corner on delicate copperhead

EVERY MIND IS AN ISLAND

IV 5.10/A4
1 set friends,
double set TCUs,
medium wires & extra RPs,
10 KBs, 5 RURPs,
25 copperheads,
bird beaks

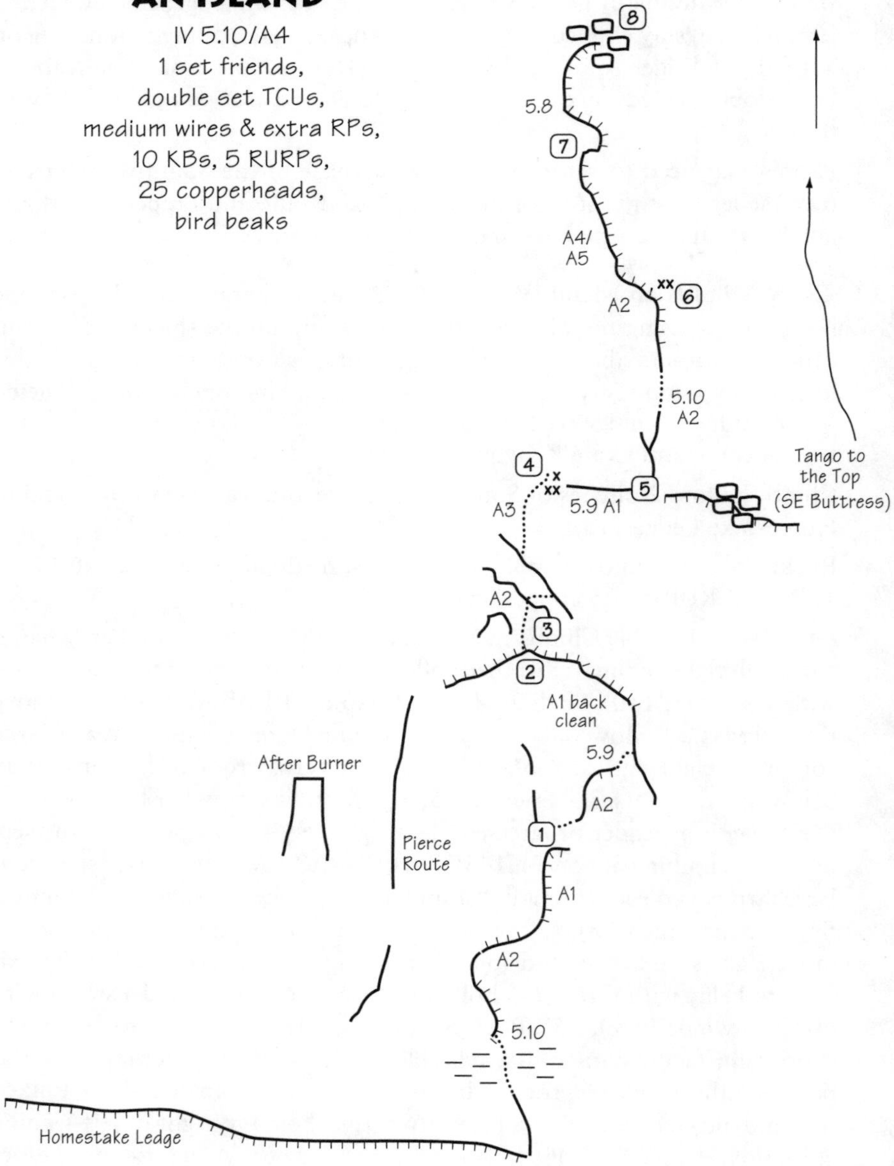

8

5.8

7

A4/
A5

A2   xx 6

5.10
A2

4   x
        xx   5
A3   5.9 A1

A2
        3

2

A1 back
clean

5.9

A2

After Burner

Pierce
Route   1

A1

A2

5.10

Homestake Ledge

Tango to
the Top
(SE Buttress)

placements to belay in alcove; 90'. **Pitch 8**—(5.8) Slide left out of alcove and up easier terrain to summit; 75'.

28. **Afterburner** (III 5.10) This excellent route ascends steep right-facing corner that begins off long traverse ledge on third pitch of the regular South Face Route. **Pitch 1-2**—(5.10a) Climb the first 2 pitches of the SOUTH FACE ROUTE and move left at top of the second pitch to chain anchors. **Pitch 3**—(5.10) Layback and jam corner to 2-bolt belay on small ledge; 150'. **Descent:** One double-rope rappel down corner, followed by two more double-rope rappels to ground.

29. **Fresh Aire** (V 5.9/+A3) **Rack:** 1 set of Friends, double set of TCUs, 10 KBs, 5 LAs, bat hooks, rivet hangers, and few copperheads. Climb the first 4 pitches of the South Face Route to Homestake Ledge. **Pitch 5**—(A3+) Step left to thin vertical seam; follow seam (aid) for 45' and work right across wall (bolts, hooks) to thin left-facing corner system; 100'. **Pitch 6**—(A3) Aid up corner system on not-the-best rock to hanging belay; 120'. **Pitch 7**—(5.9+/A2) Continue up corner system moving right to 2-bolt belay (same belay as for CENTRAL AIRE); 150'. **Pitch 8**—(5.9 or A3) Same last pitch as for CENTRAL AIRE. Either aid up right-leaning corner or free climb arete on right (pro in horizontal cracks); move up and right to overhang; go left around overhang to top of wall; 130'.

30. **Central Aire** (V 5.10+/A4) **Rack:** 1 set of Friends to #3 (doubles of #3.5 and #4), double set of TCUs, wires, and RPs, 5 KBs, 5 RURPS, 10 copperheads, bird beaks. This route climbs the steep left side of the south face with three difficult aid sections on the first 5 pitches, followed by sustained free climbing on last 3 pitches to the summit. From the base of the Southwest Buttress traverse down and right and then step up and right (exposed 5.7) to ledge with large trees. **Pitch 1**—(5.10+/A1) Traverse right past junipers and up into thin left-facing corner; (free and aid) to belay stance; 100'. **Pitch 2**—(A3) Climb right (A2) and then left past a rivet along left-leaning seam to base of flake; 80'. **Pitch 3**—(5.9+) Layback and jam flake, moving right on top to good belay stance; 100'. **Pitch 4**—(5.8/A3+) Nail vertical seam and thin horizontals; leave aid gear at tree and free climb left-facing corner (5.8+), moving right on top to exposed belay ledge; 150'. **Pitch 5**—(5.10+/A4) Work right across ever-thinning weakness to left-facing corner; crank up corner to boulder ledge; 140'. **Pitch 6**—(5.10+) Move belay to far left side of boulder ledge, layback thin flake and follow long left-facing dihedral; move right at top of dihedral to belay stance; 165'. **Pitch 7**—(5.9+) Climb up and left past dark colored ledge and into thin left-facing corner, stem up corner to 2-bolt belay; 130'. **Pitch 8**—(5.9 or A3) Aid left-facing corner or free climb arete on right (pro in horizontal cracks); climb right to overhang and move left around overhang to top; 130'. **Descent:** See SOUTH FACE ROUTE.

CENTRAL AIRE

V 5.10+/A4
1 set Friends to #3,
doubles of #3, #3.5, #4,
double set TCUs, wires & RPs,
5 KBs, 5 RURPs,
10 copperheads,
bird beaks

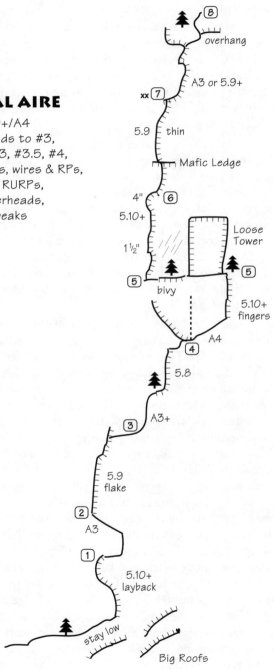

31. **Southwest Buttress** (IV 5.9+ to 5.10+) "I've climbed the Southwest Buttress five times and have never done the same route twice," says Ivan Pyatt. This statement attests to the adventure to be had on the Southwest Buttress of Flathead.

Following no single weakness, this popular route ascends the broad and highly fractured buttress for 6-8 pitches. The route has been climbed via many variations up to 5.10+, with most variants converging upon a final left-facing dihedral below the summit (See photo). **Descent:** See SOUTH FACE ROUTE.

DRUMMONDAREA

MULKEY GULCH

OVERVIEW

Mulkey Gulch is privately owned land about 45 miles east of Missoula and about 8 miles west of the small community of Drummond off Interstate 90. The drainage is split into Wet Mulkey and Dry Mulkey gulches. Dry Mulkey has the most developed routes and is described here. It is essentially a small canyon tending to run northwest by southeast containing limestone outcrops of various heights (with the 250-foot Mulkey Tower being the tallest). The outcrops come in varying degrees of rock quality and angles—from beautiful slabs of smooth gray rock featured with pockets and edges to overhanging chert-studded towers that are of questionable reliability.

Most of the thirty-plus established routes in Mulkey Gulch are reliant on bolts for protection. However, many of the bolted faces will accept Tri-Cams or TCUs for protection in pockets and slots. Without the use of this gear many of the routes become runout, especially on easier sections. Almost all of the routes have fixed rappel anchors at their end. The steep hillsides are littered with limestone scree, and erosion is already a concern; walking off from the tops of the formations generally is not recommended.

Amazingly, many of the routes in Mulkey Gulch are fairly moderate. There are several 5.8s, a good selection of 5.9s, and the majority are 5.10. For honemasters, there are also some 5.11 routes to warm up on before trying the handful of 5.12s that have been established. **Warning:** There are many loose blocks, and rockfall may occur. Wear a helmet and be careful!

A standard rack should include a wide selection of wired stoppers of all sizes, small (TCUs), and medium-sized cams and nuts, quick draws, and extra slings for clipping into belay/rappel anchors. Two ropes are required to descend from some climbs.

▲ -

Brad Hutcheson submitted the text, photos, and maps for this section. He extends a personal "thanks" for all the help and support to Shawn Peretto, Richard Plummer, Ivan Pyatt, Chris Randolph, and Jim Semmelroth, who were patient with the endless phone calls and questions about Mulkey Gulch. Without their help this would not have been possible. Yo dudes! Thank you!

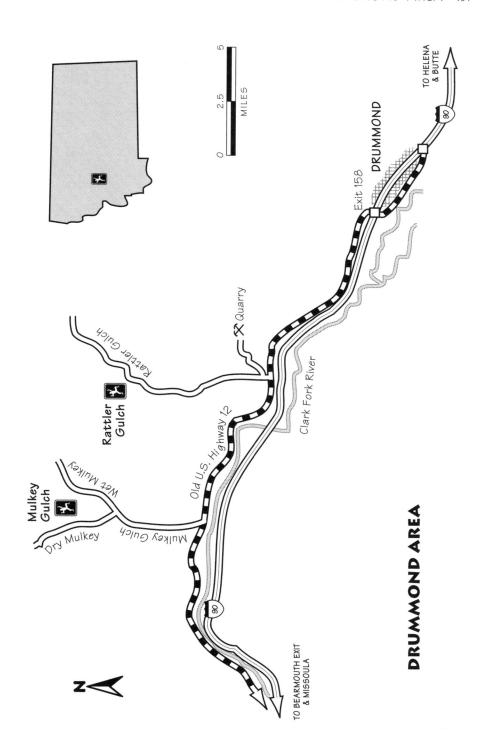

DRUMMOND AREA

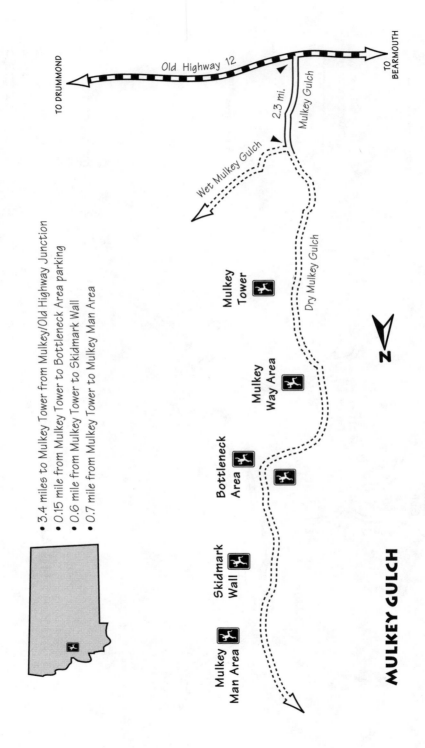

TO DRUMMOND

Old Highway 12

TO BEARMOUTH

2.3 mi.

Wet Mulkey Gulch

Mulkey Gulch

Dry Mulkey Gulch

Mulkey Tower

Mulkey Way Area

Bottleneck Area

Skidmark Wall

Mulkey Man Area

- 3.4 miles to Mulkey Tower from Mulkey/Old Highway Junction
- 0.15 mile from Mulkey Tower to Bottleneck Area parking
- 0.6 mile from Mulkey Tower to Skidmark Wall
- 0.7 mile from Mulkey Tower to Mulkey Man Area

N

MULKEY GULCH

The climbing season in Mulkey Gulch begins in March and ends in November on a normal year. Snowfall and temperatures can affect this by extending or cutting the season short. During the summer shade can be found in some areas, and with the narrow canyon walls the late afternoons can be cooler as the sun disappears over the ridge.

It is possible to camp in undeveloped spots up either Dry Mulkey or Wet Mulkey Gulch roads. No waste facilities or water are available. **Please remember that this is private land; treat the area with respect and keep it clean.**

The Bearmouth Chalet is located about 35 miles east on I-90 from Missoula at the Bearmouth exit (Exit 138). This is about 10 miles before the Mulkey Gulch turnoff on the old highway. Services are listed in "Camping" below.

Drummond is the closest town, about 8 miles east of Mulkey Gulch right off I-90. Drummond is a small ranching community and is not especially tourist oriented. But full services are available here, and the town folk are friendly.

Climbing history: This area is fairly new in terms of development. The first climb went up in 1991 (*Mulkey Man 5.10d*) and was established by Ivan Pyatt and Rafael Grana. By 1992 other climbs were beginning to appear. Richard Plummer became involved with Pyatt and Shawn Peretto (along with a handful of other activists), and the Skidmark Wall began to see attention. Pyatt and Plummer's efforts have contributed greatly to the big-number ratings on this wall and the Mulkey Man area. Since 1992 one person's contribution stands out clearly. Shawn Peretto could be called the "Mulkey Man." He has been involved with most of the new routes in Mulkey Gulch. Peretto, along with various partners, has established more routes than all other activists combined.

Trip Planning Information

Area description: 1- to 2-pitch routes on limestone fins and towers on private timber land in a narrow canyon.

General location: About 45 miles east of Missoula and 8 miles west of Drummond.

Camping: Undeveloped camping up either Dry Mulkey or Wet Mulkey Gulch roads. No waste facilities or water are available; **please remember that this is private land; treat the area with respect and keep it clean.** The Bearmouth Chalet, (406) 825-9950, has gasoline, a bar, a restaurant, some basic grocery supplies, beer, rooms for rent, and a campground; rooms start at $17.85/night; campground fees are $8/night for tent camping (showers and laundry facilities available) and $12/night for complete RV hookups. Drummond has full services.

Climbing season: March-November, but snowfall and temperatures can shorten or extend the season.

Restrictions and/or access issues: All climbing is on private property, so please treat the area with respect. At this time, the land owners are not opposed to climbing and it is important to maintain good relations. Do not block the narrow road with your vehicle when visiting this unique place. Stay on main trails when possible and pick up all refuse.

Guidebook: *The Rock Climber's Guide to Montana,* Falcon Press.

Nearby mountain shops, guide services, and climbing gyms: Pipestone Mountaineering (retail, rental, and instruction), Missoula; The Trailhead (retail and rental), Missoula; Hold-On (climbing gym, retail, rental, and instruction), Missoula; University of Montana indoor climbing wall, Missoula.

Finding the rocks: From Missoula take I-90 east about 35 miles and get off at the Bearmouth Exit (138). Turn left onto the frontage road, go north under the freeway, cross the river, and turn right/east and follow the old highway for about 10 miles. Watch for a small sign marking the left/north turn up Mulkey Gulch. Mulkey Gulch road is easily missed if not paying attention; it is the next turnoff after the well-marked turn to the ghost town of Garnet. From Drummond access the old highway at the Pintler Scenic Route exit on the west end of town. Go west on the old highway, which parallels the interstate, for about 8 miles.

From the Mulkey Gulch turnoff follow the dirt road, staying left at the junction of Dry and Wet Mulkey roads at 2.3 miles. Watch for a 250-foot-tall formation on the right of the road about 3.4 miles after leaving the old highway. This is the Mulkey Tower. Park at any of the several pullouts to climb here.

MULKEY TOWER

The tallest formation in Mulkey Gulch (250'). A 5-minute approach will give access to any of the sixteen routes located here.

1. **Sharp Shit** (5.10) Located uphill, around to the right of the smaller wall, at the right base of Mulkey Tower; 4 bolts; 50'; chain rappel anchor.

2. **Ryobi Crack** (5.10a) Sustained route downhill and around to the left of SHARP' on the same buttress. Starts at small ledge and goes past 2 bolts to a crack that accepts larger TCUs; continue past 2 more bolts to the top; 4 bolts, gear; 60'; chain rappel anchor.

3. **Choss Link** (5.9) Starts from the ledge system above RYOBI'. Access the start by climbing RYOBI' or by walking around to the right past climbs #1 and #2 and traversing in from the ledges above that formation; bolts; 65'. **Descent:** rappel from the anchor and then rappel again from RYOBI's anchor. Single rope needed for both rappels.

4. **Fester** (5.9) Starts just left of CHOSS' and continues past bolts to the same anchor. (See Choss Link for approach information); bolts; 65'. **Descent:** same as for CHOSS'.

5. **Hanta-Virus/Cave Route** (5.11) Starts on right side of large cave located on ledge about 25' from ground, toward right side of Mulkey Tower. Climb-

Photo by Brad Hutcheson.

MULKEY TOWER, MULKEY WAY AREA, & NORTH AND SOUTH SIDES OF THE BOTTLENECK AREA

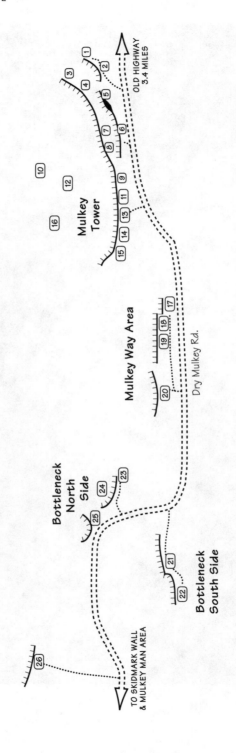

ing directly to the cave is not recommended; to get to cave traverse in from the left past the start of HONEY HUNTER (scary!); bolts; 75'. **Descent:** Rappel from chain anchors back to the cave. Downclimb, traversing left past HONEY HUNTER to get back to ground.

6. **Honey Hunter** (5.9+) Starts on small ledge left of HANTA-VIRUS. To access ledge scramble up from left side on rock and dirt ramps. There is a pine tree with a hemp rope tied to it to help ascend the steeper rock ramp; bolts, gear (#1 Camalot useful to protect entry moves to the first bolt); 70'. **Descent:** Rappel to start and downclimb ramps to the ground.

7. **Sacrificial Bat** (5.10d) Long, sustained route starts from ledge above HONEY' belay. Either climb HONEY' to gain start or traverse in from left from diagonal ramp that extends to base of LINK-UP; ascend bolt line (there are several awkward long reach clips!); bolts, gear (TCUs useful at start and in the fingertip seams farther up); 155'. **Descent:** A double-rope rappel from chains gains ledge at start of the climb. Then either scramble over to anchor for HONEY' or downclimb the diagonal ramp out left to the ground.

8. **Trad Route** (5.9) **Not recommended.** Starts to the left of SACRIFICIAL' on same ledge (See SACRIFICIAL' for approach and descent information). Follows a vague line on gear and bolts to the same anchor as SACRIFICIAL'. Watch for loose rock; 155'. **Descent:** See SACRIFICIAL'.

Photo by Brad Hutcheson.

9. **Mulkey Marathon** (5.11a/b) Fine bolted route takes a near-direct line toward summit of Mulkey Tower; first route located to right of LINK-UP. From parking area walk up the scree slope to the immaculate grey slab (follow the well-established trail); traverse right and up onto the diagonal ramp about 45' to start; follow bolts up a small slab to a small triangular roof (crux) down low; continue up through steeper orange rock to chains; bolts, gear (TCUs and some wired stoppers useful); 150'. **Descent:** Double-rope rappel.

10. **Mulkey Tower** (5.8) Second pitch variant to MULKEY MARATHON. Follow corners and cracks directly to summit of tower; start at chains at top of MULKEY MARATHON; watch for loose rock—especially near summit anchors; gear; 85'. **Descent:** Rappel back to MARATHON' top anchor then rappel (double rope) 150' to base.

11. **Dancing With Mom** (5.11b) Shares same start (2 bolts) with LINK-UP. From parking area walk up trail through scree slope to base of nice gray slab; there will be two obvious bolted lines in middle of this slab; right line is start of LINK-UP; climb past first 2 bolts then step right and head toward small roof, passing another bolt; follow bolts above the roof to ledge belay; bolts, gear (selection of TCUs and camming units useful for belay anchor); 80'. **Descent:** Take "chossy" (loose rubble) traverse left on ledge to gain chain anchors for routes 13, 14, and 15; single-rope rappel.

12. **Kid Tested Mother Proof** (5.10b/c) Located on ledge above finish of DANCING'. This highly regarded pitch follows a line of bolts, gear (TCUs useful); 90'. **Descent:** Double-rope rappel from chain anchor.

13. **Link-Up** (5.9) Fun bolted face route. See DANCING' for approach to slab. Take right bolt line by a small vertical corner system; bolts; 80'. **Descent:** Rappel from chain anchor.

14. **Peretto Bro's** (5.10c/d) 2 pitches (or 1 long pitch) left of LINK-UP. **Pitch 1**—(5.10a) Bolts; 80'; chain anchor. **Pitch 2**—(5.10c/d) Climb straight up over anchor toward a leaning crack; follow crack up and across it left onto face (crux) and easier ground and ledge; bolts (#0 TCU useful before reaching first bolt); 70'. **Descent:** Single-rope rappel from chains to anchors at top of pitch 1; single-rope rappel from chains to ground.

15. **The Pouting Game** (5.8) Starts left of PERETTO'; A-hard-to-see first bolt begins upward journey; bolts, gear (some TCUs are useful up higher); 80'; anchor same as pitch 1 of PERETTO'. **Descent:** Single-rope rappel from chains.

16. **Good to the Last Climb** (5.10c) Highly recommended. Starts at anchors at the end of first pitch of PERETTO' (also end of routes 13 and 15). From chain anchors go up and right to ledge with chains (same anchors for KID TESTED'); bolts; 90'. **Descent:** Double-rope rappel to ground.

MULKEY TOWER
LEFT SIDE

85'
16   90'
10   150'
12
5.10
5.10b
14
5.10+
16   80'
12
5.11b
5.11-
11
9
13
15   14

Photo by Brad Hutcheson.

MULKEY WAY AREA

This is the smaller, broken-up and discontinuous cliff band that is just beyond the Mulkey Tower. Use the same parking spot as for the 'Tower. The Mulkey Way Area is located on the same side of the road and is an easy 5-minute approach to the climbs of choice. The four established routes here are close together. *Mulkey Way* (5.10a/b—130') ascends the tallest, continuous formation. All the other routes in this area are to the right of this climb.

17. **Fear of Flying** (5.10a) This is the right-most climb in this section. Approach the Mulkey Way formation and follow the improved trail right, to the base of a small corner capped by a roof. Ascend the face and arete, pull the roof, and continue to easier ground; 7 bolts, gear (larger TCUs useful); 80'. **Descent:** Single-rope rappel from chain anchors at ledge.

18. **Conrad Burns** (5.9) Follows crack in corner left of FEAR'; Pull over roof at top of crack and clip 4th bolt on FEAR'; continue up FEAR' to chain anchor; gear; 80'. **Descent:** Single-rope rappel from chain anchors.

19. **Redurtnilana** (5.10b/c) Name read backwards refers to route 18. Located left of CONRAD', This route follows thin corner/arete up and over the roof to easier climbing. 6 bolts, gear (large TCUs or #1.5 Tri-Cam useful); 80'. **Descent:** Single-rope rappel from chain anchors.

Photo by Brad Hutcheson.

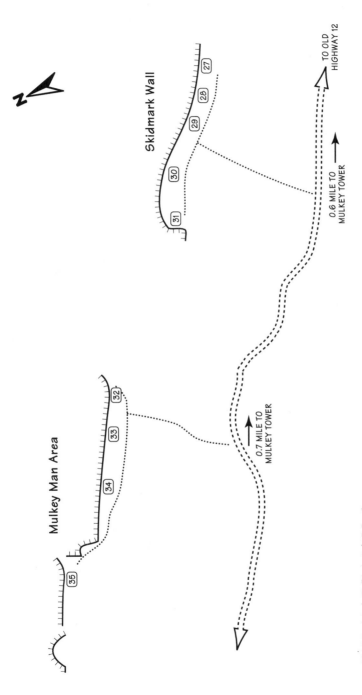

N

Skidmark Wall

31
30
29
28
27

TO OLD
HIGHWAY 12

0.6 MILE TO
MULKEY TOWER

0.7 MILE TO
MULKEY TOWER

Mulkey Man Area

32
33
34
35

**SKIDMARK WALL &
MULKEY MAN AREA**

Photo by Brad Hutcheson.

20. **Mulkey Way** (5.10a/b) This bolted route ascends the center of the Mulkey Way Tower (the tallest formation in this section); 11 bolts; 130'. **Descent:** Double-rope rappel from homemade hangers.

BOTTLENECK AREA

This is the name given to encompass the formations on either side of the road where the canyon narrows down and sharply turns after the Mulkey Way Area. The pullout for this area is about 0.15 miles beyond the parking areas for the Mulkey Way Tower. The climbs on the left/south side of the road are centered around the unnamed but striking tower with a beautiful corner that catches the eye when approaching the parking spot. The routes on the right/north side of the road are all readily visible, being quite close to the road.

BOTTLENECK-SOUTH SIDE

21. **Wet Dreams** (5.10c) Deceptive and sustained, following obvious beautiful corner of striking tower visible from road; bolts, gear (optional TCUs useful); 70'. **Descent:** Single-rope rappel from chain anchors.

22. **Gear Battle** (5.8) Located around the corner to the left of WET DREAMS. Sustained climbing along crack system that begins on right corner of face; before reaching summit step right at ledge with loose blocks to gain chain anchors on face above; gear; 75'. **Descent:** Single-rope rappel from chain anchor.

Variant (5.9) Begin in corner of WET' and ascend crack (loose) straight up into thin cracks above; continue to GEAR' anchor (essentially climbs the rappel line from the anchors); standard rack; 75'. **Descent:** Same as for GEAR'.

BOTTLENECK AREA-NORTH SIDE

23. **Green Dragon** (5.11b) Located on first formation on right side of road after parking area; 6 bolts (optional TCUs useful to protect start); 60'. **Descent:** Single-rope rappel from chain anchor.

24. **Greenough's Garden** (5.8) Follows obvious crack in corner left of GREEN'; gear; 50'. **Descent:** There is no fixed anchor at this time; scramble off tower. (Scary.)

25. **The Domino** (5.10a) Aptly named, this fun route climbs a formation that borders road at the "bottleneck" proper and ascends line to beneath the "domino"; a 2-bolt/fixed-biner anchor is beneath the "domino"; 4 bolts; 40'. **Descent:** Single-rope rappel from 2-bolt anchor.

26. **Clovis Man** (5.8+) Located on right/north side a short distance up road beyond Bottleneck Area; easily recognized by brilliant orange rock over a gray, chert-studded slab to right; bolts; 70'. **Descent:** Single-rope rappel from chain anchor.

SKIDMARK WALL

This high-quality wall is about 0.6 mile beyond the parking area for the Mulkey Tower. Located on the right/north side of the road, this clean gray wall has a distinctive black water streak down its left side. Since it is uphill and partially hidden by trees, it is easily missed. There is no convenient parking below the crag, so please park either farther up or down the road; **do not block the narrow access road.**

27. **Wipe It on The Curtains** (5.7) Right-most climb on the Skidmark Wall; 4 bolts; 65'. **Descent:** Single-rope rappel from chain anchor.

28. **Easy Like Your Mama** (5.10b/c) Next climb left of WIPE'; ascend face, cross ramp, and continue up to fixed anchor; bolts; 75'. **Descent:** Single-rope rappel from chain anchor.

29. **Skid Mark** (5.11b) First route established on the wall (Considered a classic); left of EASY' and ascends face to same anchor; bolts; 75'. **Descent:** Single-rope rappel from EASY' anchor.

30. **The Prick** (5.11d/.12a) Located left of SKID'; bolts; 70'. **Descent:** Single-rope rappel from chain anchor.

31. **Fatty Nipple** (5.12 b/c). Farthest left on wall; steep line; bolts; 60'. **Descent:** Single-rope rappel from chain anchor.

MULKEY MAN AREA

This area consists of two separate but close together walls. About 0.7 mile up the canyon beyond the Mulkey Tower (a scant 0.1 mile past the Skidmark Wall) is a small pullout below the crags. The approach uphill from the parking area takes about 5 minutes.

32. **"Project"** (5.hard+) Line of bolts on far right that lead to same anchor as MULKEY MAN (see below).

33. **Mulkey Man** (5.10d) Located to left of PROJECT, this route is perhaps one of the best in the canyon; follow black streak; 6 bolts; 75'. **Descent:** Single-rope rappel from chain anchor.

34. **Master at Arms** (5.12d/.13a) Starts to left of MULKEY MAN; bolts; 80'. **Descent:** Single-rope rappel from chain anchor.

35. **Crimpers for Christ** (5.12a) Highly recommended. Not located on the same wall as the other Mulkey Man Area routes. Go up around corner and left of previous climbs to an interesting-looking gray wall with a distinctive arch on its left side; route is located at far right end of this wall; gray face on "not-so-bomber" protruding orange chert; bolts; 80'. **Descent:** Single-rope rappel from chain anchor.

RATTLER GULCH

OVERVIEW

The fins or "ribs" that jut from the hillsides in Rattler Gulch are composed of 300 million-year-old Madison limestones. The east-west tending ribs, which were partially quarried years ago, extend up the hillsides on either side of the road. The north and south sides of the ribs are steep walls, 80 to 100 feet high and graced with edges, pockets, small chert knobs, and vertical seams. Located on the southern slopes of the Garnet Range about 48 miles east of Missoula and 5 miles west of Drummond, Rattler Gulch has become a popular destination for beginner climbers as well as "hone masters." The area receives little precipitation, has easy access, and routes are graded from 5.4 to 5.12.

Climbing on Rattler's steep walls often requires patient technical prowess as most of the routes are thin and sustained. Certainly the Diver's Wall is an exceptional standout among the other areas. This steep north-facing wall sports seven difficult and sequential face climbs from 5.11a to 5.12+, demanding finger strength, balance, and precision footwork. Diver's Wall is in the shade most of the day and remains cool even during summer months. The Sidewinder Wall has a southern exposure with well-protected moderate routes offering a fun alternative to the extremes of Diver's Wall.

Fixed anchors—high-grade expansion bolts (3/8" x 3" with 3/8" x 3.5" bolt rappel anchors)—are the predominant form of protection. A rack of quick draws will suffice for most routes at Rattler, but **a standard rack** for Rattler should include a few cams and wired stoppers (for some routes) to supplement 8-10 quick draws, slings for clipping anchors, and a single 165-foot rope. Climbs, except where noted, end at chain anchors. It is necessary to lead most routes to set up for toproping because the anchors are often below the rib tops due to loose and unpredictable rock. Scrambling on the ribs is not recommended.

WARNING: Because limestones vary in quality be extremely cautious: never trust a single anchor point for rappelling, and always backup crack protection when possible; *always wear a helmet.* Loose rock may be dislodged by a leader or when retrieving rappel ropes.

Climbing history: Rattler Gulch was the first limestone climbing area developed near Missoula. In 1990 Gray Thompson and Tobin Kelley managed to put a huge lasso around the top of Diver's Wall to remove loose rock and began toproping lines. Ivan Pyatt teamed up with them to establish the first notable lead climb at Rattler (*The Cannon,* 5.11). Soon the word was out about the new area. Other route development included: the thin, crimpy *Sidewinder* (5.11) by Jim Semmelroth; the moderate and popular *Snake Eye* and *Shredder* by

▲ –

Rafael Grana, with help from Randall Green, Tobin Kelley, and Ivan Pyatt, provided the manuscript and maps for this section.

Randall Green; *Don't Put Your Hand In It* and *Steppin' Out* by and David Jones; *Orange Peel* by Gray and Lily Thompson; the test piece *Damage* (5.12+) by Pyatt and Jim Durkin, as well as several more high-standard lines on Diver's Wall; Kyle Austin developed the two routes on Toad Rib (*Kiss The Toad* and *Mean Streak*); and Pippin Wallace established *St. Louis Direct* on Rock In Between.

Ethics: Most of the routes have been toproped with fixed anchors being placed prior to lead ascents. High-grade concrete expansion bolts (3/8" by 3 to 3 1/2") have become the fixed anchors of choice; for rappel stations it is preferable to use two long bolts with heavy duty or high-tensile chains or welded cold shuts. The limestone is dense and often hard, and the climate relatively dry, so well-placed bolts last a long time. Use care and discretion when placing fixed anchors. Because of growing concerns over visual pollution caused by fixed anchors, all anchor systems should be camouflage painted to match the color of the rock.

Chipping/manufacturing or gluing on holds is not tolerated. If a climb is too difficult to ascend without resorting to these debasing tactics leave it for future generations to try.

A group of Missoula-area climbers recently repaired some of the existing trails. Please stay on established trails to prevent further erosion.

Trip Planning Information

Area description: Sport routes on limestone fins exposed in a narrow gulch.

General location: About 48 miles east of Missoula and 5 miles west of Drummond.

Camping: No established campgrounds at the gulch. No camping is allowed on private land south of the BLM gate. The Bearmouth Chalet has rooms for rent (starting at $17.50/night) and campground facilities with showers for $8/night. Drummond has full services.

Climbing season: Nearly year-round because of the relatively dry climate. Best season April-October; south-facing walls may be hot in summer, but dry and warm in fall and winter. North-facing walls are cool and enjoyable during hot weather.

Restrictions and/or access issues: Most of the rocks are on BLM land. But the southern boundary is thought to be on or near the Diver's Wall fin. Do not park on private property south of Diver's Wall. Pullouts near the gate and up the road slightly offer limited parking. Be aware of truck traffic; park well out of harm's way and respect private property rights.

Guidebook: *The Rock Climber's Guide to Montana*, Falcon Press, 1995.

Nearby mountain shops, guide services, and gyms: Pipestone Mountaineering (retail, rental, and instruction), Missoula; The Trailhead (retail and rental), Missoula; Hold-On (climbing gym, retail, instruction, and rental), Missoula;

University of Montana indoor climbing wall, Missoula.

Finding the area: From Missoula go east on Interstate 90 about 35 miles and take the Bearmouth Exit (138). Turn left on the frontage road, cross under the freeway, go over the Clark Fork River, and turn right/east and follow the old highway for another 13 miles. Turn left/north onto the dirt road at the BLM sign marking Rattler Gulch. Stay left at the "Y" intersection with the quarry road. Drive through the open range (private land—watch for livestock on road) for about 2 miles to the rocks. Park past the gate. **Do not park on the private land adjacent to and south of the first outcrop (Diver's Wall).**

From Drummond access the old highway at the Pintler Scenic Route exit on the west end of town. Go west on the old highway, which parallels the interstate, for 5 miles to the Rattler Gulch road. Turn right/north (see above).

DIVER'S WALL

Diver's Wall refers to the north side of the first rock rib on the west side of the road. The south side is orange-red and disappointingly rotten. But the north side is solid and clean, with numerous challenging routes. The route descriptions begin on the left/east side of the wall and progress west/right.

1. **Flight of the Bumblies** (5.12a) Left-most route on wall; follows a thin crack/seam; 4 bolts, gear to 2"; 60'; bolted rappel anchor.

2. **Bottom Feeder** (5.11d) Next route right of 'BUMBLIES on steep wall split by thin cracks/seams; 6 bolts; 60'; bolted rappel anchor.

3. **Gumby Killer** (5.11d) Third route from left; ascends steep bulge to upper face; 9 bolts; 80'; bolted rappel anchor.

4. **Damage** (5.12c/d) Fourth route from left; ascends line through right side of bulge and straight up on thin edges; 9 bolts; 80'; bolted rappel anchor.

5. **Me and the Devil** (5.12b) Ascends steep face 10' right of DAMAGE; 9 bolts; 80'; bolted rappel anchor.

6. **The Cannon** (5.11c) Indistinct cannon-shaped flake near right side of wall; steep face through bulge; 8 bolts; 80'; bolted rappel anchor.

7. **The Sleeper** (5.10d/.11a) Right-most of routes on wall near large break; climb past break through bulge; 6 bolts; 65'; bolted rappel anchor.

ROCK IN BETWEEN

This rib is the second formation north of Diver's Wall. Only one route to date has been developed on its narrow west prow.

8. **St. Louis Direct** (5.9) Interesting arete problem that ascends west end of narrow rib between Shredder and Diver's walls; 5 bolts; 50'; 2-bolt-sling anchor.

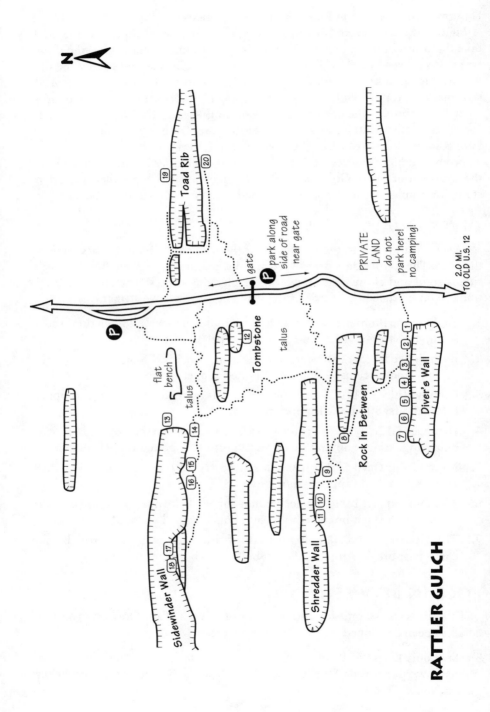

N

Toad Rib

19
20

gate

P park along
side of road
near gate

PRIVATE
LAND
do not
park here!
no camping!

2.0 MI.
TO OLD U.S. 12

P

flat
bench

talus

Tombstone

12

talus

13

14

16 15

17

18

Sidewinder Wall

1

2

3
4
5
6
7

Diver's Wall

8

Rock In Between

9

10
11

Shredder Wall

RATTLER GULCH

SHREDDER WALL

Next large fin/rib of rock north of Rock In Between. The east end of the south face is discontinuous and blocky. But midway along the south side is a short steep wall that gives way to an alcove below a longer face. Approach by wandering along paths north from Diver's Wall or west through the talus from the road.

9.   **Chumley** (5.11-) Line of homemade hangers on short wall right of STEPPIN' OUT. Thin, sharp edges; 4 bolts; 30'; 2-bolt anchor.

10. **Steppin' Out** (5.10a/b) Left/west of short wall on right side of face above alcove; take care to avoid large semi-detached flake right of crux near top; 9 bolts, gear (medium-sized wired stoppers or cams useful); 80'; shares anchor with SHREDDER.

11. **Shredder** (5.10b) Excellent, sharp-edged face climb up center of face above alcove; 10 bolts; 85'; chain anchor on ledge just below top of fin.

TOMBSTONE

North of Shredder Wall and close to the road stands a solitary tower resembling a large tombstone. This aptly named formation will surely be a fitting memorial for those attempting to climb it.

12. **Newt** (5.11-) Dangerously loose. **Not recommended.** Wired stoppers and cams useful to supplement bolts. **Descent:** Rappel and pray tower stays together.

SIDEWINDER BUTTRESS

This is the northern-most of the large fins that stand above and west of the road. The east end, closest to the road, has been quarried away, creating a triangular face. A steep talus slope (refuse from the old quarry) descends from the wall to a bench just above the road. Hike to the bench and follow a steep path up the south side of the talus. Take care to not dislodge loose rocks on the approach.

One route ascends the manmade east face of the fin, but most routes are on the south-facing wall. The majority of the moderate climbs are on this wall. Near the middle of the south face is a small dished out face or bowl with two excellent beginner leads.

13. **Bivi's** (5.10) Ascends right side of manmade (blasted) east face; bolts, gear to 3"; 95'; chain anchor.

14. **Sidewinder** (5.11a/b) Thin face climb that snakes up east end of south face characterized by line of angle-iron hangers (soon to be replaced with Petzel hangers); 6 bolts; 75'; 2-bolt anchor with ratty slings (soon to be replaced with chains) 2/3 up wall.

15. **Orange Peel** (5.8) Moderate face climb left of SIDEWINDER; bolts; 70'; shares SIDEWINDER anchor.

16. **Zelonish Gully** (5.4 R) Face and gully left of ORANGE PEEL; this sporty line angles right up the face taking line of least resistance; 4 bolts, gear; 150'; no fixed anchor. **Descent:** downclimb ramp east of SNAKE EYE or rappel from tree on top to ORANGE PEEL anchor.

17. **Snake Eye** (5.8) Right-most line on the bowl. Scramble up 30' past sizable junipers growing from the cliff to a comfortable ledge. Follow bolt line to ledge with small tree below summit; 7-8? bolts; 75'; chain anchor.

18. **Don't Put Your Hand In It** (5.8-) Left-most of routes in upper bowl, follows a vertical break in face; 5 bolts, 1 fixed pin, gear (medium stopper or cam useful); 75'; shares anchor with SNAKE EYE.

TOAD RIB

Of all the developed fins at Rattler, this rock has the most potential for new routes. The north side is predominantly smooth and steep. The south side is steep but has shredder texture. The average height is about 50'. Approach via paths through the timbered slope on the south side or via the talus on the west and northwest side.

19. **Kiss the Toad** (5.10b/c) About midway on north side of fin, pumpy and sustained; 4 bolts; 50'; chain anchor.

20. **Mean Streak** (5.11+?) Directly across from 'TOAD on the south side of the fin. Mostly 5.10 with a hard section midway up (which is even harder now due to a broken hold; bolts; 45'; chain anchor.

SouthWest

SW

REGION

Aaron Lefohn having *Second Thoughts* at Right Rock. *Photo by Randall Green.*

HELENAAREA

SHEEP MOUNTAIN

Overview

The granite domes and boulders on the southeastern slopes of Sheep Mountain are the most popular crags in the Helena area. Located south of Helena just a few miles in Lump Gulch, the exposed rocks on Sheep Mountain are part of the Boulder Batholith. The quality of the rock generally is superb with a rough texture and many natural fracture lines. The routes here are crack and face climbs typical of granite domes. Some parts of the domes are low-angled and slabby, while other aspects will be overhanging and highly textured. Some cracks are beautiful lines that cleave large expanses of solid rock replete with sharp edges and restrictions seemingly made for nuts and chocks, while others are incipient, flaring, and discontinuous. A few bolted sport routes exist, as do as several routes of mixed variety, requiring experience in gear placement for lead climbing. Because the tops of most rocks here are accessible by scramble routes, it is relatively easy to set up toprope anchors for practice climbing on many routes.

Four distinct formations are the main attractions here: Devil's Thumb (a.k.a. See-Through Spire) is a solitary spire on the western flank; Left and Upper rocks—the upper-most formations—Upper Rock is the highest and split by an obvious chimney system; Middle Rock is a slabby dome with prominent roofs on its eastern side; and Right Rock is the largest blobby domelike formation adjacent to Middle Rock on the eastern flank of the mountain. Numerous smaller formations are scattered throughout the area, offering countless bouldering and toproping problems.

A **standard gear rack** for Sheep Mountain should include a wide selection of wired stoppers from small RP/HBs and up, TCUs, nuts, cams, slings, and quick draws.

▲▲ ---

Randall Green (with help from Chris Alke, John Alke, Van Alke, Bill Bucher, Tom Lund, Jaime Johnson, Scott Payne, Sonny Stewart, and Jim Wilson) provided the information for this section.

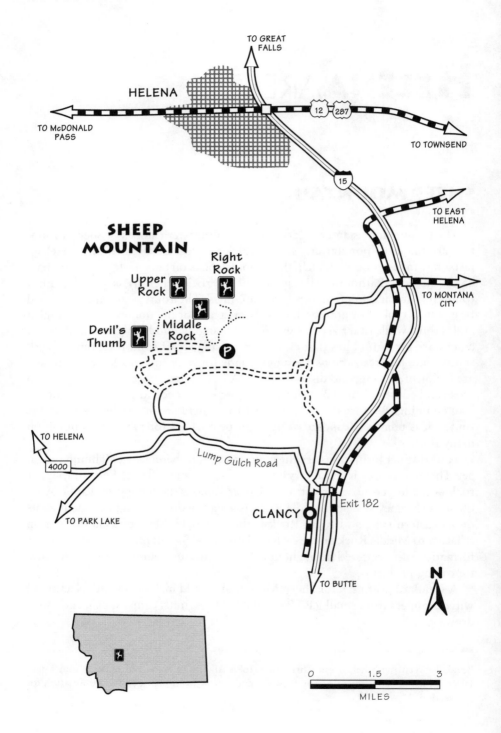

Climbing history: Although some technical ascents occurred on these rocks prior to the 1970s, there is no documented climbing history of the area. Recollection of known technical ascents began in the early 1970s when Bill Bucher and Dave Stiller began exploring the obvious crack lines on Left/Upper and Middle rocks. Later Stiller organized and taught climbing classes at Sheep Mountain, sparking the interest of others, such as the Alke brothers—Chris, John, and Van—and others.

Chris and Van Alke soon pushed the area's difficulty standards to new heights, establishing many of the early 5.9s. Sonny Stewart, Jim Scott, and Terry Kennedy joined the action and climbed some of Sheep Mountain's first 5.10s and 5.11s in the early 1980s. Bolts were used during this time to protect some blank sections between cracks. It wasn't long before this group had climbed most of the obvious lines and established the hardest crack climbs in the area. *Nemesis* and *Intensive Care*, 5.11 finger cracks on Devil's Thumb, were first free climbed by Stewart during this time, and Kennedy freed *The Myth* (5.11) on Middle Rock. Also during this period an unnamed overhanging finger crack located on a boulder near the Right Rock parking area was free climbed; it remains as one of the hardest routes on the rocks to date at 5.11d/.12a.

In the mid to late 1980s, Jim Wilson (with help from Scott Payne and Jim Nyman) established several new routes, mainly on Right Rock; and Jaime Johnson and Mark Pearson established a few new 5.10 climbs at Devil's Thumb. At the end of the decade and into the 1990s, Wilson added the aptly named *Multiple Screamer*, a 5.11 friction route on Right Rock, which has become one

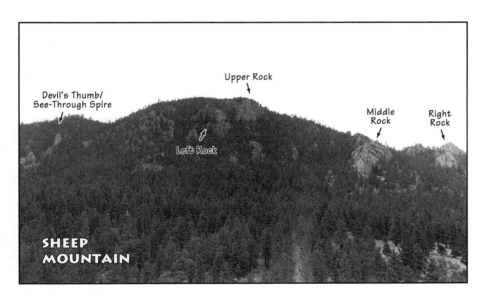

Photo by Randall Green.

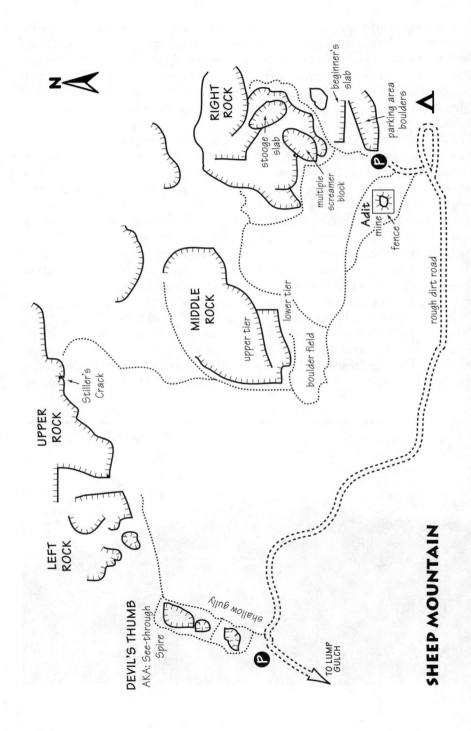

N

RIGHT
ROCK

beginner's
slab

stooge
slab

multiple
screamer
block

parking area
boulders

Adit

mine
fence

rough dirt road

P

MIDDLE
ROCK

upper tier

lower tier

boulder field

UPPER
ROCK

Stiller's
Crack

LEFT
ROCK

DEVIL'S THUMB
AKA: See-through
Spire

shallow gully

P

TO LUMP
GULCH

SHEEP MOUNTAIN

Stiller's Crack at Upper Rock, Sheep Mountain. *Photo by John Alke.*

of the area's test pieces. More recently, Payne has followed through with development of several more popular 5.10 and 5.11 routes on Right Rock.

Ethics: Although most of the routes were done on-sight from the ground up, some of routes have been toproped with fixed anchors placed prior to lead ascents.

High-grade concrete expansion bolts (3/8" by 2 to 3" or longer) have become the fixed anchors of choice; for rappel stations use two long bolts with heavy duty or high-tensile chains. The granite is quite hard and the climate relatively dry, so well-placed bolts last a long time. Only place bolts when absolutely necessary and use care and discretion when placing all fixed anchors. Because of growing concerns over visual pollution caused by fixed anchors, all anchor systems should be camouflage painted to match the color of the rock.

Chiseling, manufacturing, or gluing on holds is not tolerated. If a climb is too difficult to ascend without resorting to these debasing tactics leave it for future generations to try.

Trip Planning Information

Area description: Granite domes, predominantly south facing; single and multi-pitch routes mostly of moderate difficulty; cracks and slabs.

General location: 15 miles southeast of Helena and about 5 miles from Clancy on the mountainside above Lump Gulch.

Camping: Several tent and car camping sites are available at the trailhead parking area. Use established fire rings, but campfire restrictions may apply during dry periods. No water is available.

Climbing season: Year-round; but snow may restrict access in winter and spring.

Restrictions and access issues: Land is managed by the Bureau of Land Management. The road is nearly impassable for low-clearance passenger vehicles. Vehicles with high-clearance, a low-gear ratio, and four-wheel-drive are recommended.

Guidebook: *The Rock Climber's Guide to Montana*, Falcon Press.

Nearby mountain shops, guide services, and gyms: The Base Camp (retail), Helena; Montana Outdoor Sports (retail), Helena; Helena YMCA (climbing gym), Helena.

Finding the area: From Helena go south on Interstate 15 toward Butte. Take the Clancy exit (Exit 182), which is about 10 miles from Helena. Turn right on the frontage road toward Clancy and go east onto the graveled Lump Gulch Road, which curves past a restaurant and bar (Legal Tender) and goes northwest. Follow Lump Gulch Road to the Sheep Mountain turnoff, which is sometimes marked by a BLM sign on the right/north side of the road (3.2 miles from the I-15 interchange). Go 0.1 mile to the "Y" intersection with an unmaintained (steep and rutted) road that climbs the timbered hillside toward the rocks. Follow this rough road for about 1 mile to the Devil's Thumb pullout. Continue another 0.7 mile to the end of the road parking area and trailhead for Right, Middle, or Upper rocks.

DEVIL'S THUMB/SEE-THROUGH SPIRE

This spire offers some of the best crack climbing on Sheep Mountain. The Thumb is the western-most developed outcrops and varies in height from about 40' on its north side to 150' on the southeast side. The rock is generally of excellent quality, steep, and split by cracks on all faces. A ledge traverses the upper portion of the northeast side just below the summit block.

Finding the rock: From the pullout hike northeast up a ridge and into a shallow gully; follow an indistinct path that turns to a more well-defined game trail, which traverses toward the northeast and goes between two smaller outcrops below the 'Thumb. Continue to the base of the spire by scrambling over and around large boulders. It is possible to scramble around the spire from any direction. **Descents:** From the summit downclimb toward the west to the "Hang Nail" rappel bolts and chains (which need to be replaced with stronger hardware). From the north ridge below the summit, it also is possible to scramble down the northeast shoulder.

SOUTH FACE

1. **Nemesis** (5.11a/b) Elegant thin, double crack on south face. Most often done in two pitches—one of 90' and one of 30'—because of rope drag due to ledges on upper section. Scramble to top of block at base of route; battle thin cracks to ramp; ascend a low-angled open book to small ledge and belay; follow steep off-hand crack to top (TCUs and many small wires—#4 RPs-#6 Rocks, doubles #2-5 Rocks—for lower section to ledge and larger nuts or Friends to #3.5 for upper cracks). **Descent:** Scramble across summit, downclimb to HANG NAIL anchors and rappel or downclimb northwest shoulder.

WEST FACE

The west face is shorter and is split by three prominent crack systems that roughly lead to the same steep ramp that goes to the summit. Scramble up a sloping ledge to the base. All three crack climbs described below are within a few feet of one another.

2. Unnamed (5.8+?) Right-most of the three cracks. Ascend offhands crack to block and hand traverse left to HANG NAIL anchors; 45'. **Descent:** Rappel from HANG NAIL chain anchor.

3. **Hang Nail** (5.8+) Obvious middle crack line. Classic, albeit short finger and hand crack on west face (medium wires and cams useful); 45'. **Descent:** Rappel from chain anchors (rap bolts and chains need to be replaced; be wary of them).

4. **Lieback Flake/Boys Are Back in Town** (5.10) Short, thin crack formed by an exfoliating flake left of HANG NAIL (small wires to medium hexes/cams useful); ends at same anchor as HANG NAIL; 35'. **Descent:** Rappel from HANG NAIL chain anchor.

NORTH FACE

Several scramble routes exist on this side. Lines are discontinuous and short but give relatively easy access to summit.

5. **Unnamed** (5.8) Obvious hand and offhand crack that splits main block of north face; 30'. **Descent:** Scramble left and downclimb blocks on left side of face.

EAST FACE

Wide crack/chimney systems split this side into three main sections.

6. **Intensive Care** (5.11+) Thin, slightly left-leaning crack on right (northeastern or up hill) side of face that leads to a sloping ledge (extra #1 and #1.5 Friends or equivalent useful); 45'. **Descent:** Scramble to northeast face and downclimb.

7. **Unnamed** (5.9) About 25' left of INTENSIVE' is a low-angled arete that forms the downhill side of the upper portion of the face; an exfoliation flake and crack splits the arete and ascends to the northeast shoulder. Grunt past a strenuous lieback at start (crux) to an easy hand crack; 45'. **Descent:** Scramble to northeast face and downclimb.

8. **Ugly Crack** (5.4/.5) Wide crack/chimney/gully that separates middle and northeastern portions of the face; right of the bolt ladder; 45'. **Descent:** Scramble off northwest shoulder.

9. **Bolt Ladder** (A1) Good practice aid route that ascends steep wall of middle portion of face; take crack gear for belay on top; 1/4" bolts; 95'+?. **Descent:** Scramble and downclimb to north and west; rappel HANG NAIL or downclimb northwest shoulder.

10. **Where Hamsters Die** (5.10-) Next route left/south of BOLT LADDER. Traverse left to end of sloping ledge to stick clip first rusty bolt hanger; climb left side of face near arete; large cams useful to protect wide crack above first bolt; climb past 2 more shiny bolts and escape left past a bolt and ascend STANDARD ROUTE to summit; 100'; gear to #4 Friend useful. **Descent:** Scramble and downclimb to north and west; rappel HANG NAIL or downclimb northwest shoulder.

Photo by Randall Green.

11. **Standard Route** (5.8) Lieback and jam offhand/fist crack that splits face left of 'HAMSTERS' and gives access to various cracks in the upper section (extra nuts and cams to 3.5" useful); 110'. **Descent:** Scramble and downclimb to north and west; rappel HANG NAIL or downclimb northwest shoulder.

12. **Babies on Fire** (5.10b) Face and crack climb that begins on lower left of east face. Bolts and fixed pins protect the face climbing at bottom (crux); above fixed pins follow arete and parallel crack system to top (mid-sized wired stoppers, hexes, and Friends useful); Belay off bollards on top; 120'. **Descent:** Scramble and downclimb to north and west, rappel HANG NAIL or downclimb northwest shoulder.

LEFT/UPPER ROCKS

Left/Upper rocks are the highest and most prominent outcrops on Sheep Mountain. A gully separates the two formations. Upper Rock's south face rises unbroken for about 150'. The face is split vertically in half by a distinct chimney system (*Stiller's Crack*).

Finding the rock: From parking area for Right and Middle rocks, hike to Middle Rock and continue northwest toward the base of the Upper Rock face. Alternative approach: See Devil's Thumb—continue hiking northeast, taking the line of least resistance up the hillside, through boulder fields and timber.

Photo by Randall Green.

Left Rock

13. **B.S. (Bucher/Stiller)** (5.7) From a ledge that bisects the face scramble left/ west to gain access to a chimney that tapers to a fist crack (extra 4" pro useful); 75'. **Descent:** Walk east and descend the gully between the rocks.

Upper Rock

14. **Bill's Crack** (5.9) Obvious crack line that splits lower west face. Approach from the gully between Left and Upper rocks; 75'. **Descent:** Scramble left and descend gully.

15. **Sunny Slab** (5.5) This route zigzags up the left side of the rock, taking the line of least resistance. From the base of the main face scramble up a left-slanting ledge to a low-angled hand crack formed by a shallow open book; follow crack past a horizontal break and merge with the big corner system on the left side of wall; step left or right at the "Y"; (extra wide pro helpful); 75'. **Descent:** Scramble left into gully between rocks.

16. **Sunset Crack Direct Finish Variant** (5.8+) Start on SUNNY SLAB and take line directly left and directly through bulge at horizontal break. **Descent:** See SUNNY SLAB.

17. **Witch's Tit** (5.8) Follows cracks left of STILLER'S and joins it at mid-height above the bulge. Finish in STILLER'S.

18. **Stiller's Crack** (5.6) Main chimney that splits Upper Rock. Squirm, squiggle, or stem past small bulge (possible to belay above bulge for 2 pitches) and follow main crack system left to top; 150'; **Variant finish:** (5.8) Go right under roof near top and follow crack through bulges. **Descent:** Walk/scramble west into gully between rocks.

19. **No-Name Crack** (5.10) About 10' left of STING on the right wall of book formed by STILLER'S chimney crack. Face cling 50' to seam/groove system to top (small wired stoppers, TCUs useful). **Descent:** See STILLER'S.

20. **Sting** (5.10) Climb low-angle ramp below crack with V-shaped roof. Pass roof on the left and climb the arete past a bolt. Go up right-facing dihedral to ledges at top (RPs, wired stoppers, TCUs, hexes, and cams useful); 165'. **Descent:** Walk off to west

    Variant: Direct finish through the roofs above exit ramp offer some 5.10 climbing.

21. **Bailout Variant** (5.8) Established during first attempt to climb STING. Climb STING to small roof and exit right, following right-leaning cracks and ramp to east shoulder; belay at 2-bolt station (1/4" bolts). **Descent:** See STING.

22. **Juniper** (5.8) Next flaky groove system that leads to a tree growing out of the face right of STING. Climb a hand/finger crack to a tree (possible to

**UPPER ROCK
(VIEWED FROM
MIDDLE ROCK)**

20

16

xx

21

5.10

5.8+

floating
chimney
5.4

5.5

5.8

5.7

5.8

15

23

17

18   20, 21   22

Photo by Randall Green.

belay at tree for 2 pitches); follow crack line behind tree up to left-slanting line to groove/ramp system and BAILOUT' anchor; 100'. **Descent:** Scramble over top and west down gully between rocks.

23. **Floating Chimney** (5.4) Right of tree on JUNIPER is a chimney formed by an exfoliation flake which ends abruptly after about 40'; continue up crack line and merge with route 18; 100'. **Descent:** See JUNIPER.

MIDDLE ROCK

The south and southwest faces of Middle Rock are multi-tiered slabs that rise for more than 200'. Climbs follow shallow and discontinuous crack lines and are mostly low angled. A couple of bolted face climbs are sandwiched between the natural lines on the middle tier (Myth Slab). Most routes are 1 pitch but can be linked up for 2 or 3 pitches. It is possible to walk off the back/ northwest side of the rock, but fixed rappel anchors are in place at the tops of several climbs.

Finding the rock: The indistinct trail for Middle Rock cuts northwest just above the fenced adit (mine hole) west of the main parking area. Continue traversing northwest into a shallow timbered gully, which leads to a boulder-strewn hillside below the main face. Work left through the boulders and traverse back right/east to the base of south face.

West Shoulder

24. **The Soloist** (5.7) Line begins on the lower northwest corner. Link a series of left-leaning, discontinuous thin cracks to the upper west shoulder (TCUs, cams, and a few small nuts useful); 100'. **Descent:** Walk off west shoulder or scramble to summit (4th class).

25. **Troll's Return** (5.6) The face/crack line between 'SOLOIST and TROLL'S DIHEDRAL. Climb cracks to join upper portion of dihedral and finish by stepping right to top of 'Myth Slab (see route 31a). **Descent:** Rappel (100') from chain anchor to base (75') to ledge above ACCESS CHIMNEY.

26. **Troll's Dihedral** (5.8) Obvious left-facing dihedral on lower left flank of south face that leads to west shoulder. Start in ACCESS CHIMNEY and continue following dihedral on left side of slab; step right at top of corner to top of 'Myth Slab (wired stoppers useful).

Lower Tier/Slab

The ledge formed by the top of the lower tier is the staging area for several routes on the Middle Tier/Slab. The Access Chimney is the cleanest and most direct way to gain the ledge below Myth Slab and the cracks adjacent to it. Most of the other routes listed here are overgrown with brush and lichen.

Descents: From the ledge downclimb one of the following routes or continue up one of the routes on the 'Myth slab or right of that.

27. **Access Chimney** (5.4) Located behind large ponderosa pine at left-most side of lower tier. Also start for TROLL'S DIHEDRAL, this shallow chimney leads to ledge at top of lower tier; 25'.

28. **Chimney Sweep** (5.4) A 30' shallow, brush-filled chimney on the lower northwest corner of the south face that leads to top of lower tier; 40'.

29. **Satisfaction** (5.5) Brush-filled crack right of CHIMNEY SWEEP that leads to ledge at top of lower tier; 30'.

30. **Jiggs** (5.3) Crack and ledge system that leads to ledge, east side of lower tier; 30'.

MIDDLE TIER/SLAB

The routes described in this section are considered single-pitch lines that extend from the ledge atop the lower tier and end at the top of The Myth Slab at a chain anchor or the ledge system that angles up and left to the west shoulder. Several second- and third-pitch variants are possible above The Myth Slab and the adjacent ledge system. Low-angled cracks and textured slabs abound, punctuated by short bulging steps. It is possible to seek difficulties as high as 5.8 but also possible to traverse around such obstacles to gain the top easily.

31. **Soft Parade** (5.9+/.10-) From top of lower tier, on left side a thin crack splits face below small roof at base of Myth Slab. Ascend crack and clip bolt over lip on left side of roof; step right to avoid difficult moves over roof; once over lip climb left to discontinuous crack and more slab climbing above; 3 bolts, gear; 85'; Myth Slab chain anchors. **Descent:** Rappel from chains or continue 4th class up west shoulder and walk off west side.

31a. **The Myth Variant** (5.11) Same start as SOFT PARADE but take direct line (one or two hard moves) past thin holds over roof; continue on SOFT PARADE.

32. **Wish You Were Here** (roof variation-right) (5.9/.10-) This line connects up with face variant finish of DELIBERATION. It shares start with SOFT PARADE; go right at first bolt over lip of roof or ascend DELIBERATION start and assault roof directly. Follow bolt line left of DELIBERATION; 6 bolts, 85'; Myth Slab chain anchor. **Descent:** See SOFT PARADE.

33. **Deliberation** (5.8+) Follow shallow left-facing corner to roof and move right to discontinuous hand crack. Crux is at short face section between cracks at mid-height (medium stoppers, TCUs and cams up to #3.5 friend useful); climb to Myth Slab chain anchor; 85'. **Descent:** See SOFT PARADE.

34. **Left Crack** (5.7-) Next crack line right of DELIBERATION. Used to be a fixed pin on lower portion; climb to Myth Slab chain anchor; 85'. **Descent:** See SOFT PARADE.

35. **Right Crack/Standard Route** (5.6) Parallel to LEFT CRACK and merges with it at mid-height; climb to Myth Slab chain anchor; 85'. **Descent:** See SOFT PARADE.

36. **Twinkle Toes Variant** (5.8+ R) Climb RIGHT CRACK and just above merger with LEFT CRACK take right-slanting seam; face climb (no pro) up to ledge system that leads to west shoulder. **Descent:** Scramble left up shoulder and through cave behind tree to walk off west side of rock.

37. **Ground Out** (5.7 R) Takes the next crack/seam line right of RIGHT CRACK. When parallel seams end face climb (no pro) up and left to gain Myth Slab chain anchor; 85'. **Descent:** See SOFT PARADE.

38. **The Mistake** (5.7) Wide squeeze chimney to offhands seam that leads to ledge with tree (large cams useful); 85'. **Descent:** Scramble left up shoulder and through cave behind tree to walk off west side of rock.

39. **Buckets Away** (5.6) Right of the wide squeeze chimney are several step-like corners that zigzag up the slab to the ledge system below a squatty tree. Take the line of least resistance. **Descent:** Scramble left up shoulder and through cave behind tree to walk off west side of rock.

Photo by Randall Green.

SOUTHEAST FACE

This face is characterized by a large, low-angled slab to the right of the Middle Tier. The slab is bounded on the right/east side with large overhangs protruding from the upper section. The slab is cleaved by several crack systems that angle diagonally from right to left. A small tree stands on the left side of the slab at about mid-height. The tree marks the beginning of several climbs.

40. **Corner Pocket** (5.5/.6) Can be done in 2 to 3 pitches. Scramble (easy 5th class) to the tree at mid-height on the left side of the slab (see pitch 1 of BLOODBERRY'); continue up large right-facing open book that bounds the left wall of the slab to a stair-step feature that breaks the left side of the book; ascend the steps and scramble to base of large bulge split by several vertical cracks and belay; continue left around bulge to easier ground and summit. **Descent:** Walk off backside and down north and east side to base.

41. **Bloodberry Jam** (5.8+) 3-pitch route up the large open book formation on the left side of the southeast slab. Possible to link with several single-pitch variant finishes. **Pitch 1**—(5.3-5.5) Scramble directly up crack and groove system to ledge with small tree on left side of slab at mid-height or follow a zigzag line of crack/ledges up lower slab to base of dihedral on left side of slab, belay on ledge below dihedral, 60'. **Pitch 2**—(5.8+) Low-angled open book merges with slightly overhanging dihedral; ascend dihedral (crack is wide at first, narrowing to hands as it steepens); pull over lip of overhang past questionable rock and chockstones to triangle-shaped sloping shelf; main route continues straight up through flaky crack and some loose rock to top or it is possible to clamber left from triangular shelf and scramble over second step, belay from blocks atop second step, 70' or continue to top. **Pitch 3**—(5.9 Classy Reunion Variant) This "not-so-classy" crack is an overhanging dihedral that goes from the north end of the triangular shelf. From the belay on self cross shelf right and ascend crack in corner that is flaky and loose in spots, belay on top, 50'. **Descent:** Walk off north side toward the east and back to base of route.

42. **Choker** (5.9) Overhanging, wide fist-to-offhands crack that splits the prominent overhang directly above the middle of the slab. **Pitch 1**—(see BLOODBERRY). **Pitch 2**—(see HOOD). **Pitch 3**—(5.9) Ascend overhanging fist and off-width crack to slab above and belay. **Descent:** Scramble up slab and traverse right to easier ground and east shoulder. Downclimb off shoulder and walk around east end.

43. **Leaning Crack** (5.6?) Ascends obvious left-leaning crack to top on southeast face right of large overhangs. **Descent:** Downclimb off shoulder and walk around east end.

RIGHT ROCK

This blobby formation is deservedly the most popular climbing area at Sheep Mountain. It is easy to get to and offers a variety of climbing types and difficulties. On a weekend, The Three Stooges Slab area often has a party sampling the moderately difficult crack and face routes, which are characteristic of this rock. It is relatively easy to scramble to the tops of many routes where fixed anchors make convenient toprope set-ups. Right Rock's predominant southern exposure makes it a warm place to climb early and late in the season.

In addition to the main attraction of the main rock, several smaller outcrops along the approach trail are worth exploring. The first major outcrop above the parking area is split on the north side by an overhanging, bad-sized hand and finger crack (5.11+/.12-) that is fun to lead or toprope. If you're looking for something less extreme, several other short cracks and face problems abound here. For easy slab climbing go farther up the trail to a inviting looking low-angled slab that is about 40' high. Several trees on its top make convenient toprope anchors; the slab is a nice place to work on footwork and friction technique.

The routes described below are listed from left to right, starting on the extreme left side of the west face.

Finding the rock: The Right Rock approach trail wanders due north from the main road and parking area (some vehicles continue up the hill on an old jeep road for another 300 yards, but it is better to park at the culdesac at the end of main road). Follow the trail from the main parking area to a large slab and boulder field below the rock. Follow switchbacks to the base of the main face.

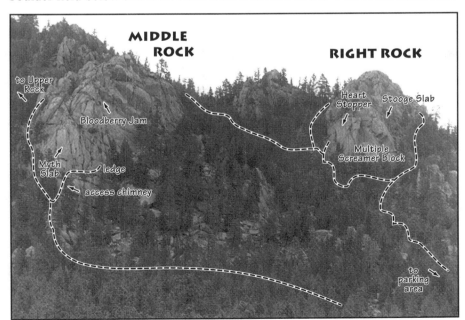

Photo by Randall Green.

West Face

44. **Mark of Zoro** (5.7) Starts in chimney formed by right side of two large blocks leaning against left side of west face. Climb chimney and step right (crux) to gain crack and flake system; 65'. **Descent:** Downclimb left into gully and walk off.

45. **Heart Stopper** (5.10b) Face and crack climb on upper west wall. Bouldery (5.9+) start follows right slanting seam to ledge with tree; face climb past bolt (crux) to horizontal crack; follow zigzag crack back right and up (RPs/HBs, small-medium wires, TCUs, #2 Friend useful) to easier face climbing near top; 80'. **Descent:** Scramble to west shoulder and walk off or rappel.

46. **Second Thoughts** (5.11a) Either begin face climbing past bolts left of DE-FOLIATOR between crack systems from atop boulders (5.9 and somewhat contrived) or start on West Face 20' right of HEART STOPPER at end of ledge, following right-facing lieback flake (5.7) to bolt line; continue up bolt line to arete that arches toward HEART STOPPER or bail out right to finish in a 5.9 crack to avoid the friction crux; 150'. **Descent:** Scramble to west shoulder and walk off or rappel from HEART STOPPER anchors.

47. **Defoliator** (5.9/.10a) Right of flaring seam (left-most of lines above a sandy ledge on north wall of cave left of huge detached block) a thin crack starts about 20' above base. Face climb past old 1/4" bolt and follow crack to

Photo by Randall Green.

bulge with flakes forming cracks (small and medium wires, hexes, and cams to 3.5" useful). Belay from blocks at top of crack; 150'. **Descent:** Scramble to west shoulder and walk off or rappel from chain anchor on good ledge to east.

48. **Fin-Again** (5.10) Next crack/seam right of DEFOLIATOR; 1-2 pitches. **Pitch 1**—(5.10) Face climb past quartz dike to tiny hole/flake (first good gear) and layback seam that angles up to squeeze chimney formed by huge detached block; use thin crack/seam for gear and chimney up to ledge at top of block. **Pitch 2**—(5.10b) Cross rubble behind huge block and ascend arching crack line (past fixed pin) to finger and hand crack that splits shallow dihedral above MULTIPLE SCREAMERS; belay from blocks at top of crack, 65'. **Descent:** Scramble to west shoulder and walk off or rappel from anchors above DEFOLIATOR.

49. **Boulder Problem** (5.11- R) Right-most of two thin-crack and groove lines on the cave wall under the Multiple Screamers block. First bolt (1/4") 15' off the ground; early ascent parties climbed thin seam to top bolt (old 1/4" bolt) and lowered off, which is **not recommended until anchor is improved**. **Descent:** Fly to hard ground at base of route if top bolt fails.

MULTIPLE SCREAMER BLOCK

This huge block is semi-detached from the main cliff. Its backside is a large chimney that tapers to a squeeze slot where the block leans against the main cliff.

WEST SIDE

50. **Multiple Screamers** (5.11c) Bolted friction face left of small tree on west side of block. Use tree to gain first holds; continue working left to edge of block, following bolt line; chain anchors at top of block, 75'. **Descent:** Rappel.

51. **The Nose** (5.9) Face and crack climb up southwest ridge of block. Begin on lower southwest corner of block; climb past 3 bolts and crack (nuts and cams to 3.5" useful) to chain anchor (easy face climbing near top is runout), 100'. **Descent:** Rappel 75' from 'SCREAMER anchor; or chain anchor above east side of block, 75'.

52. **Flame Out/Muscle Screw** (5.11a/A0) Steep, pumpy face climb on east side of Multiple Screamers block. Aid past first bolt to positive face holds; pumpy and slightly runout between bolts; 50'; chain anchors. **Descent:** Rappel from chains.

53. **Toprope Flake** (5.10 R) Exfoliation flake 20' right of FIRE DRILL leads to a chain anchor on middle of face. This route has a desperate start. Not

recommended as a lead climb due to the unprotected entry moves, it is best to climb another route to Multiple Screamer block and rappel to the chain anchor at top of flake to set up a toprope.

54. **Bloody Knuckles** (5.10b) Finger crack that splits the wall directly above the top of Multiple Screamer Block (first 20' fingers) and joins the easy chimney finish of RICH MAN-POOR MAN; a nice second pitch for routes on the block; 45'. **Descent:** Rappel to block from chain anchors at top.

SOUTH FACE

55. **Rich Man-Poor Man** (5.8+) 1- or 2-pitch line that ascends line through bombay chimney on left side of South Face. **Pitch 1**—(5.8) Follow seams directly below chimney to detached flake (hand crack); squeeze through bombay (horn offers some protection as well as small cracks in back of chimney); escape left under roofs and belay at fixed pin to avoid rope drag or continue. **Pitch 2**—(5.8) Step left and ascend chimney/flake system on west side to slab and chain anchor. **Descent:** Make two single-rope rappels; one from top of slab to Multiple Screamer Block; another from chains on east side of west wall slightly below top of Multiple Screamer Block.

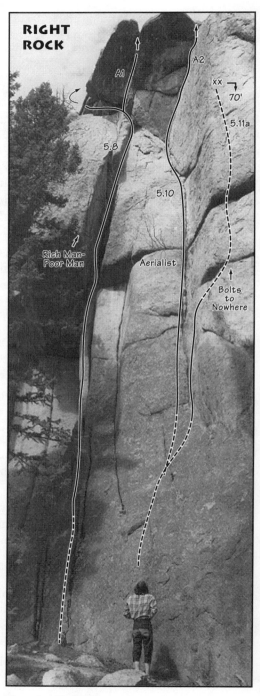

RIGHT ROCK

A1

A2

xx
70'

5.11a

5.8

5.10

Rich Man-
Poor Man

Aerialist

Bolts
to
Nowhere

Photo by Chris Alke.

56. **Aerialist** (5.10/A2) Crack and groove system left of BOLTS TO NOWHERE. Ascend seams to first roof; climb out to bolt and aid under right roof above crack to join up with CURLY and Stooges Slab anchors (RPs/HBs, TCUs, #1-3.5 Friends, #11 hex. **Descent:** Rappel from Stooge anchor and downclimb (5.4) east side of Stooge ledge.

57. **Bolts to Nowhere** (5.11a) An enticing face climb right of AERIALST that ends in blank wall above two horizontal cracks. Boulder to sloping shelf and ascend detached triangular block; follow bolts past horizontal breaks; 70', 3 bolts, gear (medium wires/TCUs useful). **Descent:** Rappel from 2-bolt-chain anchor.

58. **Gentle Touch/Pint of Blood** (5.11a) Face and crack climb right of BOLTS TO NOWHERE. Start at same place or slightly right of 'BOLTS; climb past bolts, gaining vertical seam/crack (crux); follow crack to Stooge ledge; belay from blocks; 3 bolts, gear (medium wires and cams/hexes); 70'. **Descent:** Downclimb (5.4) slab/crack at east end of ledge.

59. **Feuding Egos** (5.10) Short face climb to Stooge ledge; 3 bolts; 30'. **Descent:** Downclimb (5.4/.5) slab/crack at east end of ledge.

STOOGE'S SLAB

On the lower southeast face is a sloping ledge that angles up and left to a small bowl-shaped slab. The Stooges Slab is bounded by air and exposure on the left and a crack/seam on the right. Right of *Feuding Egos* is a easy (5.4/.5) groove that leads to Stooges Ledge. The slab is about 75' high with a chain anchor on top, making it an ideal toproping area. It is possible to scramble around the east side up a gully that leads to the top of the slab.

60. **Left Stooge—"Curly"** (5.8) Face climb on rough rock up left edge of Stooge bowl; 4 bolts, gear (medium-sized nuts or cams useful); 75'. **Descent:** Scramble up and left to top of upper gully and walk off east or rappel to Stooges Ledge from chains.

61. **Middle Stooge—"Moe"** (5.10a) Thin, low-angled crack in middle of bowl leads to friction climbing past bolts to chain anchor; 4 bolts, gear (small-med. wires, TCUs useful); 70'. **Descent:** See LEFT STOOGE.

62. **Right Stooge—"Larry"** (5.9) Thin, right-slanting crack on right side of bowl leads to friction climbing past bolts (crux) or continue up right cracks to ramp (5.8); traverse left at ramp to anchor; 3 bolts, gear (medium wires, TCUs useful). **Descent:** See LEFT STOOGE.

63. **Corner Crack** (5.5/.6) Crack system right of Stooge's Slab ends on ramp below and right of anchors. Ascend crack and ramp to anchors; gear to 3.5" (extra slings useful); 75'. **Descent:** See Left Stooge.

Upper Cracks/Seven Sisters

Along the north wall of the access gully that leads to the top of the midlevel slab (Stooges area, etc.) are seven short cracks. These clean lines are great practice climbs, which can be led or toproped. A fixed chain anchor is set above the three most popular cracks. It is possible to continue scrambling to the head of the gully and cut back right/east on a ledge system to the anchors.

64. **Left Crack** (5.6) Flaring crack that is left-most on the wall; medium to large nuts and cams useful; 60'. **Descent:** Rappel from chain anchor or scramble left and down gully.

65. **Middle Crack** (5.8) Flaring parallel jam cracks. Start in left crack; bear hug and jam both cracks through a bulge and continue up easy ground to anchors; medium to large nuts and cams useful; 60'. **Descent:** Rappel from chain anchor or scramble left and down gully.

66. **Right Crack** (5.7) Left-leaning crack that is right-most off the sandy ledge in the upper gully. Take medium to large nuts and cams useful; 60'. **Descent:** Rappel from chain anchor or scramble left and down gully.

Summit Block

67. **Clam Shell Slab** (5.7) Scramble east past the access gully for the Upper Cracks and take a climbing traverse back left to base of summit block; follow a low-angled ramp to crack through clamshell-shaped slab to left shoulder below summit. **Descent:** Downclimb and walk off north side around to east side.

68. **Summit Dihedral** (5.4/.5) Scramble up ramps above the Upper Cracks to a shallow vertical dihedral; climb dihedral and scramble to top; 75'. **Descent:** Downclimb and walk off back side and descend west-side gully.

Parking Area Boulders

These are the first outcrop encountered above the main Right Rock parking area. The south side is low-angled and split by several gully cracks that give easy access to the top. The north side is steeper and offers many short problems.

69. **Desperation** (5.11+/.12-) Overhanging bad-sized finger crack on north side of outcrop; gear (extra small-medium nuts, TCUs, and small Friends); 25'; 2 anchor bolts on top. **Descent:** Walk off east end or scramble off south side of outcrop.

BEAVER CREEK-REFRIGERATOR CANYON AREA

EYE OF THE NEEDLE

OVERVIEW

If you're looking for a semi-alpine adventure not too far from civilization and with an easy approach, the limestone cliffs in Beaver Creek Canyon offer some fine multi-pitch routes. Located in the Big Belt Mountains just 30 miles northeast of Helena near Refrigerator Canyon and the Gates of the Mountains Wilderness, the 500-foot Eye of the Needle offers a variety of climbs. Access is possible in most passenger vehicles via a well-maintained gravel road. The approaches to the climbs are typically 10- to 15-minute hikes.

The climbing is on limestone (part of the Madison formation), which was created by seabed sediments. Thrust faulting and erosion of these sedimentary layers created unique formations that are exposed in the upper Beaver Creek drainage and elsewhere in the range. The rock varies in color with slate grays, chocolate browns, rusty reds, and dingy whites. The gray rock tends to be more compact and best suited for climbing, although some of the brown rock also is compact and has texture suitable for face climbing. Routes vary from low-angled slabs to steep walls graced with edges and pockets; a few incipient and discontinuous cracks are thrown in for variety. But few continuous natural crack lines exist. Even the lower angled slabs offer an abundance of edges and texture (meaning a feel of 100 grit sandpaper). The higher-angled rock often has sharp edges and pockets. Holds can be very sharp; pockets and cracks may have teeth, and sharp edges abound to abuse a rope, your clothing, and your skin. But the climbing moves are often superb and well protected.

Fixed anchors—high-grade expansion bolts are the predominant form of protection, but a standard rack of nuts and camming devices is a necessary addition on many routes.

To avoid a cut foot from a sharp rock when fording Beaver Creek, it is advisable to take a pair of wading shoes. The creek may vary from a bone-chilling knee-deep plunge in spring to a soothing ankle-deep foot bath in summer and fall.

Climbing history: Most of the routes here were established during the summer of 1994 by various climbers from Helena and Bozeman. Scott Payne and Randall Green established the existing multi-pitch routes on the north slab; *Batteries Not Included* and the first pitch of *Bassackwards* have become "must-do" classics. Although *Batteries Not Included* is a bit sporty for its moderate

▲ -

Randall Green, with help from Scott Payne and Hunter Coleman, provided the information for this section.

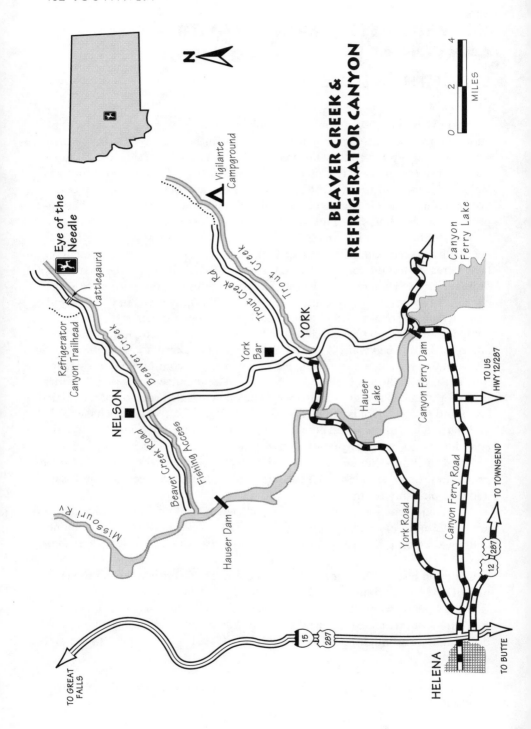

BEAVER CREEK &
REFRIGERATOR CANYON

Hunter Coleman sampling a *Forearm Flambé*. *Photo by Randall Green.*

grade of 5.8, all the difficult sections are well protected. Green's *Forearm Flambé*, on the west face, also has become popular.

Aaron Lefohn added *Walk on the Ocean*, a surprisingly good crack line on the east side, and *Dances with Roofs*, a steep face route near the creek. Green, Bill Dockins, and Kristen Drumheller established a three-pitch sport route (*This Ain' Nuthin'*) up the overhanging west face.

Ethics: Although some of the easier natural lines were done on sight from the ground up, most of the routes have been toproped with fixed anchors being placed prior to lead ascents.

High-grade concrete expansion bolts (3/8" by 3 to 3 1/2") have become the fixed anchors of choice; for rappel stations use 2 long bolts with heavy duty or high-tensile chains or welded cold shuts. The limestone is dense and often hard, and the climate relatively dry; well-placed bolts last a long time. Use care and discretion when placing fixed anchors. Because of growing concerns over visual pollution caused by fixed anchors, all anchor systems should be camouflage painted to match the color of the rock.

Chipping/manufacturing or gluing on holds is not tolerated. If a climb is too difficult to ascend without resorting to these debasing tactics leave it for future generations to try.

WARNING: Because limestones vary in quality be extremely cautious: never trust a single anchor point for rappelling, and always backup crack protection when possible. *Always wear a helmet*; loose rock may be dislodged by a leader or when retrieving rappel ropes.

Trip Planning Information

Area description: Prominent limestone buttress on north slopes above creek; single and multi-pitch routes on low-angled slabs and steep faces.

General location: 30 miles northeast of Helena in the Big Belt Mountains.

Camping: Car camping areas abound along the creek about 0.25 mile east of the spire just off the Beaver Creek road near the creek; bring drinking water or a filter for creek water; use existing fire rings and be extra cautious about open fires during dry periods.

Climbing season: April through October, but south and west facing routes may be dry in winter.

Restrictions and access issues: Land is managed by the Forest Service and is outside of the Gates of the Wilderness Area. Parking is limited to pullouts along the main road or at the Refrigerator Canyon trailhead.

Nearby mountain shops, guide services, and gyms: The Base Camp (retail and instruction), Helena; Montana Outdoor Sports (retail), Helena; Helena YMCA (climbing gym), Helena.

Finding the rock: Eye of the Needle stands on the north-facing slopes of Beaver Creek Canyon about 0.2 mile past the Refrigerator Canyon trailhead.

Susan Zazzali on the third pitch of *This Ain' Nuthin'*. *Photo by Randall Green.*

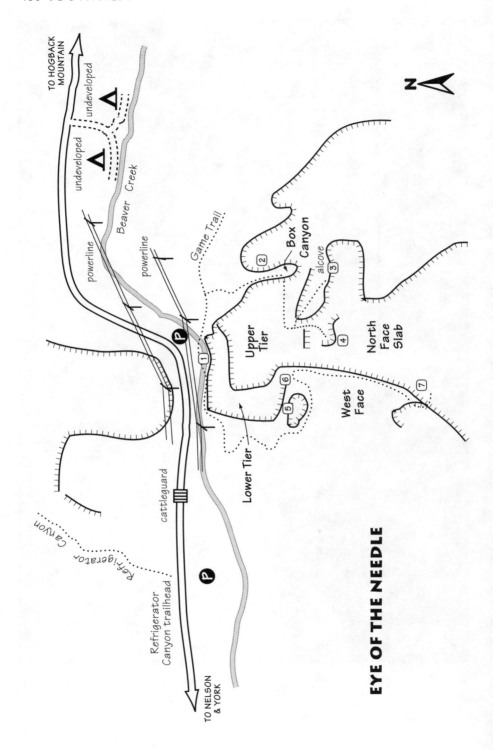

EYE OF THE NEEDLE

EYE OF THE
NEEDLE

West Face

Upper North Slab

cave

alcove

xx

Walk
on the
Ocean

5.9+

2

xx

5.11

Dances
with
Roofs

1

Beaver Creek

Photo by Randall Green.

From Helena go east on the paved York/Canyon Ferry Road (County Highway 280); Custer Street becomes Canyon Ferry Road at Montana Avenue. Cross over Interstate 15 and follow signs to York. Once across the York Bridge (Hauser Lake), the road narrows and follows a canyon to the small community of York (16 miles from Helena). Turn left onto a graveled and washboarded road at the York Bar and go north toward Nelson about 7.3 miles. At Nelson ("the [self-proclaimed] cribbage capital of the world") take the right-hand fork and head east up Beaver Creek Canyon about 4.4 miles. The Eye of the Needle comes into view just past the Refrigerator Canyon trailhead. Continue beyond the trailhead parking area across a cattleguard to one of the pullouts near the base of the northeast corner of the spire.

North Face—Lower Tier

Routes are directly across the creek from the pullout. Cross Beaver Creek and traverse along base of wall to routes. Routes may be difficult to get to during periods of high water.

1. **Dances with Roofs** (5.10+/.11-) Face climb that ascends a bluish indention in left third of the lower tier; first bolt may be redundant during periods of highwater; 6 bolts; 60' to chain anchor. **Descent:** Single-rope rappel from chain anchor or walk off east side of buttress.

North Face—East Side Box Canyon and Upper Tier Slab

Cross Beaver Creek and ascend a faint game trail on the east side of the spire. Watch for a path that cuts right where a small dead tree lays across the trail. Follow the faint path across the hillside under the support wire for the nearby electric transmission tower and up a steep slope. The access path ends in a small box canyon just above a crack route called *Walk on the Ocean*. Scramble right/ west onto ledges that lead to the lower north shoulder of the buttress. From the shoulder scramble up until the main slab begins.

2. **Walk on the Ocean** (5.9+) Located on lower nose of left box canyon wall. Short, right-leaning crack that starts out thin fingers and widens to hands; gear (TCUs and nuts and cams to 3" useful); 60'. **Descent:** Single-rope rappel from chain anchor at top of crack.

3. **Bassackwards** (5.10) 2-pitch face climb on left side of north slab. Route begins 150' left of BATTERIES NOT INCLUDED; a ledge traverses east/ left 30' below starting point for BATTERIES'. Scramble across an exposed ledge with small trees and up a short gully to a comfortable alcove above the box canyon. **Pitch 1—**(5.9-) Face climb right past two bolts to avoid alcove overhang and ascend clean slab to cave; 7 bolts (take long slings for bolts below cave if merging with BATTERIES); belay from cave with tree;

Photo by Randall Green.

75'. **Pitch 2**—(5.10) Go left from cave and climb a steep left slanting line to the gully left of summit block; 7 bolts, gear (TCUs and medium-sized cams useful); 100'; welded coldshut rappel anchor at base of gully and on right wall of elongated summit block. **Descent:** Double-rope rappel to cave with trees; single-rope rappel from tree to lower alcove (start of route).

4. **Batteries Not Included** (5.8) 2-pitch climb to North Summit of North Face. From north shoulder scramble to base of upper slab and belay from small tree on right/west side. **Pitch 1**—(5.8) Mixed crack and face climbing mostly straight up to a chain anchor slightly above and right of cave; 6 bolts, gear (#3 and #3.5 Friends, #0 TCU, small and medium stoppers useful); 140'. **Bypass variant** (5.7) goes left at third bolt, following a undercling flake to an alcove/cave with trees growing from it; 4 bolts, gear (extra small and medium cams and nuts useful); 110'. **Pitch 2**—(5.8) From chain anchor, face climb straight up slab toward summit, following right-hand edge near top; 9 bolts; 150' to ridge; anchors set in Eye of the Needle below ridge top; 165' rope is just long enough for belay leash to ridge top for belay. **Descent:** Two double-rope rappels to shoulder; rappel through hole below leaning block (chain anchor located below ridge top); rappel from semi-hanging stance (chains) in middle of face to shoulder of ridge and base of route.

Recommended variant: Combine the first pitch of BASSACKWARDS and the upper pitch of BATTERIES' from the chain station at mid-height. Traverse right from last bolt on BASSACKWARDS first pitch to cave and continue up right wall of cave past 2 bolts to chain station; 150'; take extra slings to avoid rope drag when traversing past cave.

West Face

The lower west face is broken into two tiers with good, high-angle rock on both cliffs of the tiers. The lower tier is a south-facing gray wall split by several horizontal cracks. The upper tier is about 75-90' high with caves and aretes of solid rock. Where the tiers meet the North Face, the wall rears back in over-hanging steps more than 120' in places. The rock is generally good on this side, too.

The upper west face, right of *Gimpy*, is solid gray and slabby up to a band of rotten rock, 75-120'. Farther up the base of the cliff, the wall becomes steeper with one bulging wall rising more than 400' high. This large face curves north-west in an unbroken line for another 300 yards. The rock here varies in color and quality.

To access this side, cross Beaver Creek upstream from a large boulder be-neath the main North Face where a pile of driftwood is lodged against the wall. A path goes from the boulder along the base of the wall, heading west. Follow a faint trail under the base of North Face cliff and ascend path on the west side of buttress.

WEST FACE

125'
xx
xx
5.11a 80' alternative
rappel/lower
xx
xx 150'
5.11c
xx
200'
xx
110'
Gimpy
Forearm
Flambé
5.11+/
5.12-
7

Photo by Phyllis Lefohn.

5. **Forearm Flambé** (5.10b) Line ascends clean gray face, which is split by several horizontal fracture lines, on lower tier of the West Face. 4 bolts, gear (#4-#12 stoppers useful); 65'. **Descent:** Single-rope rappel from chain anchor.

6. **Gimpy** (5.10c) Single-pitch face and crack line that ascends large prominent dihedral that extends to lower shoulder of upper North Face. Belay from alcove at base of dihedral; start in corner then face climb on good rock right of dihedral proper past 4 bolts; at mid-height climb steep crack in dihedral corner to avoid section of bad rock on right (crack is solid and takes small to medium-sized cams); finish on left side of dihedral up steep gray face (crux) to small ledge just below shoulder; 8 bolts, gear (medium-sized cams helpful to protect section between second and third bolt); 110'. **Descent:** Double-rope rappel from chain anchor just below ridge or scramble up to ridge and walk down east side trail.

7. **This Ain' Nuthin'** (5.11+/.12-) 3-pitch line that ascends bulging West Face to north summit. Line begins at bottom of "V" formation on main face (about 200 yards uphill from GIMPY) and roughly follows the left-most gray stripe through a bulging wall to a slight alcove dish and then onto a nose feature through upper bulges. **Pitch 1**—(5.11+/.12-) To avoid rotten rock at base of wall scramble uphill between a large boulder and wall to gain a ledge 25' above ground, belay from bolts in back of cave; climb left off ledge and over bulge to gain access to main face (thin and sustained); go left as difficulty eases and climb toward left end of horizontal flake with bush; go past bush up block to belay chains; 13 bolts: 120'; **Single-pitch variant:** Go right as difficulty eases toward ledge at right end of horizontal flake with leaning pillar; 11 bolts; 110'. (Double-rope rappel to base. If you change your mind and want to continue, it is possible to traverse the ledge/horizontal flake 60' (past 4 bolts) to gain belay for pitch 2). **Pitch 2**—(5.11c) Ascend steep line (crux directly above belay) that arches right to alcove dish high on face, sustained ; 12 bolts; 130'; 2-bolt belay for final pitch is 30'left of chain rappel anchor. **Pitch 3**—(5.11a) From 2-bolt belay, line ascends steep nose up and arches right below bulge; 11 bolts to welded coldshuts; lower off (80') to rappel chains or continue on easier ground to upper rappel chains (medium cams useful for upper section); 120' to summit ridge chain anchors. **Descent:** Three double-rope rappels to base of West Face (note of caution: all three rappels have free hanging sections; to reach final anchors rappel below ledge until it is possible to get hold of rock to climb up to anchor); **Optional descent:** From summit scramble down ridge and rappel through Eye of the Needle down BATTERIES'.

NOTES:

Dwight Bishop pulling over the roof on a route near Butte. *Photo by Andrew C.G. Denton.*

BUTTEAREA

OVERVIEW

Butte, Montana, was and still is a mining town. Gold was discovered in 1864, then came silver, and finally copper when the gold and silver ran out. By World War I, the city's population swelled to more than 100,000. Twenty thousand were mine employees. In the 1950s, open pit mining came to Butte and "the richest hill on earth" began to disappear. The one landmark that stands out in Butte now is the open mine pit, a mile wide and a mile deep. Butte's landscape is still dotted by old mine headframes, elevators that carried miners more than a mile below ground.

Today, Butte, the "All America City," is in transition to a more diversified economy. There are historical attractions throughout the city to help visitors learn about its background. Outside of town you can enjoy fishing, camping, hiking, mountain biking, kayaking, and, of course, climbing during spring, summer, and fall.

Three of the many fine places to climb in the Butte area are at Spire Rock, Dragon's Back, and the Homestake Pass area. The rock of all three areas is granite of the Boulder Batholith.

If you're interested in specifics, the rocks are identified as Butte quartz monzonite, an equigranular rock consisting of 35 percent plagioclase, 30 percent potassium feldspar, 20 percent quartz, and 15 percent hornblende and biotite, with minor accessory minerals. Around Butte the rock includes areas with crystals of potassium feldspar up to ten inches in length.

The peculiar blocky nature of outcrops at Spire Rock and Homestake Pass is due to the weathering of regularly spaced jointing patterns in the rock.

For hardy souls, climbing can be done here year-round. The summer months are the warmest. However, it can snow any month of the year in the mountains of Montana, especially on the Continental Divide. In the winter it can be 40 degrees below or 50 degrees above. The best time to climb though is June through October. The days will be warm to hot, 50 to 70 degrees, and the nights are

▲ -

Dwight Bishop, author of *A Climber's Guide to Butte,* provided the maps, photos, and majority of the text for this section. Jim Wilson and Brad Hutcheson provided additional information and valuable review comments.

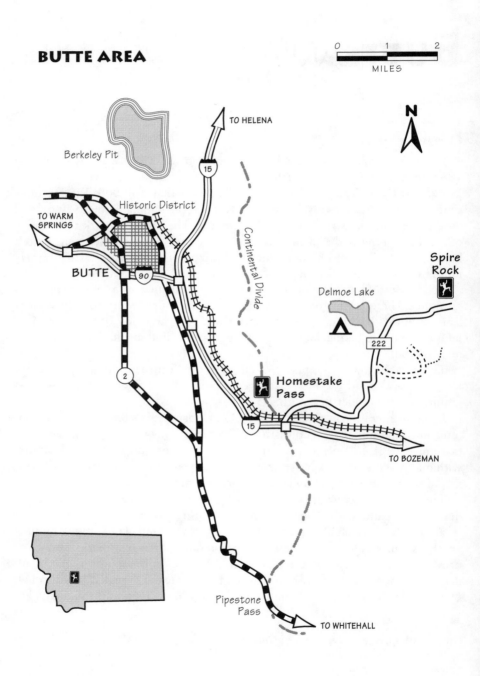

cool. For all the areas covered here, the elevation is around 6,000 feet.

All services are found in Butte. A good place for a shower is at the YMCA, 4040 Paxson Avenue in Butte; (406) 494-3605.

A **standard gear rack** for the Butte area should include a good selection of small to large nuts, chocks, cams, quick draws, and extra slings. Always look at climbs and plan ahead.

Climbing history: Climbing began here in the 1960s, and, unfortunately, what records were kept were lost. Montana Tech then had a mountaineering club that used the crags to train for exploits outside Butte. At that time, there was a climber's cabin located in the Humbug Spires; the cabin has since burned down.

The only evidence left now of that time are the rusted pitons you will find here and there. But around the middle 1970s, Bill Dockins, John Gogus, and others started to pioneer new routes and pushed the standards into the hard 5.10 range. Before Gogus left, he put up possibly the hardest route of the early 1980s, *Hot Wings* (5.11b). Dwight Bishop continued the trend and has since pushed the standards through 5.12. Bishop and others such as Jim Wilson have established many fine routes on Homestake Pass and Spire Rock. Around 1986 the limits started to increase again, pushing to 5.13 by 1990. Now with the influx of climbers from all over, each area offers unlimited climbing in just about every grade.

Trip Planning Information

Area description: High-quality granite spires and crags—Split Pinnacle, Gillette Edge, Town Pump, Hot Wings, Dragon's Back, and Spire Rock—offering crack and face climbing in a mountainous setting on the Continental Divide.

General location: Crags on the west side, summit, and east side of Homestake Pass off Interstate 90, 10 to 22 miles from Butte and 80 miles west of Bozeman or south of Helena.

Camping: Primitive and developed USDA Forest Service campgrounds within a short drive of each area.

Climbing season: July and August are the only times not likely to get snow.

Restrictions and/or access issues: Be cautious when pulling off and on the interstate highway to avoid being a hindrance to the fast and safe flow of traffic. It is not only dangerous to cross the interstate but also is illegal. A $50 fine may be assessed for crossing at unauthorized areas. Also use caution when crossing the old railroad tracks on Homestake Pass.

Other guidebooks: *A Climber's Guide to Butte,* by Dwight Bishop; available in most climbing shops in Montana.

Nearby mountain shops, guide services, climbing gyms: Pipestone Mountaineering, Butte (retail, instruction, and guide service), featuring an indoor climbing wall and free advice on where to go and what to do; Great Divide Cyclery, Butte (right next door to Pipestone Mountaineering; besides working on your mountain bike they can fill you in on the best places to go riding or climbing).

Emergency services: St. James Community Hospital, 400 S. Clark, Butte, MT, (406)782-8361. For any emergency call 9-1-1. Both Butte and Whitehall have a search and rescue. They have little experience with rock, but as I can attest, they are capable of getting you out safely. They can be notified through 9-1-1.

Other nearby climbing areas: Roof Rock is located east of Spire Rock. Fish Creek and Roadside Rocks are located on Montana Highway 2 between Butte and Whitehall. Rock Resorts is just above the chain removal area on the west bound side of I-90 below Homestake Pass.

Attractions: In Butte, the Berkeley Pit viewing stand, World Museum of Mining at Montana Tech, Copper King Mansion, Arts Chateau, Headframes, Our Lady of the Rockies, and St. Lawrence Church. Contact the Butte Silver Bow Chamber of Commerce, 2950 Harrison Ave., Butte, MT 59701, (406)494-5595. Don't forget to stop in Butte for a pasty; ask anyone in Butte for Nancy's bakery location on Continental Drive.

Outside Butte there are many ghost towns: Cable, Gold Coin Mine, Highland City, and Southern Cross. Lewis and Clark Caverns State Park off MT 2 near Whitehall is probably the most colorful cavern in the United States.

HOMESTAKE PASS

OVERVIEW

The rocks described here include all the developed crags—including Rizenzubi, Split Pinnacle, Gillette Edge, Town Pump, and Hot Wings—east of the rest area on I-90 to Dragon's Back. The climbs are short, 40' to 60', have an easy approach, and offer a good mixture of difficulty. The granite is coarse and solid for smearing but a little painful for finger jams. **Descents:** Either walk off or rappel.

Finding the rocks: If you are coming from the east on I-90 go past Whitehall and Pipestone then continue to the top of Homestake Pass to the west-bound rest area. When coming from Butte, it is best to go to Exit 241 (Pipestone interchange) and get back on the interstate west-bound lanes and park at the west-bound rest area on I-90 on top of the pass. It is unsafe and inadvisable to cross the interstate from the east-bound rest area. From the west-bound rest area cross over the small creek to the north and climb the hill to the railroad tracks above.

Camping: It is best to drive another mile west on I-90 and take the exit marked for Homestake Lake. There is no camping allowed at Homestake Lake, but 0.5 mile past the lake are some excellent areas for camping. There are no services at these locations.

HOMESTAKE PASS

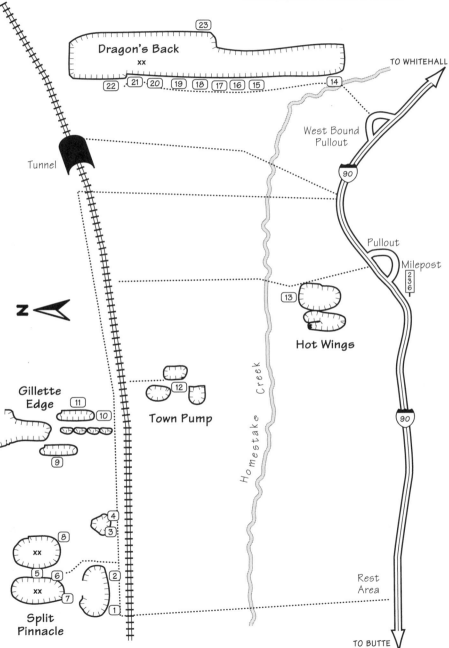

RIZENZUBI ROCK

This graffiti-christened face is located on top of the hill north of the rest area. It is near the railroad tracks below Split Pinnacle. Three short routes are located on the south face of Rizenzubi Rock, and two more routes are on the next formation east along the tracks.

1. **Rizenzubi Left** (5.9) Face climb on the far left side of the Rizenzubi graffiti; 2 bolts, gear (small stoppers, TCUs useful); 30'. **Descent:** Walk off back side or rappel from chain anchors.

2. **Rizenzubi Right** (5.9) Face climb on far right side of the graffiti; 2 bolts, gear (small stoppers, TCUs useful); 30'. **Descent:** Walk off back side or rappel from chain anchors.

Photo by Dwight Bishop.

SPLIT PINNACLE

Photo by Dwight Bishop.

3. **Twist of Fate** (5.11) Short bolted face line on left side of next formation east of Rizenzubi Rock; 3 bolts; 35'. **Descent:** Rappel from chain anchors.

4. **Cleavage** (5.9) Face line that ascends wide groove right of 'FATE; most often lower 35' is climbed to chain anchor shared with 'FATE, but it is possible to climb another 70' above the chains to top (5.8) another set of chains; 3 bolts, gear (small stoppers, TCUs useful on top section); 100'. **Descent:** One double-rope rappel from top chain anchor or two single-rope rappels from chain anchors.

Split Pinnacle

Split Pinnacle is located on top of the hill north of the rest area. From I-90, this formation is visible past the rest area heading east. It is made up of two 80' boulders separated by a 3' gap.

Once on top of the railroad tracks north of the rest area continue east on the tracks for another 0.5 mile. Turn north up the hill between *Rizenzubi* and *Twist of Fate* until you reach Split Pinnacle. **Descent:** Rappel off the bolts on top. Bring some slings to back up the rappel if needed.

5. **Cracksters Unite** (5.8) Inside gap there are two cracks; ascend hand crack on east pinnacle; take standard gear rack; 60'. **Descent:** Rappel off top bolts.

6. **Dark Shadows** (5.10) Crack directly opposite CRACKSTERS UNITE on western pinnacle. Follow finger-hand crack until it starts to fade out then move left on to vertical face; face climb past bolts in a line that curve up and left to top; 3 bolts, gear; 60'. **Descent:** Rappel off top anchor bolts.

7. **All Your Own Moves** (5.10a/b) Climb southeast corner of west pinnacle; 4 bolts; 60'. **Descent:** Rappel off top anchor bolts.

8. **Lotta Balls** (5.9+/.10a) Located on south face of east pinnacle is a flake with a bolt to its right; climb past flake and up friction face; 4 bolts; 60'. **Descent:** Bring some extra webbing to back up rappel slings.

Gillette Edge

Continue down the tracks past Split Pinnacle for another 0.5 mile. These are the obvious rocks that appear too thin to support your weight, hence the name Gillette Edge. **Descent:** Either rappel or walk off.

9. **S-Crack** (5.10) One of the more popular routes. Located on west side, the crack is obvious; gear (small stoppers useful); 70'. **Descent:** Walk off south end.

10. **Gillette Edge** (5.7) This route will bring you to grips with the Gillette Edge. Climb far south crack to very summit; once on edge there is no place for

Photo by Dwight Bishop.

gear until belay point, which is slings wrapped around a horn; 80'. **Descent:** Rappel off horn.

11. **Sweet Lisa** (5.12b) Face route that starts on east side. Taller climbers seem to have a little easier time on this reachy route; 4 bolts; 75'. **Descent:** Walk off top.

TOWN PUMP

This formation is named for the Town Pump gas stations that dot Montana's interstates and the pumped feeling you will have upon the completion of the main route.

Located 300' east of Gillette Edge on the south side of the tracks, the face of this formation cannot be seen from the tracks. You must descend the hill to see the climb. **Descent:** Climb off the back side toward the tracks.

12. **Town Pump** (5.10b) Start of this hand crack is the crux and has defeated many a 5.10 climber; gear; 65'. **Descent:** Climb off back side toward the tracks.

HOT
WINGS

5.11b

13

Photo by Dwight Bishop.

Hot Wings

Hot Wings started the rise of standards around Butte in the early 1980s. Continue walking east on the tracks for 0.3 mile past Town Pump. Look across to the interstate and down to see a crack that is curving and winglike. In early spring the base of *Hot Wings* will be wet from the overflowing creek.

13. **Hot Wings** (5.11b) Start is overhanging and angled with crux just below open pod two-thirds up; gear (#3 Friend with extra #2 Friends useful); 50'. **Descent:** Walk off.

DRAGON'S BACK

Overview

The top of the Dragon's Back is visible from the I-90 west-bound turnout. The shape of this large formation is unmistakable and aptly named. It offers some of the finest moderate routes on excellent granite. Most of the routes are either cracks, faces, or a combination of the two, ranging from 50' to 200'.

Finding the crag: Dragon's Back is located on top of Homestake Pass 2.4 miles east of the rest area on I-90. To get to the turnout for Dragon's Back continue east to the Pipestone exit (Exit 241) and turn off here; get back on the interstate and head back west for 7.6 miles. Park off I-90 on the west-bound side just above Dragon's Back. **Use extreme caution pulling off and on the interstate highway to avoid inhibiting the safe flow of traffic.** From the pullout hike down the hill and cross Homestake Creek to the base. All the routes listed here, with the exception of Slipperman, will require a standard rack. **Descent:** The recommended descent is done in two single-rope rappels off the west face by way of bolt anchors. Please sign in on the register on top to make your presence known.

Camping: It is best to go 4 miles west on I-90 to Homestake Lake to camp. Primitive camping sites are past the lake.

South Nose

14. **Proboscis** (5.8) A fine 3-pitch mixed crack and face route. **Pitch 1**—(5.7) Start on the southwest side and follow easy cracks up a dihedral to the ridge line and a ledge with a big tree; 80'. **Pitch 2**—(5.8) Climb on top of blocks and follow the hand crack for 50' up the ridge line. **Pitch 3**—(5.8+) Continue following the crack up the ridge line until you run out of rope. **Descent:** Rappel off bolt anchor down west face.

15. **Power Pusher** (5.9) 2-pitch route that starts 150' north of PROBOSCIS at base of a tree. **Pitch 1**—(5.7) Follow left-facing corner for 50' then go right and continue up right-facing corner. **Pitch 2**—(5.9) Follow hand, fist crack in corner to top; 60'. **Descent:** Although climb stops at top of pitch 2, you

still have one more pitch to do to get off. You can either do last pitch of PROBOSCIS (5.8+) or continue around to east face and climb EVENING STROLL (5.8). **Descent:** Rappel down west face.

DRAGONS BACK

Photo by Dwight Bishop.

16. **The Ramp** (5.6) Same start as TOUCH & GO but stay right all the way to top. **Descent:** Same as for PROBOSCIS.

17. **Touch & Go** (5.10) Ascends right-facing corner thatbecomes steeper and steeper with holds slowly disappearing; gear (medium stoppers useful); 60'. **Descent:** Same as for PROBOSCIS.

18. **Hot Rod of Love** (5.9+) Second bolted face right of SLIPPERMAN. Face climb past bolt to big ledge with a tree. Continue up thin lieback crack to top; bolts, gear (thin nuts useful); 60'. **Descent:** Same as for PROBOSCIS.

19. **Adrenaline Pumper** (5.9) Start right of SLIPPERMAN. Follow a short left-slanting crack part way up face; continue above it past bolts to chain anchor at tree; either continue to top by doing second pitch of OWL' or descend; 3 bolts, gear; 70'. **Descent:** Rappel from chain anchor.

20. **Slipperman** (5.11) classic edgy face climb is located 15' right of OWL'; climb is finished halfway up face; crux is just past last bolt; 4 bolts; 70'. **Descent:** Rappel from chain anchor.

21. **Owl Dihedral** (5.8) 2-pitch climb. Continue along ledge system from start of PROBOSCIS to north until you reach prominent right-facing dihedral. Take standard rack. **Pitch 1**—5.8 follow dihedral up to tree of mixed climbing; about 70'. **Pitch 2**—5.8 continue for 40' more to top. **Descent:** Rappel (single rope) back down route following bolt anchors.

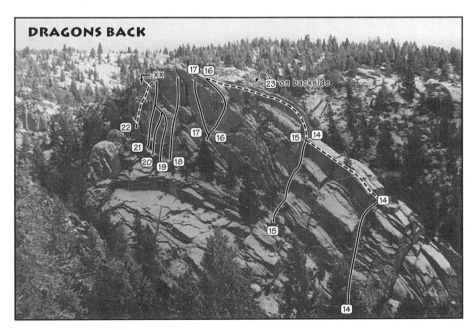

DRAGONS BACK

Photo by Dwight Bishop.

22. **Bishop's Surprise** (5.7+) Long mixed climb. From OWL' continue north for about 30'; gear placements may not be obvious; belayer will be squeezed between rock walls; gear; 160'. **Descent:** Rappel down SLIPPERMAN.

23. **Evening Stroll** (5.8) Approach by first doing first two pitches of PROBOSCIS then downclimb or rappel (30') or downclimb to east side; climb first left-facing corner to top for 80'. **Descent:** Rappel off West Face down SLIPPERMAN.

SPIRE ROCK

OVERVIEW

This is by far the most popular crag around Butte. Within this small area, the climbs are concentrated, approach is easy, and there are climbs of all types, (place your own gear, clip and go, or mixed). Climbs range from 30' to 200' high on excellent granite. Cracks, friction, edges, roofs, laybacks—it's all here.

Spire Rock is divided into two rock formations, named the King and the Queen. Unless otherwise noted, a standard rack will allow adequate protection on all of the routes listed.

Finding the rock: From I-90 take the Pipestone exit (Exit 241) 16 miles east of Butte and travel 5.4 miles north on Forest Service Road 222 to Delmoe Lake. At 5 miles you can see the Spire Rocks straight ahead. At 5.4 miles there is a dirt road to the right, which may or may not have a sign posted for Spire Rock. Follow this road up and around to the east side of Spire Rock. The final approach road is rough, so many people park right after the turn and walk straight up to the Queen or King.

Camping: This is an excellent area for camping and climbing. You can camp slightly past the turnoff for Spire Rock. Most campers drive around to the back side and camp there. Please be sure to use the same campsites others have used instead of establishing new ones to lessen the impact to the area. Be sure to bring water with you since there is none available around the area.

KING

The King is the northern outcrop of Spire Rock and is the largest with the longest routes. For descents off the King walk off the east face or rappel either the west face or south face with two 80' rappels. Several bolted rappel stations are located at various points along the top of the crag.

NORTH FACE

Although several climbs are located on this face, which is somewhat problematic to get to, only one is highly recommended. It is best to climb a route on the south or west face and descend the steep gully on the north side to the base of the wall. Locate a large chimney with an obvious chockstone lodged in it.

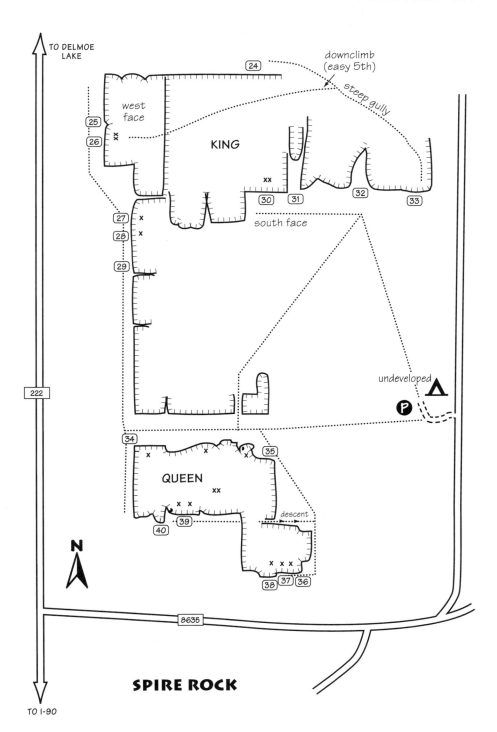

TO DELMOE
LAKE

downclimb
(easy 5th)

steep gully

24

west
face

25

26
xx

KING

xx

30   31   32   33

27   x

28   x

29

south face

undeveloped

P   ⛺

34

35

QUEEN

xx

x x

39
40

descent

38   37   36

x x x

N

8635

SPIRE ROCK

222

TO I-90

24. **Psycho Babble** (5.8) Finger-to-hand crack right of chimney (Esophagus); a hand-fist crack is on the right (Extra Space); gear to 3.5"; 75'. **Descent:** Scramble west or south along top to rappel anchors on west (see AERIAL BOOK) or south faces (see CATABOLISM).

WEST FACE

25. **Aerial Book** (5.9) 2-pitch climb with prominent right-facing dihedral that starts about 75' left of WHITE LINE. **Pitch 1**—(5.8) Go up face over a small roof to a tree belay on a 5'-wide ledge about 80' up. **Pitch 2**—(5.9) Follow the right-facing dihedral 20' north of WHITE LINE's second pitch to top either by laybacking or hand jamming. **Descent:** Rappel from chain anchors (double rope) located 30' to the east.

26. **White Line** (5.8) Another classic 2-pitch route. Obvious crack that bisects upper part of west face. **Pitch 1**—(5.8) Start up a right-facing dihedral with a large bush up about 15'. Follow dihedral straight up to a headwall (crux); belay at same tree as for AERIAL BOOK. **Pitch 2**—(5.8) Continue straight up vertical hand-finger crack. **Descent:** Same as AERIAL BOOK.

27. **Frick** (5.9+) Several bolted 1-pitch face routes are located together on West Face. This route and FRACK are classic sport routes at Spire Rock. Frick is first bolt line located 100' to the right of WHITE LINE; 4 bolts; 60'. **Descent:** Rappel from chain anchor.

Photo by Dwight Bishop.

28. **Frack** (5.9) This is located directly right of FRICK. Both climbs end at same chain anchor; 4 bolts; 60'. **Descent:** Same as for FRICK.

29. **Doo Doo Man** (5.9+) 4th bolted climb to the right/south of FRICK and goes all the way to the top of formation; 6 bolts, gear (stoppers and Friends useful); 190'. **Descent:** Either take the long walk around the rock or carry an extra rope for the double rappel back down the route, or from the top of the formation walk over to welded cold shuts above FRICK and make two rappels (25-30' to FRICK chains and 60' to ground).

SOUTH FACE

The south face of the King is divided into three sections by two prominent water troughs. These are important for locating the following climbs.

30. **Catabolism** (5.12b) Bolted face located 100' left of southwestern water trough and below South Face rappel line. Clip bolts that protect crux at about 30', then continue up the face for another 40' to the top; 3 bolts, gear; 70'. **Descent:** Rappel off 2-bolt anchor.

31. **Pipeline** (5.9 probably a sandbag rating) Many a 5.10 climber has backed off this one. Start up western-most prominent water trough until it gets vertical; ascend first crack to right of trough with an old piton in it; crux is getting past piton and then continuing up crack where difficulty eases to 5.8; standard gear rack; 130'. **Descent:** Walk west for about 50' then walk

Photo by Dwight Bishop.

toward edge and look for chain anchors. As you rappel off keep looking to right for second set of chain anchors; be sure to anchor yourself in as your partner rappels down to you.

32. **Limelite** (5.10b) One of the favorite climbs on south face of Spire Rock. Start just left of south-most eastern water trough on south side; angle slightly left then step right into a left-facing corner; follow corner to an overhang with a large bush to its left (#7 stopper useful); gear (#3 Friend, small stoppers useful); 165'. **Descent:** After topping out head west past first water trough about 20' to 2-bolt rappel station. Approach edge of the cliff (use caution) to see anchors. A small bush is located next to them.

33. **Walk-about** (5.8) Starts next to pine tree and ascends green pillar, taking path of least resistance (stepping left when difficulty increases); 160'; gear. **Descent:** See descent for PIPLINE.

QUEEN

The Queen is the smaller formation on the south side. It is easily descended by scrambling through a break on the southeast side.

NORTH FACE

34. **Wabbit** (5.7) This is the western-most crack (hands) on north face of Queen; 70'; take a standard rack. **Descent:** Walk off eastern side.

35. **Dreamweaver** (5.9) Crack climb located on northeast corner of Queen with a pine tree on either side; gear; 45'. **Descent:** Walk off eastern side.

SOUTH FACE

All these climbs have toprope bolt anchors. The Queen's south face favorite spot for climbing instruction. About 40' high, a standard rack will supply adequate protection.

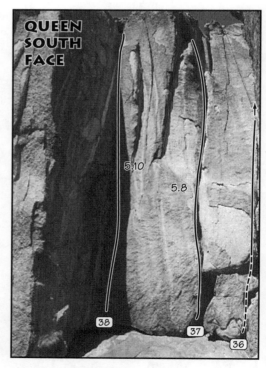

Photo by Dwight Bishop.

36. **Beginners Lead** (5.7) Located around east side of Queen on south side. Scramble to a right-facing corner (CRUISE CONTROL). Beginners Lead is second crack to the right; either ascend hand crack or face climb to left or right, using crack for placing gear; 45'. **Descent:** Walk off eastern side.

37. **Automatic Pilot** (5.8) Great finger-hand crack between CRUISE CONTROL and BEGINNERS'; gear; 45'. **Descent:** Walk off eastern side.

38. **Cruise Control** (5.10c). One of the area's test pieces; hand tooff-hands crack left of AUTOMATIC PILOT; gear (medium stoppers and several #2 and #3 Friends useful); 40'. **Descent:** Walk off the eastern side.

39. **Nuclear Energy** (5.12d) Very fingery face climb located on south face (but not same face as CRUISE CONTROL). From on top of Queen a gap leads down to this section of South Face. A large chockstone blocks the way; scramble under chockstone to reach an area with several overhanging bolted climbs. This route is the third bolted climb from right. A few dynos and a one-finger pull-up is required; 2-bolt anchor on top; 2 bolts, gear (Friends useful); 40'. **Descent:** Walk off eastern side.

40. **Dead Children's Glee Club** (5.11a) Located on same face as NUCLEAR ENERGY; second hand to off-width crack to west; gear (extra #3 Friends useful); 40'. **Descent:** Walk off the eastern side.

Photo by Dwight Bishop.

HUMBUG SPIRES

WEDGE

OVERVIEW

The Humbug Spires are a result of the southern rift of the Boulder Batholith that extends from Helena through Butte and Whitehall to Dillon. Like the northern region of this batholith, good crisp granite is predominant and abounds in more than fifty spires sprinkled along the west to southwest flank of the range. About one-fifth of these spires are in the 300- to 600-foot range, the Wedge being the largest.

The Humbug Spires resemble monolithic structures more than the blocky formations exposed near Butte, which look more like fortresses. If the granite of the Humbugs has any flaw, it's the scaly and grainy nature of some of the more decomposed areas. Overall, long crack-groove systems dominate the bigger spires intermixed with expansive faces full of shallow scoops and liberally spaced chicken heads.

One semi-alpine gemstone of good rock stands out among the rest. Standing 450 and 600 feet tall on its west and southern aspects respectively, the Wedge guards the head of a remote valley. Climbing the Wedge is more of an alpine rock experience and requires an effort to reach it, separating it from the typical crag scenes closer to roads and towns.

Most routes on the Wedge follow crack systems, but some of the newer routes venture out onto the wonderful friction faces, protected by bolts and the occasional nut placement or sling draped over a horn.

A **standard rack** for the Wedge should be well stocked with crack gear ranging from the smallest wired stoppers (including RP/HB nuts) to large cams (#4 Friend/Camalot, etc.), quick draws, slings, and biners. The crack systems are excellent for nuts and camming units. Be sure to bring extra shoulder-length slings. Take two ropes for the descent or plan to downclimb some 5.2 terrain after a shorter rappel.

Climbing history: Route development began in the 1960s, involving some of the most adventurous and bold Montana climbers of that time. Clare Pogreba, Ray Martin, and Jim and Jerry Kanzler pioneered the first routes of the Wedge— *Butter Knife* (5.8-), *Southwest Face* (5.8), *The Mutt and Jeff* (5.8), *West Face* (which eventually went free at 5.9), *West Face Direct* (5.9+, by Terry Kennedy), *Gandalf* (5.10, in which Pat Callis was recruited), and the *Dogleg Crack* (possibly Montana's first 5.11, which was led by Jim Kanzler). Clare, Ray, and Jerry were killed with two others in an avalanche on Mount Cleveland in Glacier

▲ –

Ron Brunckhorst, author of *Big Sky Ice*, and owner of Reach Your Peak guide services, and Donnie Black, Dwight Bishop, and Brad Hutcheson provided the information for this section.

National Park, cutting short the number of new routes they would surely have done. Ron and Gerald Brunckhorst added *Exit 99*.

The newer classics have been added by Donnie and Penny Black (and friends), Dwight Bishop, David Bassler, and Brad Hutcheson. Some of these excellent routes include the *Spellcaster* (5.8+), *Bovine Intervention*, *Tiny Tim*, and *Scrooge* (all 5.10).

The Humbugs is yet another awesome crag area with much unpublished climbing history. Many formations in the Humbugs received lots of attention: The Nose, Baldy, Arch Rock, and others had many routes. But lots of them have been lost to obscurity. These other formations were more accessible at the time because access was possible from the west (you could drive to within a 15-minute walk of most of these formations).

Ethics: Generally the Humbugs have been regarded as a very "traditional-style" climbing area (meaning most routes were climbed from the ground up with minimal fixed anchors used). Even some of the hard friction climbs were

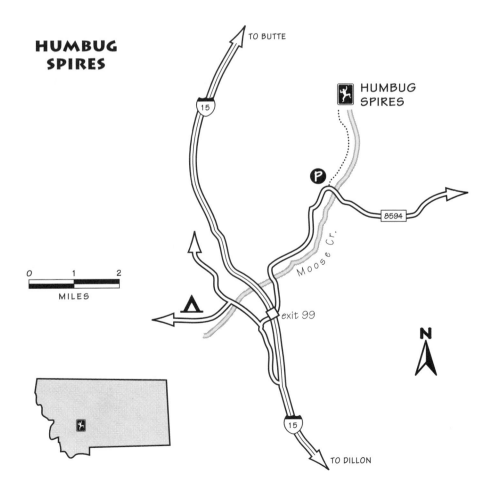

drilled on lead. Recently some of the longer new friction/face climbs went in from the top down. Although there was initially some controversy over the ethics of this, the routes were nevertheless classic and stayed with part of the traditional theme of the Wedge—being a multi-pitch endeavor. Even the newer generation of routes aren't sport climbs (the "new" generation of climbers in the Humbugs should keep in mind that power drills are prohibited). They require nut placements to supplement the bolts, which are well spaced and located where they're "really" needed. With this in mind, routes on the Wedge will be limited in respect for the rock, its rich history, and the sake of the pristine setting.

Trip Planning Information

Area description: Multi-pitch routes on a granite spire in a semi-alpine setting; elevation 7,000 feet.

General location: In the Moose Creek drainage of the Humbug Spires Wilderness Study Area, which is about 26 miles south of Butte and 39 miles north of Dillon off Interstate 15.

Camping: All services are available in Butte and Dillon. An undeveloped camping area is located between the Moose Creek trailhead parking lot and the creek. Camping spaces are limited here; an outhouse is available at the parking lot. Numerous other undeveloped camp spots are along the first 1.5 miles of the trail. Also, the Wedge (4-mile approach) has some fine camping near its base and at the remains of a cabin where a spring is located. To be safe, boil or filter

Looking up the southwest-south face of the Wedge. *Photo by John Alke.*

the water from the spring and from Moose Creek.

Climbing season: July and August are best for climbing in the Humbug Spires. May, June, September, and October can have fine weather, too, but aren't as dependable. Since most of the routes face south and west, climbing the Wedge can be comfortable in cooler weather.

Restrictions/access issues: The spires are part of the Humbug Spires Wilderness Study Area, managed by the Bureau of Land Management. Power drill use is prohibited. A new trail was recently built, providing a more defined access route to the spires. No-trace guidelines apply.

Guidebook: *More Climbs in Butte*, by Kurt Krueger and Keith Calhoun, has a one-page topo and map devoted to the Wedge. This pamphlet may be available at climbing shops in the Bozeman, Butte, and Missoula areas.

Nearby mountain shops, guide services, and gyms: Pipestone Mountaineering, Butte (they have an indoor climbing wall and offer classes and guided trips); Reach Your Peak Guiding and Instruction (Ron Brunckhorst), Bozeman.

Finding the area: From Butte go west on Interstate 90 to the I-15 interchange. Take I-15 south toward Dillon for 26 miles to exit 99 and drive the narrow, graveled Moose Creek Road about 3 miles to the Moose Creek parking lot. The new trail to the Wedge is a 4-mile hike on a good tread, gaining about 1,000 feet. (No getting lost like in the old days.) From the parking lot follow the signed and marked trail along Moose Creek about 1.5 miles to a fork; take the right fork up a tributary to where it veers east up and over a low ridge and into the upper drainage beneath the Wedge. The rock will not be visible until you are within 0.25 mile, just before reaching the base of the hill that the Wedge sits on. Look for a spring and the remains of the cabin. A short distance beyond are some good tent sites.

The following route descriptions begin on the Northwest Face and progress to the right, facing the cliff. **Standard descent:** From the east shoulder, which can be reached from the summit via a 4th-class traverse), make a double-rope rappel from three poor bolts to the ground or a single-rope rappel and scramble down the east side on easy (5.2) terrain.

Northwest Face

This face is shorter and steeper than the West and South faces and is separated from them by a slight arete or corner.

1. **Eagle Dance** (5.11b) 5 pitches on the Northwest Face, joining TINY TIM for a couple pitches to the summit. Starts below an eagle nest 50' uphill from the northwest corner. Each pitch is short but technical. Take a standard rack. **Pitch 1**—(5.10a) Climb a corner to an eagle nest, then step left and belay; 80'. **Pitch 2**—(5.10b) Step back to the nest and work up face above; 60'. **Pitch 3**—(5.10a) Continue up cracks to a large ledge; 60'. **Pitch 4**—(5.11b) A single bolt (long reach) placed on lead marks the starting

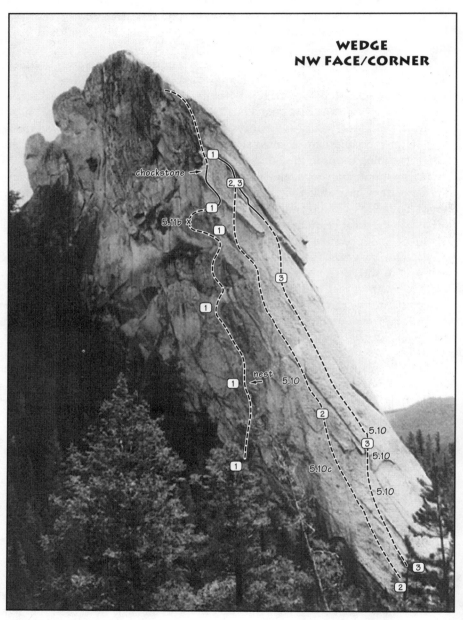

WEDGE
NW FACE/CORNER

chockstone →

5.11b x

nest
←

5.10

5.10

5.10c

5.10

5.10

Photo by Dwight Bishop.

HUMBUGS
WEDGE NW FACE/
ARETE

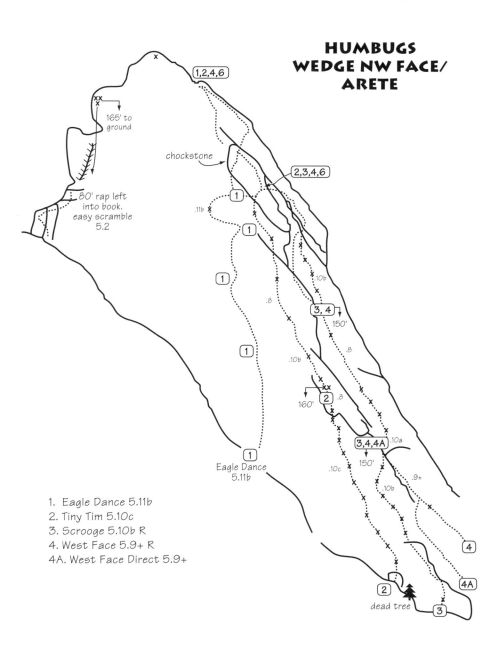

165' to ground

chockstone

80' rap left into book. easy scramble 5.2

1,2,4,6

2,3,4,6

.11b

1

1

1

1

.10b

.8

3, 4

150'

.8

1

.10b

2

.8

160'

3,4,4A

.10a

150'

.10c

.9+

.10b

Eagle Dance 5.11b

4

2

4A

dead tree

3

1. Eagle Dance 5.11b
2. Tiny Tim 5.10c
3. Scrooge 5.10b R
4. West Face 5.9+ R
4A. West Face Direct 5.9+

point; the "good" jugs above are all down sloping, so don't hesitate or stop; traverse up and right to a vertical crack that turns horizontal; follow crack to a corner; 80'. **Pitch 5**—(5.9) Climb straight up under a chockstone; belay from chockstone; 80'. **Pitch 6-7**—(5.7-5.4) Climb the last two pitches of TINY TIM to top. **Descent:** See standard descent described above.

WEST FACE

The awesome West Face of the Wedge is a huge slab that emerges from a timbered hillside, extending from a toe hidden by the trees to a spirelike summit. Three parallel cracks/seams run diagonally upward right to left toward a thin line of roofs at 175'. The first or right-most (southwest) crack, which literally is a seam for the first 120', is only one of the three main cracks that connect up to and through the overhang.

The anchor beneath the overhang is common for *Scrooge*, the *West Face Route*, *West Face Direct*, and other variants using the second or middle (shallow, discontinuous hand crack/trough) or the third, left-most (northwest) crack (thin, discontinuous seam). Slightly left of the northwest crack is a curving flake (*Scrooge*) also rising right to left. Fifty feet farther left is the northwest corner/arete (*Tiny Tim*).

The West Face offers clean crack climbing in a wonderful environment. The only problem is its imposing first 100' slab of decomposed rock is poorly protected, with occasional chicken heads for draping slings or questionable gear placements in seams.

2. **Tiny Tim** (5.10b/c) Excellent friction/face route. Set of stoppers, camming units from 3/4" to 3", and 12 quick draws useful. **Pitch 1**—(5.10) Start near standing dead tree at corner of northwest face. Climb from boulder onto face (2" gear useful), then up and right to first of 11 bolts, leading to hanging belay with fixed anchors; 165'. **Pitch 2**—(5.10) Continue on face past 2 bolts, trending left onto incredibly featured NW face; 2 more bolts protect next 60' of moderate climbing covered with fragile horns; At 100' you intersect first of 2 diagonal cracks rising right to left; climb across each crack (good gear, 3.4" to 2" cams) then 2 more bolts protect last 30' of fun ramps and roofs; small crack (1") is located at 155'(165' rope just barely makes it), offering protection for a traverse right to join SCROOGE, WEST FACE, and MUTT AND JEFF. **Pitch 3**-(5.8) MUTT AND JEFF et. al. final pitches—Climb past a few 5.7 moves above the belay to the easy (runout) face leading to summit. **Descent:** See above.

3. **Scrooge** (5.10b R) Flake and face line that intertwines WEST FACE ROUTE, using common belays but alternate climbing. Set of stoppers, camming units from 3/4" to 3", shoulder length runners, and 10 quick draws useful.

   Pitch 1—(5.10) Start at uprooted dead log near wall. Climb bouldery start

(20') with 1 bolt to gain discontinuous curving flake and good protection for next 40'; 6 more bolts protect upper headwall leading to common belay with WEST FACE below roof; 160'. **Pitch 2**—(5.10- R) Work right under roof and pull overhang via chicken heads or use the crack of the West Face and angle right, following widely spaced bolt line (5.8) to hanging belay; 150'. **Pitch 3**—(5.10) Continue up toward wide bowl between upper SOUTHWEST FACE and west arete, passing one last crux before merging with WEST FACE for last 40' to slab belay (gear needed, see WEST FACE), which funnels up and in close to the finish of WEST FACE crack/seam and TINY TIM, following bolt line. **Pitch 4-5**—MUTT AND JEFF final pitches— Climb past a few 5.7 moves above the belay to the easy (runout) face leading to summit. **Descent:** See above.

4. **West Face** (5.9+ R) Variety of starts have been used for this route, but all (except SCROOGE) converge at about 120' where the right or uppermost of 3 parallel cracks/seams split the headwall below an overhang. The final thin crack to the belay offers exciting and well-protected climbing. Standard rack (RPs useful). **Pitch 1**—(5.9+) Original start near toe of buttress is slightly right of 1st parallel crack/seam in a low-angle scoop. Friction climb up, trending left toward chicken head (attach runners) at 50' and 80' (broken off); 3/8" bolt protects crux traverse left into 1st crack/seam (5.9, but whew! No worry of a ground fall...); finally at 120', seam accepts excellent small wires (midsized RPs, HBs especially useful) and provides an exciting 5.9+ crux finish; by 150' crack widens to about 4" where SCROOGE converges; anchors are at 160', but a gear belay can be set at 150'. **Pitch 2**— (5.9) Above overhang, wall is split by crack (left of SCROOGE bolt line) with solid 5.9 finger locks, then becomes a left-facing book with flaring 1"- 2" crack and ample foot holds; 5.7 for next 60'; at about 100' route intersects a right-leaning thin hand crack (hard to see from ground); a steep beginning leads to easier broken ground; gear belay can be set where desired (at 160' route intersects left-leaning crack (pitch 3); a 2-anchor belay to right serves SCROOGE and WEST FACE; gear to 2.5" (small wires useful). **Pitch 3**—(5.8 R) Follow left leaning crack toward west arete until loose, decomposed cracks lead up and right and offer marginal protection for traverse right into wide bowl where SCROOGE joins; slabby steps lead up and left (some gear placements) toward where routes 2, 3, 4, and 6 merge; gear belay with wires (1/2"to 3/4"). **Pitch 4-5**—MUTT AND JEFF final pitches (see below)—(5.7 to 5.3/.4) Climb past a few 5.7 moves above the belay to the easy (runout) face leading to summit. **Descent:** See above.

4a. **West Face Direct** (5.9+) Single pitch direct start variant to WEST FACE route; Standard rack (RPs useful). Begin right of SCROOGE on lowest of three left-slanting seams; Near end of seam, face climb up and right on knobs to a second left-slanting hand crack; transfer to the third seam/crack (takes small stoppers and RPs), to the anchor beneath overhang. Continue up WEST FACE or rappel 160' to ground.

5. **Dogleg Crack** (5.11a) 1-pitch variant start to either MUTT AND JEFF or SOUTHWEST FACE. Standard rack (extra camming units from 1/2" to 1" and double rope useful to avoid rope drag). Follow obvious dogleg line on the extreme right side of West Face; climb the lower crack (80' very sustained) to the long traverse right (it is possible to belay near end of traverse crack to avoid rope drag); continue right past end of crack that extends up face and across to right-facing corner and up to the belay near an old 1/4" bolt (there are numerous places to set a gear belay in this area). Continue to top.

6. **The Mutt and Jeff** (5.8) Classic 5-pitch route that ascends the part of BUTTER KNIFE on the south face and then up a slab and left of the Cyclops Eye. Standard rack to 5". **Pitch 1**—(5.7) Ascend flake at base of wall and crack/seam up slab, passing 2 horizontal bolt placements to gain crack above; at about 80' look for small horns and knobs leading 20' left to a corner and broken ledge system above (an old bolt may be found here). **Pitch 2**—(5.8) Fairly sustained; take left-leaning crack system under Cyclops Eye to hanging belay. **Pitch 3**—(5.8) Main crack is wide but 5.9 finger crack left offers a nice variant to where crack system joins ridge. **Pitch 4**—(5.7) Blocks lead up and left side of wide, rat-infested crack/chimney (3"to 4" gear useful); continue left toward intersection with west arete until convenient to climb up and back right onto easier summit slabs; numerous points for belay. **Pitch 5**—(5.3/.4) Climb easy (runout) slab to summit. **Descent:** See above.

7. **Southwest Face**—a.k.a. Old Aid Line (5.8) 4-pitch route that shares same start with MUTT' but takes crack line along right side of Cyclops Eye (big roof in upper portion of face. Standard rack. **Pitch 1** (5.7) Ascend flake at base of wall and crack/seam up slab, passing 2 horizontal bolt placements to gain crack above; at about 80' look for small horns and knobs leading 20' left to a corner and broken ledge system above (an old bolt may be found here). **Pitch 2**—(5.8) Follow cracks, flakes, and pass right of roofs via obvious slot/chimney system (crux) along right side of Cyclops Eye; there is a small belay stance (semi-hanging; TCUs and small Tri-Cams very useful here) above bolt ladder, which is 1/4" studs (use wires over studs for protection). **Pitch 3**—(5.8) Friction climb last portion of chimney/slot and go right at its end to steep hand crack; belay at end of crack. **Pitch 4**—(5.7) Continue up and left to corner/crack system to join MUTT' on summit ridge or continue up and right to hand crack to belay in bowl.

7a. **Bovine Intervention (5.10)** A good last pitch variant. Look for bolts on face above the third belay; climb past 4 bolts to the summit ridge in 1 pitch.

8. **Butter Knife** (5.8-) 2 pitches along left side of unusual knife-like flake that marks the start. Standard rack. **Pitch 1**—(5.7) Start same as MUTT' but

instead of traversing left half way up first pitch continue up crack to a stance at about 150' up. **Pitch 2**—(5.7+/.8-) Continue up widening crack, passing a bulge to gain a large platform/ledge system and two belay bolts. Do two double-rope rappels, starting from anchors 20' below ledge or do the combination link-up of the SOUTHEAST CHIMNEY.

8a. **Southeast Chimney Variant** (5.8) Climb 2 pitches of BUTTER KNIFE to Balcony Ledge. **Pitch 3**— Traverse 100' right to another large ledge (a section of downclimbing is involved here). **Pitch 4-5**—(5.7) Continue up a chimney and steep crack (5.7) to a notch on the east ridge. **Pitch 6**—(5.8) Wonderful friction climbing; clip the bolt on the top of the block above; then climb to top of block and clip hidden bolt out around corner on face; downclimb 10' or so and swing out left around corner onto face (crux) and follow three bolts up and left to summit ridge; a double rope is advised for a weaker second. Beware of the ancient 1/4" bolts that need to be replaced; fortunately the old bolt at the crux has been replaced by a 5/16" bolt.

9. **Spellcaster** (5.8+) At corner of Southeast Face nearly 100' right of start for 'MUTT AND JEFF lies a large boulder, forming a chimney between it and the main wall of the Wedge. Spellcaster ascends the wall inside this wide chimney. BALCONY DIRECT (below) enters from above and shares common belays. Standard rack. **Pitch 1**—(5.8+) Ascend friction and flakes to a bolt and crack above; easier climbing past another bolt ends at a 2-bolt belay anchor (BALCONY DIRECT merges here); 150'. **Pitch 2**—(5.8+) Climb to first bolt on face and then up and left, gaining crack that runs to top of the Butter Knife "balcony"; a 2-bolt belay is 20' below top balcony and just left of crack. Continue to top via GANDALF or rappel (two double-rope rappels starting from anchors 20' below Balcony Ledge).

10. **Balcony Direct** (5.9) 2-pitch route around right (east) of the large block that forms corridor and start of SPELLCASTER. Light rack of wires and camming units plus quick draws. **Pitch 1**—(5.8) Start from the uphill side of large boulder. Step into upper end of chimney/decomposed trough; slant left past 3 bolts to anchors of SPELLCASTER (short pitch). **Pitch 2**—(5.9) Slant right and up, passing a roof at mid-rope, then traverse right onto final headwall and "balcony" ledge of BUTTER KNIFE; 9 bolts. Continue up GANDALF, or SOUTHEAST CHIMNEY, or rappel (two double-rope rappels).

11. **Gandalf** (5.10c R) 2-pitch route starts almost directly above end of BUTTER KNIFE'S last pitch. Standard rack with RPs. **Pitch 1**—(5.10c) Take left seam crack midway up the main crack system, then seams for a long pitch to a belay. **Pitch 2**—(5.10) Go up face with marginal pro to crack/seam on right (almost hidden) and a face with a bolt, for another long pitch. A very respectable climb. **Descent:** Standard descent route.

Photo by Keith Calhoun, courtesy of Brad Hutcheson.

HUMBUG SPIRES
THE WEDGE

2. Tiny Tim 5.10c
3. Scrooge 5.10b R
4. West Face 5.9+ R
4A. West Face Direct 5.9+
5. Dogley Crack 5.11a
6. The Mutt and Jeff 5.8
7. Southwest Face 5.8
7A. Bovine Intervention 5.10+
8. Butter Knife 5.8
8A. Southeast Chimney Var. 5.8
9. Spellcaster 5.8+
10. Balcony Direct 5.9
11. Gandalf 5.10c R
12. Exit 99 5.8-
12A. Variant 5.8-

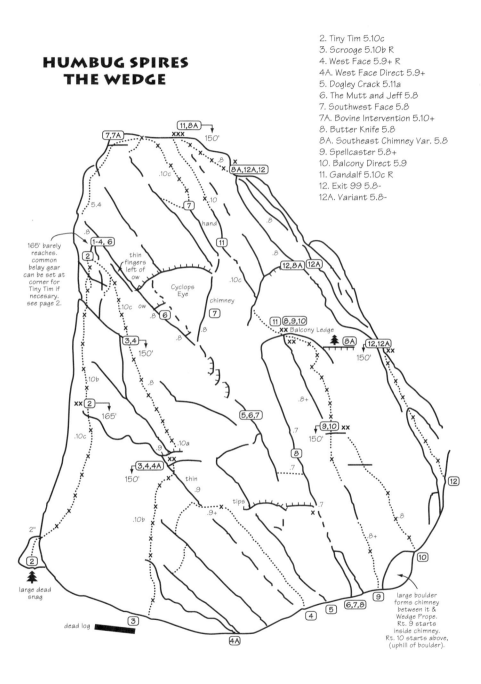

165' barely
reaches.
common belay
gear can be set
at corner for
Tiny Tim if
necesary.
see page 2.

large dead
snag

dead log

large boulder
forms chimney
between it &
Wedge Prope.
Rt. 9 starts
inside chimney.
Rt. 10 starts above,
(uphill of boulder).

12. **Exit 99** (5.8-) 2-pitch direct start to SOUTHEAST CHIMNEY. 6 quick draws and standard rack. **Pitch 1**—(5.8) Start on blunt friction arete found almost directly beneath chimney pitch of SOUTHEAST CHIMNEY; climb 140' past 6 bolts to an anchor (a couple of marginally slung horns could reduce the runout). **Pitch 2**—(5.8-) Traverse left on a short ramp and follow easy 5th-class terrain to big ledge beneath SOUTHEAST CHIMNEY. **Pitch 3-6**—See SOUTHEAST CHIMNEY VARIANT. **Descent:** Standard descent route.

12a. **Variant** (5.7/.8) Fun variation starts at end of pitch 1 of EXIT 99. **Pitch 2**—(5.7) Climb broken terrain up through cracks and blocks for 150' to belay right of SOUTHEAST CHIMNEY. **Pitch 3**—(5.8) Climb nice thin crack on arete above and right of SOUTHEAST CHIMNEY to belay at notch on East Ridge. **Pitch 4**—(5.8) Same as last pitch for SOUTHEAST CHIMNEY. **Descent:** Standard descent route.

NOTES:

Pat Callis on *The Fugitive. Photo by Bill Dockins.*

BOZEMANAREA

OVERVIEW

Several climbing areas are within a 30-mile radius of Bozeman, and all the areas have relatively easy access. The rock types include limestone, schist, and gneiss, with single- and multi-pitched crack lines as well as bolted face climbs. More than 230 climbing routes have been established in the Bozeman area. This section is a mere sampling of the great climbing opportunities here. Dozens more good climbs and first ascent histories of each area are chronicled in *Bozeman Rock Climbs*, second edition, by Bill Dockins. Anyone wishing to really get to know the climbs and climbing areas in the Bozeman area should also pick up a copy of Dockins's book.

The areas described here are: Frog Rock in Rocky Canyon (Bozeman Pass); Practice Rock in Hyalite Canyon; Squaw Creek Road limestone, Gallatin Tower, and several of the main formations in Gallatin Canyon; and Neat Rock along the Madison River.

Climbing history: The first known technical ascents in the Bozeman area occurred in Gallatin Canyon on Gallatin Tower and the adjacent formations across the river. But prior to 1965 little or no records were kept on who climbed what first or in what style in Gallatin Canyon or elsewhere in the area.

In the late 1960s, Jerry Kanzler and Barry Frost established the first 5.9 on Gallatin Tower while Brian Leo and Chuck Rose were aid climbing new routes that later became classic free climbs. Development at the local crags languished because most of the climbers from the area were busy exploring bigger cliffs and peaks elsewhere. Few new routes were established around Bozeman until the mid-1970s when a host of new activists burst onto the scene.

Jim "Rathole" Kanzler, Terry Kennedy, Doug Randall, Jack Tackle, John Kravetz, Tom Ballard, Dougal McCarty, Steve Jackson, Gary Skaar, and Mindy Shulak were a few who pushed the free climbing standards through the 5.10

▲ - ▲

Bill Dockins, author of *Bozeman Rock Climbs*, gave permission to use excerpts from his book (1995 revised edition) and added invaluable assistance in compiling and reviewing this section. The climbing history section is a brief summary of the *Bozeman Rock Climbs* Introduction and Climbing History chapter written by Pat Callis with additional contributions from Dockins.

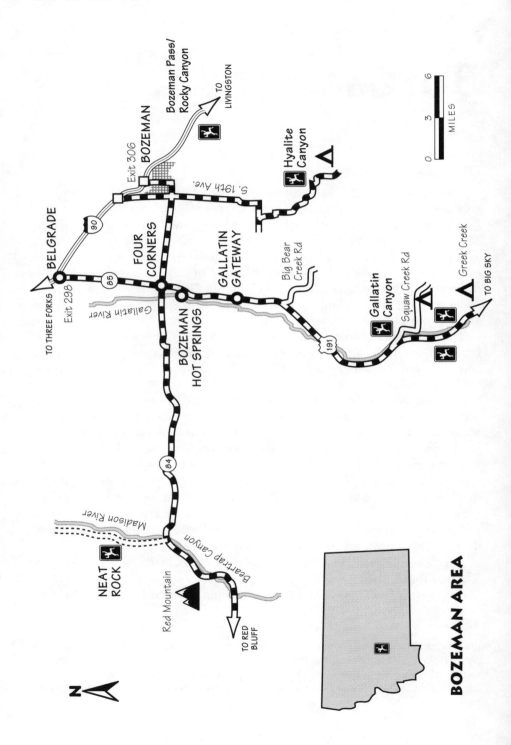

BOZEMAN AREA

level to 5.11. Several new hard routes were developed at the Tower and in Hyalite Canyon during this time.

In 1977 the area received another burst of new route energy, which extended into the 1980s, by Dockins, Peter Boveng, Kim Keating, Tom Jungst, and Pat Callis. Many new lines were established during this period. In the ensuing years many more difficult and bold routes were developed, some on seemingly blank faces by Dockins, Tom Kalakay, Kristen Drumheller, Alex Lowe, Jim Scott, and Scott Wade. Also, Jim Scott, Van Alke, and David Gerhart began exploring areas farther from the popular crags, developing many nice routes. Lowe and Dockins elevated the standards to 5.12 with routes like *Cardiac Arete* and *The Fugitive*.

More recently, several routes of high standard have been established on the limestone cliffs in Rocky Canyon (Bozeman Pass), initiated primarily by Tom Kalakay and Tom Jungst in 1987. The limestone cliffs along Squaw Creek Road as well as the gneiss formations in Gallatin Canyon have seen many new quality lines of high standard climbed, too. Major contributors to the recent flurry of new routes are: Meg Hall, Mike Kehoe, Robert Müller, Rand Swanson, Dockins, Drumheller, Callis, Lowe, and others.

Trip Planning Information

Area description: Area offers single- and multi-pitch routes on limestone and gneiss. Climbing opportunities vary as does the rock; there are some bolted sport routes and a plethora of natural and multi-pitched climbs, all with relatively easy access.

General location: Within a 30-mile radius of Bozeman. Practice Rock in Hyalite Canyon is about 10 miles south of Bozeman on Forest Road 62; Gallatin Canyon climbs are about 25 miles southwest of Bozeman and 13 miles north of Big Sky on U.S. Highway 191; Neat Rock is about 29 miles west of Bozeman on Montana Highway 84. See individual area overviews for more specific information.

Camping: Car/tent camping just off the road along the Madison River near Neat Rock; Beartrap Recreation Area offers developed campsites; USDA Forest Service campgrounds are located in Hyalite Canyon south of Practice Rock; and several developed Forest Service campgrounds are located near Gallatin Tower going south toward Big Sky; fees required.

Climbing season: March through October; the season is shorter for areas at higher elevations; but during dry, sunny spells in November and February the southwest walls of Squaw Creek Road and Neat Rock (lowest elevation) with its south-facing wall can be warm and dry.

Restrictions and access issues: All the routes described in this section are on public land. Treat all areas with respect. Fixed anchors on new routes should be used only when absolutely necessary and painted to match the rock to minimize visual impact.

Other guidebooks: *Bozeman Rock Climbs*, by Bill Dockins, second edition, 1995.

Nearby mountain shops, guide services, and gyms: Northern Lights Trading Company, Bozeman; The Great Outdoors, Bozeman; Montana State University climbing gym, Old Gym, Bozeman; Peak Adventures (instruction, guide service), Big Sky; Reach Your Peak (instruction, guide service), Ron Brunckhorst, Bozeman.

ROCKY CANYON (BOZEMAN PASS)
FROG ROCK

OVERVIEW

The limestone cliffs in Rocky Canyon on the way to Bozeman Pass are the closest developed crags. Frog Rock is a limestone buttress on a steep, timbered flank of Chestnut Mountain, which is visible on the skyline west of town. The frog-shaped buttress is on the south side of Interstate 90 just a few miles up toward the pass. Frog Rock's limestone seems different from any other limestone area described in this book. In addition to the characteristic positive edges of Madison limestone, several routes on the Frog are laced with pockets that are often crystal lined.

As you drive east up the pass look for a large black stain on the lower northwest face of the rock. Several good routes are concentrated on or near this

Photo by Randall Green.

distinct feature. The routes on Frog Rock are one- to two-pitch sport climbs from 5.8 to 5.12 and are well-equipped with lead protection bolts and chain rappel anchors. The longer routes require two ropes for the rappels. Because the climbs are in the shadows most of the day, it is a good place to go during the summer months. Winds often buffet the buttress.

Finding the rock: From Bozeman take I-90 east about 6 miles to a pullout on the right (2.3 miles past the Bear Canyon Road interchange) overlooking the creek and the railroad. **Be cautious turning off and on I-90** to avoid being a hindrance to the fast flow of traffic. (If you miss the pullout, it is only 1 mile farther up the highway to the Trail Creek Road interchange where you can return on the west-bound lane to the Bear Canyon Road interchange and start over.) Park well away from the highway across from a red-stained rock cut on the railroad right-of-way. Cross the tracks; **use extreme caution** because this is a busy freight route with several trains passing through here each day. Just left of the wide red stain on the cut bank are two logs across the creek. Once across the creek, a well-used path traverses west across the steep timbered slope to an avalanche gully. Follow the gully to the base of the wall. It takes about 30 to 45 minutes for the approach.

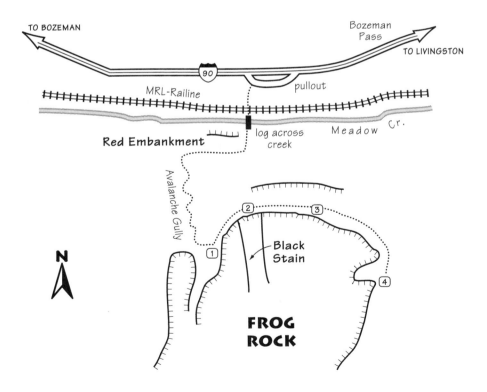

1. **Femoral Attraction** (5.10) Steep, textured face on a west-facing wall right of SERVUS. From the head of the main approach gully scramble right up to base of west wall. Route follows line right of large flakes in middle of wall; 15 bolts; 165'. **Descent:** Double-rope rappel from chain anchors.

2. **Servus** (5.10-) Can be done as a 1- or 2-pitch route with a second pitch variant; the line roughly follows the prominent black stain on the northwest face. From head of approach gully scramble (unprotected 5.3) 25' to 30' up to ledge at base of black stain. **Pitch 1**—(5.8) Ascend steep face graced with large, crystal-lined pockets to a large ledge; 7 bolts; 150'; chain anchor. **Pitch 2**—(5.10-) Move left 25' and follow right-slanting bolt line up steep face that ends with an easy slab (may want gear on slab, especially if wet; **Direct Variant**—Pitch 2 (5.10-) Climb directly above the rappel chains and join the route at the second or third bolt); 10 bolts; 165'. **Descent:** Double-rope rappel from any set of chain anchors. **Amber Variant**—Pitch 2 (5.9) From top of pitch 1 of SERVUS go left 40' and follow bolt line to left side of upper slab (either belay below steep block at double bolt station on slab or take long slings or double rope to avoid rope drag when assaulting final block; 12 bolts (runout on slab); 150'. **Descent:** Double-rope rappel from chain anchors on top of block (variant finish up slab to SERVUS pitch 2 anchors).

3. **Mean Streak** (5.12b) Thin overhanging line above ledge 60' left of SERVUS and directly below a prominent cave. From upper part of gully follow path leading left/east to wide ledge that crosses base of north face; 7 bolts; 60'. **Descent:** Single-rope rappel from chain anchors.

4. **Virga** (5.12a) Severely overhanging face near the left-most skyline of the rock. From top of gully traverse left up to ledge that crosses the north face, continue east past MEAN STREAK and scramble up to base of severely overhanging wall; 7 bolts; 65' (note of caution: if lowering from anchors it is best to clip last bolt to avoid damage to rope on arete's sharp edge. **Descent:** Single-rope rappel from chain anchors.

HYALITE CANYON
PRACTICE ROCK
OVERVIEW

Located only about 10 miles from Bozeman, Practice Rock is a popular crag. The routes here are good leads and can be toproped as well. It is the first of two small cliffs on the northeast side of Hyalite Canyon. The west face is fractured at odd angles and streaked with orange and yellow lichens; its north wall has more vertical crack lines and is much darker. A pinnacle separated from the main west wall by a chimney leans against the left side of the west face.

Photo by Bill Dockins.

Bring a gear rack well stocked with wired stoppers (including small RP/HB nuts) and cams (small to medium-sized Tri-Cams as well as TCUs and Friends). Hexentrics also work well in some situations. Carry quick draws and extra slings.

Finding the rock: Go south from Bozeman on South 19th Avenue to Hyalite Canyon Road (FR 62). Practice Rock is about 3 miles from the junction on the left/east side of the canyon. From the turnout follow the left-most trail through a talus slope that ascends the steep hillside to the rock.

NORTH WALL

5. **The Fiver** (5.8) Crack route in middle of steep north face; 50'. **Descent:** Rappel from anchors at Raven's Nest Ledge or continue another pitch on WIZARD'S WELL to top.

6. **Wizard's Well** (5.9+) Continuation of 'FIVER or THEORETICALLY; from the ledge continue up to the left corner of roof; traverse left past a bolt to crack system that leads to top; 40'. **Descent:** Walk off the backside or rappel route (2-ropes).

7. **Theoretically** (5.10) Discontinuous finger and hand crack that leads to the Raven's Nest Ledge left of the right edge/arete of the north wall; 50'. **Descent:** Continue on WIZARD'S' and walk off back side or rappel (2-ropes).

WEST WALL

8. **Practice Wall** (5.11) Line on face left of a pinnacle; face ends in steep, shallow dihedral; 5 bolts and gear (small to medium wire and cams to 2" useful). **Descent:** Double-rope rappel from 2-bolt anchor.

9. **Cardiac Arete** (5.12) Arete on northwest corner of pinnacle; 5 bolts, gear (#0.5 Flex Friend useful near top); 65'. **Descent:** Rappel off anchor on top of pinnacle.

10. **Pinnacle Standard Route** (5.6) Main dihedral on south face where Pinnacle meets main face; second pitch can be added above Pinnacle. Follow dihedral past square flake sticking out of crack (crux) and continue up widening crack and chimney to top of Pinnacle; 75'; gear (standard rack to 4"). **Pitch 2 VARIANT** (5.5)—Step across "void" from top of Pinnacle onto upper west face; easy climbing broken with some scrambling to top. **Descent:** Single-rope rappel from anchor at top of Pinnacle or walk off back side from summit of main face.

11. **Jerry's Route** (5.8) Face and crack line right of wide crack in middle of face right of Pinnacle; line crosses right-slanting parallel cracks extending to top of orange-white face and follows right-leaning shallow dihedral and face above; 65'. **Descent:** Rappel from anchor above ledge at top.

12. **Rosebush Crack** (5.9-) Right of the prominent crack (Strawberry Crack) on south face, which tails off in height from left to right. This crack system goes through a bulge (crux, but well protectable) then straight up past a rosebush to a good belay ledge; 60'. **Descent:** Rappel or walk off right, following a good ledge system.

GALLATIN CANYON
GALLATIN LIMESTONE—SQUAW CREEK
(STORM CASTLE MOUNTAIN)

OVERVIEW

The first cliffs encountered as you enter Gallatin Canyon are crumbly brown limestones on the east side of the river. But as you venture farther into the canyon, the quality of the rock improves as the rock color changes to a yellowish brown streaked with gray. The good rock is a compact, thin-layered horizontal strata that offers steep faces with an abundance of edges and blocky roofs. The routes are of fairly high standard and protected mostly with bolts. But in addition to a rack of quick draws take along an assortment of wired stoppers and cams for a few routes with discontinuous cracks.

Chain anchors are set for rappels at the tops of each route. Double ropes are necessary on several lines that exceed 100 feet.

Finding the rocks: Take US 191 west and then south from Bozeman or MT 85 south from Belgrade to Four Corners junction, just north of Bozeman Hot Springs. Here MT 85 merges with US 191, which winds through Gallatin Canyon.

From Bozeman go about 20 miles on US 191 to Squaw Creek Road. Turn left/east off the highway onto Squaw Creek Road, which immediately crosses the Gallatin River via an old cement arch bridge. From the bridge, the main group of developed cliffs—**Wildebuttress**—is 0.7 mile south. Follow Squaw Creek Road to the right/south for about 0.8 mile to a pullout and park. The approach trail wanders through a clearcut above the road. Backtrack from your vehicle until you see the path ascend the bank. The easy walk takes about 10 minutes to reach the base of the cliffs.

WILDEBUTTRESS

The following descriptions start from the right side (facing the wall) and progress left.

13. **Wildebeast** (5.11c) Located on wall right of large book formation with several small roofs; steep face with small roofs; 12 bolts, gear (#3 or #4 Rocks useful); 120'; chain anchors.

14. **Wilde Dreizehn** (5.11a) Right-hand wall of open book formation; gray rock is split by a discontinuous crack with a small tree growing from it; 13 bolts and gear (medium wires); 130'; chain anchors.

Photo by Randall Green.

15. **Bonehead** (5.10b) Begins at a U-shaped indent in the cliff wall (flat area) left of the large open book formation; 6 bolts; 60'; chain anchors.

16. **KaChing'** (5.11b) About 100' left of BONEHEAD is another open book indent in the cliff. Follow a short dihedral to a small overhang and face above; 10/11 bolts, gear (small assortment of nuts useful); 130'; chain anchors.

GALLATIN GNEISS FORMATIONS

OVERVIEW

If limestone face climbing is not to your liking then go deeper into Gallatin Canyon. About 25 miles southwest of Bozeman and 13 miles north of Big Sky, elegant looking towers, fins, and faces jut skyward on both sides of the highway. The rock, which seems like overcooked sandstone, is gneiss that is almost like quartzite in places.

Gallatin Tower is the dominant formation on the west side of the canyon; the Watchtower, The Waltz, Black Line, and Skyline buttresses dominate the east side. Multi-pitched climbs abound here, offering distinct challenges for climbers of varying ability and experience levels. Dockins says that "despite the unusual, somewhat tricky nature of the climbing, the canyon lures you back again and again to climb."

Bring a **standard gear rack** well stocked with wired stoppers (including small RP/HB nuts) and cams (small to medium-sized Tri-Cams as well as TCUs and Friends). Hexentrics also work well in some situations. If you plan to do many routes here, bring all the crack gizmos you own. Gear placements can vary from textbook-classic nut placements to technical, tricky opposition and camming placements. The rock can vary from clean, solid, and sticky to dirty, loose, and slippery. Wearing a helmet is a good idea because loose rock is abundant on many ledges. And it is often prudent to have two ropes to avoid rope drag on routes with roofs or zigzags and to provide safe escapes from some routes on the larger formations.

GALLATIN TOWER

The Tower is the largest cliff on the west side of the highway. At first glance, its jumbled-looking dark gray mass is not inspiring nor does it resemble much of a tower when viewed from the road. But closer inspection reveals deep hues of blue and gray rock contrasted with a marbling of white veins. The top of the tower actually is separated from the hillside it juts from by a 50' cleft or notch.

Descents from the summit are via two single-rope rappels: one down to the base of the notch, and one more down slabs to the south face. It is possible to scramble off north from the first two pitches of several routes that intersect a large horizontal break that cuts across the lower third of the wall.

GALLATIN CANYON GNEISS FORMATIONS EAST SIDE

Spare Rib

Skyline Buttress

Ashes of Stone

Pineapple Buttress

Tango Tower

Watch Tower Lower Tier

The Waltz

Fish Face

Black Line Buttress

B.O. Buttress

No Rest for the Weary

Photo by Bill Dockins.

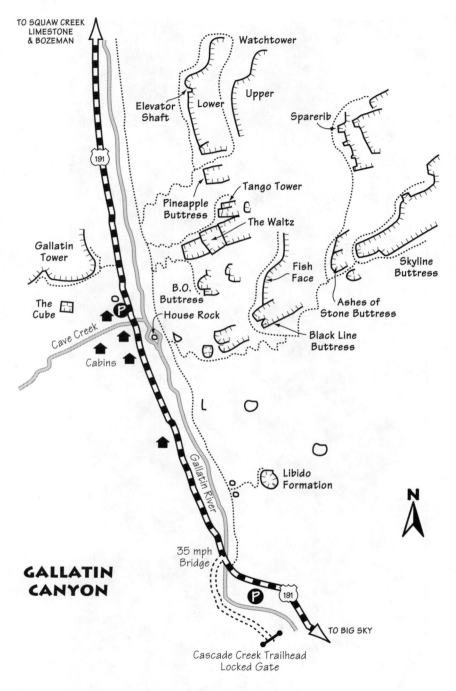

TO SQUAW CREEK
LIMESTONE
& BOZEMAN

191

Watchtower

Elevator
Shaft

Lower

Upper

Sparerib

Tango Tower

Pineapple
Buttress

The Waltz

Gallatin
Tower

B.O.
Buttress

Fish
Face

Skyline
Buttress

The
Cube

House Rock

Ashes of
Stone Buttress

Cave Creek

Black Line
Buttress

Cabins

L

Gallatin River

Libido
Formation

N

**GALLATIN
CANYON**

35 mph
Bridge

P

191

TO BIG SKY

Cascade Creek Trailhead
Locked Gate

Map courtesy of Bill Dockins, *Bozeman Rock Climbs*, 1995 edition.

Finding the rock: Take US 191 west and then south from Bozeman or MT 85 south from Belgrade to Four Corners Junction just north of Bozeman Hot Springs. Here MT 85 merges with US 191, which winds through Gallatin Canyon. From Bozeman it's about 25 miles to a pullout on US 191 across from the main formations, which are past the Squaw Creek limestone cliffs going south. Park in the turnout on the west side of the road just past the tower. Walk along the highway north to the talus slope at the base of the tower. Follow a faint trail marked with cairns up to the east face and along the south side.

17. **Orange Crack** (5.11-) The first pitch of this route (5.9) offers it all—face, thin crack, to offwidth. Start on face holds, climb to top of square-topped pillar, and follow thin crack to ledge and wider crack system left to belay ledge; 140' (4" cams useful). From large horizontal break in face continue up steep (5.11-), blocky roofs to easy (albeit unprotected 5.7) slab above to join STANDARD ROUTE for final pitch to summit (easy to walk off north after first pitch but not after second pitch). **Descent:** See STANDARD ROUTE.

18. **Tigger** (5.10-) Thin crack and right-facing dihedral left of ORANGE CRACK. Optional belay ledge with detached block at top and left of lower dihedral; 2 crack variants possible above ledge; TIGGER continues up right-facing dihedral above ledge; 140' (small wires and nuts to 2" useful). From large horizontal break continue another pitch on slab (5.7 R) to join STANDARD ROUTE for final pitch to summit or at top of first pitch scramble north and walk off side of tower. **Descent:** See STANDARD ROUTE.

19. **Thing In Between** (5.9) Crack line through roofs between TIGGER and FIRST BEST (gear to 1"); once past final roof, continue on TIGGER or variants of FIRST BEST; 140'; From large horizontal break in face continue another pitch on slab (5.7 R) to join STANDARD ROUTE for final pitch to summit. **Descent:** See STANDARD ROUTE.

20. **First Best** (5.10-) Left-facing dihedral that leads to optional belay block used by TIGGER and THING'; continue up TIGGER or a left-most crack variant to large horizontal break in face. Continue another pitch on slab (5.7 R) to join STANDARD ROUTE for final pitch to summit. **Descent:** See STANDARD ROUTE.

21. **Standard Route** (5.8) Classic 3- or 4-pitch route to summit of tower. Standard rack with extra slings and nuts/cams to 3.5".

    Pitch 1—(5.6-5.7) Several variants are possible; scramble to ledges, follow a right-leaning double crack or a shallow left-facing dihedral to a flat ledge with chain anchor; 40'. **Pitch 2**—(5.8) Follow cracks to prominent left-facing open book that splits entire face; belay at large horizontal break; 100'. (pitch 2 and pitch 3 may be combined—165'). **Pitch 3**—(5.7) Continue up open book to ledges at base of final chimney and overhanging

Photo by Bill Dockins.

face. **Pitch 4**—(5.7) Traverse left and face climb into chimney, following lefthand crack system to blocks.

Recommended variant direct finish (5.9+) Follow finger and hand cracks that split overhanging wall above belay; scramble to summit. **Descent:** Rappel from chains on northwest corner (50') to base of notch; scramble and walk southwest across terrace to rappel chains hidden below a boulder; rappel (85') down southwest corner to base of tower.

22. **Soft in the Middle** (5.11c) Left-facing dihedral around corner on main south face. Climb dihedral past small overhang to ledge and continue up steep face; 4 bolts, gear (small-medium wired stoppers useful); 70'. Descent: Rappel from chain anchor.

23. **Bowling for Buicks** (5.12a) Sustained face line (named for once-trundled boulders that nearly took out a car on the highway below) near left side of south face; 5 bolts, gear (small-medium wired nuts useful); 65'. **Descent:** Rappel from chain anchor.

THE CUBE

The Cube is a 50'-high square block south of Gallatin Tower.

Finding the rock: It is a pain in the...to traverse from the trail along the south side of Gallatin Tower. It is better to hike straight up the hillside to the rock from the pullout on the highway south Gallatin Tower.

24. **Like Pablo** (5.10) Thin crack line on right side of north face. Follow crack to ledge just below summit; gear; 40-50'. **Descent:** Downclimb backside of The Cube.

25. **Evergreen Arete** (5.11b) Line on overhanging east face. Start 4' left of corner, climb to ledge, and hand traverse to corner and north face; finish up and right on slab; 5 bolts, gear (small-medium wired stoppers and RPs useful); 60'. **Descent:** Rappel from 2-bolt anchor.

26. **Straw Man** (5.12b/c) Face line in middle of east face. Ascend a short dihedral to sloping ledge; exit overhanging face by going left and up slab; bolts, gear? 60'. **Descent:** Rappel from EVERGREEN' anchor.

LIBIDO AREA

Libido is a small outcrop about 0.5 mile south of the main east-side formations. It has a clean north face and large roof facing the river.

Finding the rock: From the parking area south of the 35-mph bridge follow the riverside trail north to a large boulder. Leave the main riverside trail and go up hill on the north side of the boulder. Follow a switchback route through talus to the base of the outcrop.

THE CUBE

Photo by Bill Dockins.

27. **Crack of Libido** (5.11-) Intimidating 10' horizontal roof split by hand crack on right side. Climb broken rock to base of roof or walk to roof via right side; follow crack out roof and up overhanging wall above (crux is turning roof); 60'; #2-4 Friends useful. **Descent:** Scramble to top and walk off to the right (fairly obvious).

28. **Butthole Surfer** (5.11+) Thin crack and face line that ascends north face of formation. Once past initial bulge follow crack to fixed pin and face climb to top; bolts, gear (small—#3 Rock—to medium wired nuts useful and #1-1.5 Friends for belay). **Descent:** Walk off left.

BLACK LINE BUTTRESS

This is the first large outcrop on the middle tier north of Libido. A deep, 10'-wide chimney forms the black line that splits the wall into two separate buttresses.

Finding the rock: From the main riverside trail at a 7' boulder take a path to the right/east and ascend the hill past a smaller blocky formation called the Glass Catcher and a larger one between Glass Catcher and Black Line Buttress. Continue past these rocks to the south side of Black Line Buttress. It also is possible to go around the west side to Fish Face.

SOUTH FACE

29. **French Lace** (5.11c) Right-most of two routes on short, light-colored face above a ledge on upper right of wall. Climb 4th class or easy 5th class up right side to ledge; short dihedral on left side is harder. From ledge surmount a boulder and ascend crack above (right-most of two parallel cracks above ledge); at horizontal break traverse left on good holds and ascend thin face holds above past bolt; finish by mostly face climbing past a thin crack slightly up and right above second bolt. **Descent:** Walk off right.

30. **If Pleiades Could Dance** (5.11b) Start shares same ledge for FRENCH LACE. Ascend crack left of boulder past overhang to horizontal crack; traverse left 8' and climb past bolts; 3 bolts, gear (RPs, wired stoppers, and nuts to 2.5" useful). **Descent:** Walk off right.

31. **White Tag Sale** (5.10) Crack and face line near left side of face right of BLACK LINE. Start about 6' right of a large fir tree; bulge leads to a crack that fades out below a bolt line; traverse left to BLACK LINE at fixed pin to avoid a 5.10 runout section below ledge (comfortable belay); traverse right and climb up to gain 5.7 crack and next ledge; 140'. **Descent:** Double-rope rappel from chain anchors on right side of upper ledge.

32. **Black Line** (5.10) Slightly right-leaning crack on left side of face. Face climb to finger-to-hand crack; at end of crack traverse right to ledge (good belay);

BLACK LINE
BUTTRESS

Photo by Bill Dockins.

from ledge traverse right and climb up to gain 5.7 crack and next ledge. **Descent:** Rappel (140') from chain anchors.

WEST FACE

33. **Raven's Roost** (5.9 R) Ascends the first prominent west-facing prow on the left side of the south face. Climb right-facing dihedral and follow middle of prow to top. **Descent:** Scramble right along ledge and rappel (140') from chain anchors at top of WHITE TAG'.

34. **Storm Rider** (5.11) Thin crack line right of southwest corner of left-hand buttress (left side of entrance to deep chimney). Follow thin crack past fixed pin (crux) to edge of narrow prow (right of WARTS') and move right on right face of prow; gear; 150'. **Descent:** Rappel north (150') from chain anchors at top of narrow prow.

35. **Callis's Warts and Corns** (5.8 R) Wanders up larger prow left of RAVEN'S'. Ascend bulge left of center; continue until possible to traverse left under white quartz crystal to gain crack; follow crack up and right and face climb up center to ledge below small overhang (optional belay) and climb higher to more comfortable ledge; climb short, easy section to top of prow. **Descent:** Rappel north (150') from chain anchors at top of narrow prow.

**BLACKLINE BUTTRESS
NORTHWEST FACE**

Photo by Bill Dockins.

36. **Diesel Driver** (5.9+ may be a sandbag) "Many climbers, especially those who have quickly reviewed the moves on a downward flyby, feel that the route is harder," says local guidebook author Bill Dockins. Look for crack splitting pink-colored face on the north side of buttress; follow crack through overhang to ledge above; short second pitch (5.8) follows crack on north face; take medium stoppers and gear to 3.5". **Descent:** Rappel (150') from chain anchors at top of prow.

FISH FACE

Fish Face is the curving wall comprised of many large flakes stacked right to left like the heavy pages of a stone book located on left/north side of Black Line Buttress. Each "page" has a narrow prow and adjoining face.

Finding the rock: See Black Line Buttress. It also is possible to scramble up the gully between the Waltz and B.O. Buttress to reach the base of the wall.

37. **Guppy Roof** (5.10+) Located on right side of wall, mostly following the right edge of face. Traverse up and right to corner that drops away below; follow corner to overhang; traverse left and over roof (reachy) at fixed pin; climb to tree and follow leaning crack to top. **Descent:** Rappel from top of BIF'.

38. **The Bif Memorial** (5.11) Next line left of GUPPY'. Ascend crack system to roof in middle of face; pass roof and go slightly right to gain crack with fixed pin; face climb past bolt and traverse right to top; 80'. **Descent:** Rappel.

Photo by Bill Dockins.

39. **Crystal Delight** (5.8+) Follows line of white crystals up right side of cliff facing river about 200' left of BIF'. **Descent:** Walk off left and scramble down gully between Fish Face and Waltz's third tier.

40. **Not in Vein** (5.6) Similar in nature to CRYSTAL DELIGHT but farther left, less steep, and easier. Follow crystal vein right of a obelisk-like boulder and the descent gully between Fish Face and Waltz's third tier.

ASHES OF STONE AREA

Named after the fallout from the Mount St. Helens explosion, *Ashes of Stone* is above Black Line Buttress. This area is a lower, semi-detached "rib" of the larger Skyline Buttress.

Finding the rock: See Black Line Buttress. Continue up hill past the southeast side of Black Line Buttress on an indistinct trail, angling left to the crest of a rounded ridge. Follow ridge to base.

41. **Maverick** (5.10) Ascends colorful wall on south side of main rib. Scramble up chimney/gully to large rotten log; climb up and left over bulge on good face holds and horizontal cracks; traverse right to open book; go up and left to short off-width crack; gear (RPs to #2 Friend useful). **Descent:** Scramble to back of rib and down right/south side.

42. **Ashes of Stone** (5.9) Face route up center of west-facing prow; 4 bolts, gear (small assorted rack for climb and belay). **Descent:** See MAVERICK.

43. **Farewell to Arms** (5.10+) Steep, sustained, and somewhat undefined line that leads to thin crack on left/north side of rib; climb good holds and aim for thin crack above; climb thin crack through bulge and easier rock to top. **Descent:** See MAVERICK.

SKYLINE BUTTRESS

Skyline is the large outcrop directly above Ashes of Stone and is characterized by several parallel fins or ribs that point toward the river.

Finding the rock: See Black Line Buttress. For routes on the south and west faces continue up hill past the southeast side of *Black Line* and *Ashes of Stone*; to reach routes on the northwest face of Skyline scramble over top of Ashes of Stone at the foot of the main ribs of *Skyline*.

44. **Crystal Caper** (5.7) Long single-pitch route on south side of third rib. Ascend crack that gradually widens and then follow west-facing open book to top. Continue up SKYLINE or rappel route (2-ropes).

45. **Skyline** (5.6) Longest route in Gallatin Canyon; 2 to 5 pitches step up the Skyline ridge. Start on north side of buttress in chimney behind a detached pillar. **Pitch 1**—Ascend chimney to notch in ridge (40') and ascend ridge, heading up and left to belay below 15' step. **Pitch 2**—Scramble two 15' steps and belay at base of larger step (50'), which is second pitch of ITHACA'); descend a steep, narrow 20' chimney to right/south side and good belay ledge below a 100' chimney. **Pitch 3**—(5.6) Ascend clean chimney, emerging through a hole onto a ledge at top. Either wander up and right about 20' to escape (double-rope rappel down CRYSTAL') or continue 2-3 pitches of ridge scrambling punctuated by some steps (5.6). **Descent:** Hike up north side of ridge, walk through slot, and descend south side.

46. **Sky King** (5.11) Righthand of parallel crack system left of SKYLINE chimney start. Follow first crack left of chimney and traverse left 10' under bulge; ascend crack above that splits section of pink rock and wide diagonal crack (can escape to chimney via diagonal crack); continue to top of step, zigzag right and then left to get into upper crack; gear to 2.5" (small wired stoppers useful). **Descent:** See SKYLINE for optional descents.

47. **Ithaca Connection** (5.9-) Hike up to a large inside corner/open book on the lower buttress and then hike up loose rock an scree a few yards before dropping down to continue walking east along the base of north face to

SKYLINE BUTTRESS WEST & SOUTH FACE

Ithaca Connection 2nd pitch

Crystal Caper

47

44

Photo by Bill Dockins.

SKYLINE BUTTRESS
NW FACE
ASHES OF STONE

to 52

52

49 48 47

51

walk-off

thin
5.10

5.9

43 42

Photo by Bill Dockins.

**SKYLINE BUTTRESS
SOUTH-SOUTHWEST FACE**

70'

48

49

50

51

Photo by Bill Dockins.

where the far left side of the book merges with the next wall. **Pitch 1**—
(5.9-) Ascend crack system to small, flat platform below largest step on
ridge. **Pitch 2**—(5.9-) Follow west-facing wall of large step past 2 bolts to
top of step. Continue up SKYLINE or climb up 20' and scramble off right/
south, following ledges.

48. **The Throwback** (5.10c) 2-pitch line left of ITHACA. **Pitch 1**—Climb first
15' of ITHICA then "wander" up and left to belay at base of chimney; 90'.
Pitch 2—(5.10+) Traverse right over a block to a discontinuous crack leading to top; 80'. **Descent:** See ITHACA.

49. **Don't Think Twice** (5.10-) Look for shallow groove and light tan-colored
rock 10' left of ITHACA' and 15' right of lowest of two trees growing out
of cracks in the lower section of the face. Ascend groove and pass bulge
(first crux); angle up and left to vegetated crack and a "suspect" flake (possible to escape right into chimney to avoid flake); 165'. **Descent:** See ITHACA
CONNECTION.

50. **Stigmata** (5.11+) Line ascends prominent flat-topped tower that leans against
the lower wall left of DON'T THINK TWICE. Follow crack up overhanging north face of tower past two "blood-red" stains; crux near top; 70'.
Descent: Rappel from chockstone behind tower.

51. **Never on Sunday** (5.10) 4-pitch route, starting about 20' left of STIGMATA
tower. **Pitch 1**—Take line of least resistance to belay in cleft behind tower;
50'. **Pitch 2**—(5.10) Climb left-facing open book that changes to right-
facing (crux) about 20' up then gets easier (4th class); belay at base of Red
Tower. **Pitch 3**—(5.7) Ascend the west face of the tower to its top. **Pitch 4**—
(5.10) Traverse right to chimney and stem up it a ways then bridge left to
and climb left wall; when good holds fade out (10') hand traverse left into
groove; continue on excellent crack, which is only a few feet right of final
pitch of SKYDIVER; gear to 3.5" (RPs, small wires, and Friends to #3
useful).

52. **Skydiver** (5.10-) Of original route, only upper 2 pitches are recommended.
Go left along base of wall and uphill until possible to cut back right on
good ledges to mid-height of face left of Red Tower to avoid loose rock and
lower portion of wall. **Pitch 1**—(5.9-) Diagonal right and up, heading toward left-facing corner formed by a huge flake; follow flake to its top and
go 10' left under a roof. **Pitch 2**—(5.10-) Climb crack and groove system
above belay ledge then work up and right into clean hand crack past bush
to top. Gear to 3.5" (small to medium wired stoppers and nuts to #3 Friend
useful). **Descent:** Scramble up Skyline Ridge until it is possible to walk off
south side of buttress.

SPARERIB AREA

Left or north of Skyline is a square-faced buttress with a number of "ribs" protruding from it toward the river. Sparerib is the prominent rib on the left side of the west wall.

Finding the rocks: See Black Line and Skyline buttresses. From the west/downhill side of Ashes of Stone go left and traverse across the talus slope to the base of Sparerib. To reach Out-of-Bounds continue northward past Sparerib and ascend the hillside to the base of the wall.

53. **Songline** (5.12b/c) Line on brown, rippled, south face of Wafer (above Sparerib). Face climb past bolt and fixed nuts to break; traverse right along break, pass a short bulge, and continue on steep face above; 3 bolts, gear (RPs, wired Rocks to #7 and small TCUs useful); 80'. **Descent:** Rappel from large tree.

54. **Zig Zag** (5.8) Look for obvious zig zag crack splitting buttress about 40' right of main Sparerib buttress. **Pitch 1**—(5.8) Ascend crack to small ledge with tree (30') and follow zig zag crack to top of rib. **Pitch 2**—Go up and left, following sandy, low-angled chimney to top. **Descent:** Walk off left or right side of buttress.

55. **Sparerib** (5.8-) "Superlative route" up tallest and most prominent clean rib/buttress on formation. Two sets of double cracks split the west face of rib. **Pitch 1**—(5.6) Ascend middle of buttress, following 2'-wide groove

Photo by Bill Dockins.

SPARERIB

53
Songline
54
55

Photo by Bill Dockins.

ending on ledge; 50'. **Pitch 2**—(5.8-) Follow righthand set of double cracks past two small overhangs to top; 150'. **Descent:** Walk off left or right side of buttress.

B.O. BUTTRESS

South of the Waltz Formation on the lower tier, the smaller B.O. Buttress is a narrow finlike feature with one prominent overhang that faces the river.

Finding the rock: See The Waltz. Continue down the Riverside Trail past the approach path to Black Line and Skyline buttresses. The paths are really very obvious and change from year to year because of deadfall trees. The path goes to the base and south side of the Waltz Formation and continues south to B.O.

56. **Densepack** (5.11-) Start in a chimney/slot and generally follows southwest corner of buttress. Layback a flake and follow thin crack system on south side of left rib. Climb chimney to short layback flake then move right onto face; follow seam and when possible traverse left to corner of buttress; crack leads to top; gear to 3.5" (RPs and stoppers and one large piece useful). **Descent:** Walk off either side.

57. **Boveng's Overhang** (5.9 R) Line that crosses left edge of slanting roof left of DENSEPACK and follows prow of rib (RPs and small wired stoppers useful). **Descent:** Walk off.

58. **Dark Horse** (5.10) Thin crack on north side of rib left of BOVENG'S. Follow thin crack to roof; surmount overhang on right side and follow cracks to top. **Descent:** Walk off.

THE WALTZ FORMATION

Large prominent finlike formation that is broken into three major steps that descend toward the river. It steps up the hill roughly in the middle of the east-side formations.

Finding the rock: Directly across the canyon from Gallatin Tower leave the main riverside trail and follow a path that switchbacks up the slope to the base of the Waltz's bottom step.

59. **The Waltz** (5.8) 3-pitch route that follows the prow of each step. **Pitch 1**—(5.7) Start on south side of first tier and traverse left on ledges to avoid lower roof; climb center of prow to top of first step. **Pitch 2**—(5.6) Follow crack near the right side of second step; downclimb the short, low-angled ramp behind top of the second step to base of next step. **Pitch 3**—(5.8) Start on right side and work up and left onto face, continuing straight to top. **Descent:** Walk off the south side from top of second or third step.

**B.O. BUTTRESS
NORTH & WEST FACES**

57
Boveng's

Dark
Horse
5.10

58

Photo by Bill Dockins.

Photo by Bill Dockins.

TANGO TOWER

Tango Tower is a steep slab that leans against the north side of the third step/ tier of the Waltz.

Finding the rock: From the main riverside trail continue a couple hundred feet past the first trail to the Waltz and ascend a switchback route up the left/ north side of the Waltz.

60. **The Fugitive** (5.12-) Mostly a face climb with a few finger locks, this single-pitch climb goes up north face of tower's lowest rib. Crux is midway up wall; after crux go right to rest ledge on arete; make a move up arete and return to crack and good face holds. Thin and strenuous; gear (many small to medium wired nuts and #1.5 Friend useful). **Descent:** Scramble off via exposed ledge system to left.

61. **Watercolor Wall** (5.11 R) Look for a colorful face uphill from FUGITIVE. Some "artistry" required to place decent protection. Start in middle of face and traverse up and left along a thin seam to a fixed RURP (likely will not hold a lead fall); continue straight up to left side of ledge; gear to 2.5" (small wired stoppers and Tri-Cams useful). **Descent:** Rappel from 2-bolt anchor.

PINEAPPLE BUTTRESS

Left/north of the third tier of the Waltz Formation, Pineapple Buttress is characterized by a slender tower of rock in the middle of the buttress.

Finding the rock: From the main Riverside trail ascend a talus slope, taking a diagonal line northeast toward the Pineapple and Bleacher buttresses and the Watchtower, or go same way as for Tango Tower.

62. **Fox Trot** (5.5) Ascends line near right side of buttress. Follow good cracks (many variants possible) to gain ledge on right shoulder of buttress below overhanging face; standard gear rack; 160'. **Descent:** Walk off to right side of buttress.

63. **Pineapple Thunderpussy** (5.9) 2-pitch route offering lots of exposure on northwest corner of buttress. Scramble up gully north of buttress until above first short tier. **Pitch 1**—(5.9) Ascend a dihedral through light-colored rock to a roof; go left around roof and continue 15' up vertical crack on north face to ledge (placing good belay anchors here requires thought). **Pitch 2**— (5.9) Climb straight above ledge until possible to traverse right to arete. **Descent:** Walk to back of buttress and descend left side.

Photo by Bill Dockins.

THE WATCHTOWER—LOWER TIER

The Watchtower is a two-tiered slab left/north of Pineapple Buttress. The prominent Elevator Shaft chimney toward the right side of the formation splits the lower face into two segments—Joker Face on the right and Mother's Day Face on the left.

It is possible to walk off either side of the lower tier; both sides require some downclimbing.

Finding the rock: From the Riverside Trail hike up talus slope below and right of the Watchtower to Pineapple Buttress and go north along the base of the face.

64. **The Joker** (5.9) 3-pitch route following crack systems right of the Elevator Shaft chimney. Locate cul-de-sac between 'Shaft and surrounding buttresses. **Pitch 1**—(5.5) Start on right side of cul-de-sac and ascend groove to wide crack and dihedral system; go past a few ledges to a grassy ledge on right; 120'. **Pitch 2**—(5.7) Face climb up and left then straight up until possible to traverse right to left-facing dihedral below roof; turn roof near an 18" chockstone and squeeze between two prominent horns to small ledge above. **Pitch 3**—(5.9) Sustained difficulties begin with 10' traverse left onto face; follow groove, flairing crack, and face to bolt; go up past bolt and left to northwest corner of buttress summit block. **PITCH 3—VARIANT/WATCH-TOWER STANDARD ROUTE** (5.8-) From ledge above horns continue up dihedral and chimney. **Descent:** Walk off left or right.

Photo by Bill Dockins.

65. **Mother's Day** (5.8+) 3-pitch route left of the Elevator Shaft Chimney. Start at chockstone-filled hand crack splitting southwest corner of buttress left of the 'Shaft. **Pitch 1**—Climb crack up 15' step, scramble past bushes and small trees to belay ledge at base of left-facing dihedral. **Pitch 2**—(5.7) Climb dihedral above ledge about 25' then traverse right into crack; follow crack to good ledge. **Pitch 3**—(5.8+) Traverse 10-15' right around corner to groove and crack on face of buttress; follow crack to roof (crux) and easier ground above. **Descent:** Walk off.

BEARTRAP
NEAT ROCK

OVERVIEW

Neat Rock is situated on the west side of the Madison River east of Norris near the north end of Beartrap Canyon. Its south- and east-facing walls make it a popular early-season crag; even in winter during spells of dry, warm weather it is possible to climb here. In spring keep a sharp lookout for rattlesnakes lounging in the sun as they emerge from winter dens.

Finding the rock: From Bozeman go west on US 191 to Four Corners and the junction with MT 84. Continue straight through the intersection on MT 84 for nearly 22 miles to the Beartrap Bridge. Neat Rock will come into view about 2.5 miles before the bridge. Turn right off the highway onto a dirt road and go north 2.5 miles (downstream) along the west side of the river to the rock. The approach is about 50' from the road.

66. **Standard Route** (5.9-) 2-pitch route about in middle of face; line tends to the left. **Pitch 1**—(5.7) Follow finger to hand crack in prominent open book (can be done in one long pitch or broken in middle at nice ledge). **Pitch 2**—(5.9-) Angle left up ramp on left side of upper diamond-shaped face; ramp turns into right-facing dihedral capped by a roof; turn overhang and scramble off left. Gear to 3". **Descent:** Walk off east-facing slabs. **Pitch 2—escape right variant:** (5.7) Avoid the roof crux of pitch 2 by going right to the slot/ chimney up the right side of the upper diamond face. **Descent:** Same as above.

67. **Brothers in Arms Variant** (5.10+) Single pitch variation of STANDARD ROUTE. Follow pitch 1 of STANDARD ROUTE to good ledge on left midway up open book. Traverse left 20' and ascend thin crack splitting a bulge (crux) and continue up through more overhanging obstacles to sloping ramp at base of diamond shaped face. Continue up Pitch 3 of STANDARD ROUTE to top. **Descent:** Walk off east.

68. **Rock Lobster Variant** (5.10+ R) Single pitch variation of STANDARD ROUTE. Climb Pitch 1 of STANDARD ROUTE to base of upper diamond-

shaped face. Follow left-leaning crack and groove up diamond face (first section is hard to protect with ledge-fall potential); climb face holds past fixed pin and gain left-leaning crack to small ledge; go up right under overhang to summit. **Descent:** Walk off east.

69. **Sunny Butterflies** (5.9+) Starts about 75' right of STANDARD ROUTE and 30' left of a detached spire. A bolt marks the start of the route. If you are unfamiliar with the rock here, an on-sight lead of this route will seem like the rating is a sandbag by a grade. Climb past bolt (crux) to ledge; mantle to stance below roof and follow a hand crack through overhang and to another ledge; continue up easy ground along a large column to base of diamond-shaped face (can easily walk off to right after first pitch). Continue up STANDARD ROUTE or ROCK LOBSTER to top. **Descent:** Walk off east/right.

70. **Steel Drivin' Man** (5.10d/.11a) Climb SUNNY BUTTERFLIES or scramble up gully to its right to a large sloping ledge below huge triangular roof. Move right past a bolt and over overlaps and up bolt line; 5 bolts. **Descent:** Double- or single-rope rappel from chain anchor (double rope gets one all the way down—single rope rappel requires some easy downclimbing gully right of SUNNY BUTTERFLIES).

Photo by Bill Dockins.

NOTES:

SouthCentral

REGION

BILLINGSAREA

GRANITE PEAK

OVERVIEW

At 12,799 feet, Granite Peak is Montana's highest point and a highly sought-after summit. It was first successfully climbed in 1923 after several previous attempts and today sees more than 1,000 attempts each year. As Pat Caffrey states in his *Climbers Guide to Montana*, "Elevation and crowds aside, the peak is unique and interesting and offers a worthwhile confrontation."

The summit is atop a flat-topped pyramid that is dwarfed by the large Granite Peak massif extending north in a great sprawling mass. The Granite Glacier clings to the lower flanks of the steep north face. The easiest route to the summit is via the East Ridge, which extends to the northwest flank of Tempest Mountain. Several other established technical routes of greater technical difficulty are on the North Face.

Route finding and weather may be the cruxes for most mountaineers attempting Granite. The elegant low-angled line of the East Ridge seduces one to think the climbing is easy. But sections are loose, exposed, and technical. Moreover, the approach is long and arduous, and the Beartooths are notorious for winterlike storms in summer. Caffrey's warning in his description for the route aptly summarizes the nature of the beast: "The route itself is neither simple or secure. Don't do Granite as your first mountain."

In an entry in *The Hiker's Guide to Montana*, Michael Sample points out that people attempt to climb Granite Peak all times of the year, but August and early September are the best choices. Even then sudden storms with sub-zero wind chills are a real possibility. Snowstorms can happen anytime, and the thunderstorms around the peak are legendary. Be prepared with warm and windproof clothing and a shelter that will hold together and stay put in a strong wind.

Two main approaches typically are used. The West Rosebud/Mystic Lake approach is shorter but much steeper and strenuous and offers an alternative

▲ –

Jerry Buck (with helpful review comments from Chad Chadwick) provided the approach and climbing route descriptions for this section.

GRANITE PEAK & EAST ROESBUD

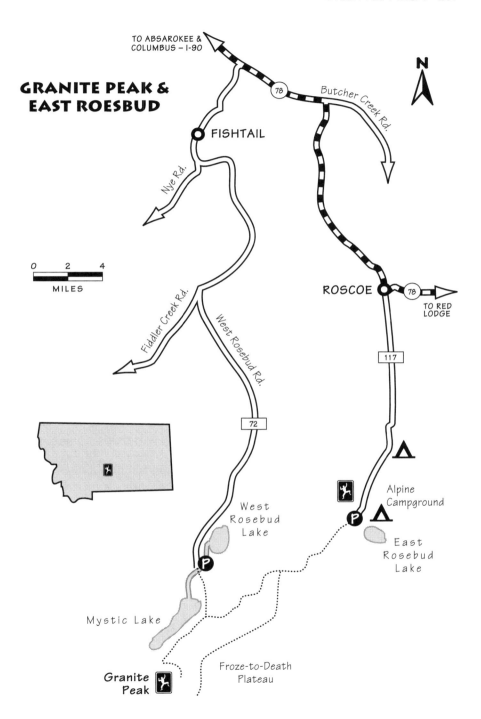

TO ABSAROKEE & COLUMBUS – I-90

N

78

Butcher Creek Rd.

FISHTAIL

Nye Rd.

MILES

0 2 4

Fiddler Creek Rd.

West Rosebud Rd.

ROSCOE

78

TO RED LODGE

117

72

West Rosebud Lake

Alpine Campground

East Rosebud Lake

Mystic Lake

Granite Peak

Froze-to-Death Plateau

approach up Huckleberry Creek. The East Rosebud Lake approach is longer but not so steep. Both approach trails lead to Froze-to-Death Plateau. Routes across the plateau are marked with cairns. An overnight base camp can be set at about 11,700 feet on the plateau on the west side of neighboring Tempest Mountain. A variant to the Mystic Lake approach from the West Rosebud up Huckleberry Creek may require two nights out but offers better shelter from winds and bad weather on the plateau.

Gear recommendations: 150- to 165-foot rope, crampons, ice axe, a few chocks/nuts, slings, and extra carabiners.

Trip Planning Information

Area description: Ridge route on the state's highest peak.

General location: In the heart of the Beartooth Mountains about 80 miles southwest of Billings.

Camping: National forest campgrounds are located near the ends of the roads at the West and East Rosebud trailheads; the campgrounds offer water, trash cans, and outhouses for a nightly fee; there is no camping in the canyons outside of designated campsites; bivy-style camping is possible on Froze-to-Death Plateau, but since it is above timberline it is important to use no-trace techniques.

Climbing season: August through September. The area gets snow early, and the snow stays late because of the elevation. Campgrounds close in mid-August so bring your own water if you plan to come late in the season.

Restrictions and access issues: Granite Peak is in the Absaroka-Beartooth Wilderness Area; all wilderness restrictions apply—no power drills, etc. Because it is a popular area use no-trace techniques and do not trundle loose rocks.

Other guidebooks: *Climbing Granite Peak* by Donald Jacobs; *Climbers Guide to Montana* by Pat Caffrey. For more information contact the Beartooth Mountaineering and Climbing Club, Billings.

Nearby mountain shops, guide services, and gyms: The Base Camp, Billings.

Finding the trailheads—West Rosebud: From Columbus drive south on Montana Highway 78 to Absarokee. Go through Absarokee and in about 2 miles take a well-marked turn to the right/west to Fishtail. Go through Fishtail and turn left/south onto the West Rosebud Road about 1 mile south of town. About 2 miles farther take another left/southeast at the sign for West Rosebud Lake. It's another 14 miles of bumpy gravel road from this point. In total it's 27 miles from Absarokee and 41 miles from Columbus. The road ends and the trail begins right at the Mystic Dam Power Station.

East Rosebud: Go to Roscoe, which is between Columbus and Red Lodge on MT 78. At the north edge of Roscoe, the road turns to gravel and heads straight for the East Rosebud trailhead. Just after you cross East Rosebud Creek about

**GRANITE PEAK
EAST RIDGE**

Photo by Michael S. Sample.

7 miles from Roscoe be sure to take a sharp right turn and continue heading south along the creek. It's 14.5 miles of gravel with one section of pavement about two-thirds of the way from Roscoe to the trailhead. Take the Phantom Creek Trailhead turn, which is on the right/west side of the road about a mile before the road ends.

Approaching the peak via Mystic Lake/Froze-to-Death Plateau (West Rosebud): From the trailhead at Mystic Lake power plant head west up the trail toward the dam (3 miles). Continue along the south end of the lake on the trail to the first turnoff. Enjoy the first section of this hike as it becomes very strenuous from here on out. At the trail junction (about a half mile from the dam) head up toward Froze-to-Death Plateau. This section of the approach can best be described as "switchbacks from hell."

Once the trail crests the plateau look carefully for cairns. Follow the cairns a few miles across to Tempest. Eventually the trail will head in a more southerly direction. Water often can be found up here in the form of springs. When you get close to Tempest contour around the west until a trail can be found leading over several boulder fields to the col between Tempest and Granite. Several mediocre tent shelters can be found along the way. Anticipate nasty boulder hopping.

Approaching the peak via Huckleberry Creek (from Mystic Lake—West Rosebud): From the Mystic Lake dam head west past the Froze-to-Death/Panther Creek turnoff. After about 2.5 miles you will come to the Huckleberry Creek Campground. From the back of the campground and on the west side of the creek take the trail up toward Huckleberry Lake. From the lake follow the trail up to Princess Lake through moderate terrain. Cross the lake via a land bridge on its south end. Head southwest toward the ridge and pick up a trail leading to Lower Snowball Lake. Pass by the string of lakes (severe scree/boulder hopping) to the north end of Avalanche Lake. From Lower Snowball Lake head up the scree field to the saddle between Tempest and Granite to pick up the east ridge.

Approaching the peak via Phantom Creek Trail (East Rosebud): Follow the trail as it climbs gradual switchbacks along Armstrong Creek for about 2.5 miles before it breaks out of the forest into a great panorama highlighted by Hole-in-the-Wall Mountain to the south. The trail continues climbing to Froze-to-Death Plateau. See Mystic Lake approach for description across plateau.

EAST RIDGE (III/IV 5.4)

The East Ridge extends from the saddle between Tempest Mountain and the summit of Granite Peak. From the saddle, climb on the south side of the east ridge toward the snow bridge (3rd class). After reaching the snow bridge (about 12,300' elevation) traverse the south side of its crest (crampons and belay recommended). Then continue traversing left toward the south and up to a prominent chimney that leads to a "V" notch. Watch for some rappel slings at the top of the notch to use on the way down.

From the "V" notch follow cairns along a ledge system up the main face. A lot of zigzag traversing will eventually lead to the ridge proper and mostly can be done with moderate 4th class moves. On the skyline a large feature called the "keyhole" can be seen. Also, look for piton and sling anchors to rappel off of on the way down.

Climb toward the keyhole once on the top of the ridge by traversing left on a ledge into a 20' chute. Some moderately easy 5th class climbing will lead to the base of the keyhole. Belay here. Once past the keyhole, it is an easy scramble to the summit. **Descent:** Downclimb route and rappel at 2-3 locations or wherever necessary.

EAST ROSEBUD CANYON

OVERVIEW

East Rosebud Canyon is an area boasting large granite faces of high quality as well as beautiful views of some of the most rugged terrain Montana has to offer. The routes lie just before the tiny hamlet of Alpine along the west side of the road. There are four large formations with smaller spires and domes interspersed throughout. Moving north to south toward the lake, the three major towers are named Tower of Incubus, Tower of Innocence, and Tower of Poor Rock. The fourth formation is The Ramp and looks like a large ramp of gray-colored rock. All the formations with the exception of the Tower of Poor Rock hold fine multi-pitch routes for experienced climbers. Several high-quality single-pitch routes are located on a smaller formation called Double Book Dome.

The climbs in this area have an alpine feel and as such hold a variety of dangers. Weather moves in and out of East Rosebud Canyon quickly and with intensity. In an hour it is not uncommon for perfectly clear sky to give way to sheets of windblown rain, dark skies, and lightning on the ridge tops. Always come prepared for storms, and remember that you will not be close to your car. A helmet is essential. There is a lot of loose rock that can be knocked off by climbers; be aware. East Rosebud Canyon is a gateway to the Absaroka-Beartooth Wilderness, so please treat it with respect and leave the beauty behind for others to discover.

Trip Planning Information

Area description: Multi-pitch and single-pitch routes on large granite cliffs and domes near the Absaroka-Beartooth Wilderness Area.

▲▲ –

Jason Taylor provided the text, maps, and photos for this section.

EAST ROSEBUD
(VIEW FROM ROAD)

The Ramp

to Double
Book Dome

Photo by Jason Taylor.

General location: 43 miles south of Columbus in the Custer National Forest.

Camping: A national forest campground is located at the end of East Rosebud road, 2 miles south of the climbing. Another campground is located about a mile after entering the national forest. The campgrounds offer water, trash cans, and outhouses for $7 a night. There is no camping in the canyon outside of designated campsites.

Climbing season: May through September. The area will get snow early because of its elevation. Campgrounds close in mid-August so bring your own water if you plan to come late in the season.

Restrictions and access issues: All climbing described is on national forest land. Be sure to park well off main road in pullouts.

Other guidebooks: None. But for more information contact the Beartooth Mountaineering and Climbing Club, 931 Ginger, Billings, MT 59105.

Nearby mountain shops, guide services, and gyms: Back Country, An Outdoor Specialty Store, Billings; The Base Camp, Billings.

Finding the area: From Columbus go south on MT 78 to the village of Roscoe, about 29 miles. At Roscoe turn west on East Rosebud Road and follow it into the canyon. The road is a mix of horrible washboard, rocky sections, ruts, and an odd section of concrete. There is a good pullout about 12 miles from Alpine immediately after the concrete ends just after a bridge that crosses the river. Down the road another 2 miles is a campground.

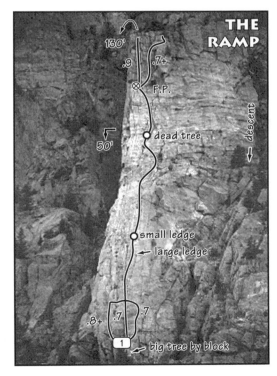

Photo by Jason Taylor.

THE RAMP

OVERVIEW

The Ramp is a fine 5-pitch climb on a formation with the same name. To access this climb park in the pullout at the end of the concrete after the bridge. Walk about 100 yards down the road just past a cattle guard. On the right look for a faint trail that heads up the mountain. If you can't find the trail, some bushwhacking may be in order. Look up at the formations and head toward the low-angle, gray-colored rock that looks like a ramp. If you do find the trail follow it until it leads you to a large rock at the edge of the valley floor (Double Book Dome). *The Ramp* is clearly visible from this vantage. The approach will take about 45 minutes.

1. **The Ramp** (III 5.7+) 5-pitch route that follows cracks up the middle of the face. Take a standard rack (wired stoppers #3-10; Friends #1/2-3 useful). To start, scramble up on a ledge with a big tree by a block at base of middle of face. **Pitch 1**—This pitch has three variations; (1a—5.8+) Traverse left from the base ledge to a dihedral. Follow the dihedral up to a belay ledge; (1b—5.7) Go straight up a clean hand crack over a small bulge to the belay ledge. (1c—5.7) Start to the right of the hand crack in a series of seams and cracks. Follow this obvious line to the right and then cut back left after going over a bulge. Continue left to the belay ledge. All variations are long and take a full rope. **Pitch 2**—Follow crack straight up over a large ledge to a smaller ledge and stop to belay. **Pitch 3**—Follow easy crack system to a ledge with a large dead tree. **Pitch 4**—Climb up to a large ledge with an old piton. **Pitch 5**—This pitch has two variations; (5a—5.9) climb directly up over a roof into a tricky hand crack and then over a second roof to the top; (5b—5.7+) climb to the right into another crack and follow to the top. **Descent:** There are two ways to descend from the top of the cliff. The most common is down the right-hand side, which essentially follows a series of ledges down the face right of *The Ramp*. To the left is a double-rope rappel into a gully. Some searching may be necessary to find hidden piton anchors. Once in the gully rappel off a tree over a small cliff into the lower gully. Be very careful of loose rock!

DOUBLE BOOK DOME

Overview

Double Book Dome is below and south of *The Ramp*. It is easily recognizable as it has two prominent dihedrals on its southeast face. To approach this formation park in the pulloff at the end of the concrete just past the bridge. Walk about 100 yards past a cattle guard. If you look to your right, you will see the obvious dihedrals of the dome. There is a faint trail leading from the road. Walk 20-30 minutes on this trail to the base of the rock.

This formation has high-quality, single-pitch routes ranging from 5.8 to 5.11. The rock is very solid, fun to climb on, and the large roofs make for some spectacular climbing. To return to the base, you can walk off the top or make a double-rope rappel. Looking at the rock from left to right, the routes are:

2. Unnamed (5.11a) This route is on the face left of the left-most dihedral. Climb over a large roof and up face; 9 bolts; bolt anchors. **Descent:** Walk off left or rappel (see route 2).

3. Unnamed (5.8) Line is on the face right of the left-most dihedral, following outside edge/arete of the right dihedral. Follow edge; traverse right over the top of a very large roof; 10 bolts; chain anchors on top. **Descent:** Rappel with two ropes from chains.

4. Unnamed (5.7) Climb crack systems inside and just right of right dihedral; gear; bolt anchors on top. **Descent:** Rappel (see route 2).

5. Unnamed (5.10c) Starts several feet right of right dihedral where left edge of a roof is fractured with a seam extending up face; 5 bolts, gear (small wires, TCUs useful); bolt anchors on top. **Descent:** Rappel (see route 2).

Photo by Jason Taylor.

APPENDIX A
FURTHER READING

Accidents in American Mountaineering, American Alpine Club.

A Climber's Guide to Butte, Dwight Bishop, 1990.

A Climber's Guide to Glacier National Park, J. Gordon Edwards, Glacier Park Natural History Association & Falcon Press, 1995.

Bitterroot Guidebook, Rick Torre, 1993.

Bozeman Rock Climbs, Bill Dockins, Second Edition, 1995.

Climbing Granite Peak: Beartooths, Donald Jacobs, 1992.

Climber's Guide to Montana, Pat Caffrey, Mountain Press, 1986.

Mountaineering: The Freedom of the Hills, 5th edition, Mountaineers, 1992.

Roadside Geology of Montana, David Alt and Donald Hyndman, Mountain Press, 1986.

Rock 'n Road: Rock Climbing Areas of North America, Tim Toula, Chockstone Press, 1995.

Stone Hill: Rock Climbs of Lake Koocanusa, Greg Stenger, 1989.

The Climber's Guide to Lolo Pass, Brad Hutcheson, 1992.

The Climber's Guide to North America (Rockies), John Harlan III, Chockstone Press, 1985.

The Trail Guide to Glacier & Waterton National Parks, Erik Molvar, Falcon Press, 1994.

The Hiker's Guide to Montana, Bill Schneider, Falcon Press, 1994.

Wild Country Companion, Will Harmon, Falcon Press, 1994.

APPENDIX B
RATING SYSTEM COMPARISON CHART

YDS	British	French	Australian
5.3	VD 3b	2	11
5.4	HVD 3c	3	12
5.5	MS/S/HS	4a, 4a	12/13
5.6	HS/S 4a	4b	13/14
5.7	HS/VS 4b	4c	15-17
5.8	VS 4c/5a	5a	18
5.9	HVS 5a/5b	5b	19
5.10a	E1 5a/5b	5c	20
5.10b	E1 5b/5c	6a	20
5.10c	E2 5b/5c	6a+	21
5.10d	E2/E3 5b/5c	6b	21
5.11a	E3 5c/6a	6b+	22
5.11b	E3/E4 5c/6a	6c	22
5.11c	E4 5c/6a	6c+	23
5.11d	E4 6a/6b	7a	24
5.12a	E5 6a/6b	7a+	25
5.12b	E5/E6 6a/6b	7b	26
5.12c	E6 6b/6c	7b+	27
5.12d	E6 6b/6c	7c	27
5.13a	E6/E7 6b/6c	7c+	28
5.13b	E7 6c/7a	8a	29
5.13c	E7 6c/7a	8a+	30
5.13d	E8 6c/7a	8b	31
5.14a	E8 6c/7a	8b+	32
5.14b	E9 6c/7a	8c	??
5.14c	E9 7b	8c+	??

Sources: *Mountaineering: The Freedom of the Hills,* 5th Edition; *Climbing Magazine,* No. 150, February/March 1995.

APPENDIX C

CLIMBING EQUIPMENT RETAIL SHOPS

Canyon Critters
175 S. 2nd
Hamilton, MT 59840
(406) 363-5270

Big Horn Wilderness Equipment
600 Central Ave.
Great Falls, MT 59401
(406) 453-2841

Montana Outdoor Sports
708 N. Last Chance Gulch
Helena, MT 59601
(406) 443-4119

Northern Lights Trading Company
1716 W. Babcock
Bozeman, MT 59715
(406) 586-2225

Pipestone Mountaineering
101 South Higgins
Missoula, MT 59801
(406) 721-1670

Pipestone Mountaineering
829 S. Montana
Butte, MT 59701
(406) 892-4994

Rocky Mountain Outfitter
135 Main
Kalispell, MT 59901
(406) 752-2446

The Base Camp
1730 Grand Ave.
Billings, MT 59102
(406) 248-4555

The Base Camp
333 N. Last Chance Gulch
Helena, MT 59601
(406) 443-5360

The Great Outdoors
25 N. Willson Ave.
Bozeman, MT 59715
(406) 585-7204

The Trailhead
110 East Pine
Missoula, MT 59802
(406) 543-6966

CLIMBING GYMS

Hold-On
235 West Main
Missoula, MT
(406) 728-9157

Helena YMCA
1200 Last Chance Gulch
Helena, MT
(406) 442-9622

Montana State University
Old Gym, Grant St.
Bozeman, MT
(406) 994-3621

Pipestone Mountaineering
829 S. Montana
Butte, MT
(406) 892-4994

University of Montana
Outdoor Recreation Dept.
Fieldhouse Annex, S. 6th
Missoula, MT
(406) 243-5172

GUIDE SERVICES

Peak Adventures
P.O. Box 427
Big Sky, MT 5916

Reach Your Peak
Ron Brunckhorst
405 S. 19th, Apt.C
Bozeman, MT 59715
(406) 587-1708

CLIMBING CLUBS AND
ORGANIZATIONS

Access Fund
P.O. Box 17010
Boulder CO 80308

American Alpine Club
710 10th St.
Golden, CO 80401

**American Mountain Guides
Association**
P.O. Box 2128
Estes Park, CO 80517

**Beartooth Mountaineering and Climbing
Club**
931 Ginger
Billings, MT 59105

APPENDIX D
GLOSSARY OF TERMS/CLIMBER JARGON

aid/artificial climbing—Type of climbing where equipment is used for upward progress (supporting body weight, used for hand and foot holds, etc.)

anchor—Secure attachment to the rock. Many different combinations exist:

artificial/gear anchors—may consist of climbing hardware placed in cracks, etc.;

fixed anchors—may be bolts or pitons permanently attached to the rock;

natural anchors—may consist of a block, keyhole in the rock, or a tree, etc.

angle piton/angle—Specific type of piton with a "V" shape cross section (see piton); removable, yet invasive—damaging the rock and possibly the piton.

arete—Sharp, narrow ridge or spur; outside corner.

bashy—Malleable hardware for extreme aid climbing (see copperheads); otherwise known as a "mashy" or a "trashy" when the cable blows out; removable, yet invasive—damaging the rock and the equipment.

beak/bird beak—Specific type of piton for extreme aid climbing; very thin and in the shape of a bird's beak (see piton).

belay—Rope handling technique to hold a climber in the event of a fall; **belayer**—person securing the rope for a lead climber; **belay anchor**—the secure attachment of the rope to the rock.

beta—Detailed description of all information about a climb.

bolt—Permanent/fixed protection device (typically commercial grade concrete expansion bolt) that is driven into a hole drilled in the rock; invasive equipment that is removable but generally left on the cliff for other climbers to use. A specially designed metal alloy "hanger" is attached so carabiners can be attached easily.

bouldering—Type of free climbing on small cliffs and boulders; generally done without protective equipment such as a rope.

buttress—Formation of rock connected to a large wall or cliff, resembling a support or reinforcement.

cam—Variety of protection devices that when placed will rotate to take a load; removable and non-invasive.

Camalot—Specific type of spring-loaded 4-cam unit; removable and non-invasive; typically heavy and expensive.

carabiner/'biner—Metal alloy snap link used in many ways for connecting points of protection, rope, and person to a belay and anchor system.

chicken head—Bump or protrusion on the rock surface about the size of a chicken's head.

chimney—Narrow cleft in a cliff generally 8 inches or wider.

chock—Removable, non-invasive wedge, nut, or cam made of metal alloy used for points of protection and anchors typically placed in cracks.

copperheads/c-heads—Malleable wedges attached to a short cable; driven into seams and shallow cracks for extreme aid climbing (see bashy).

crack—Split, break, or fissure of various width and depth in rock.

dihedral—Rock formation resembling a two-sided open book or inside corner.

edge—Small indentations or steps in the rock used for hand and foot holds.

face—Feature of a cliff or mountain; also a type of climbing technique where the texture of the rock is used for holds.

fixed hardware—Permanent protection equipment placed in the rock (i.e. bolts, fixed pitons, nut or cam that is too stuck to remove without damage; see anchors).

flash—To free climb a route/pitch without falls, hangs/rests, or prior knowledge of the climb.

free climbing—Type of climbing where equipment is used only for protection, not for upward progress or to support body weight; may be done without a safety rope and belay (see free solo climbing).

free soloing—To climb alone without a rope or any protective hardware (see solo climbing).

Friend—Specific type of spring-loaded 4-cam device; removable and non-invasive.

gear—Equipment used for protection (invasive and non-invasive apparatuses; see anchors).

hangdogging—Type of climbing where leader free climbs from one point of protection to another, resting or supporting body weight on the equipment.

HB (Hugh Banner)—Specific type of protection wedge/nut made of metal alloy and equipped with a short loop of cable; removable, non-invasive.

hook—Specific type of metal hooks of various shapes and designs for extreme aid climbing on the texture of a cliff face; removable and non-invasive.

jam—Technique involves wedging parts of the body—fingers, hands, feet, etc.—for ascending cracks. The size/width of the crack dictates type of technique required.

jug—Large "thank God" hold.

knifeblade—Specific type of thin piton (see piton).

layback/lieback—Technique using counterforce; pulling with the hands while pushing with the feet.

lead—Situation where a climber goes first up a pitch, attached to a rope and belayer and placing protection along the way.

lost arrow—Specific type of piton named after the Lost Arrow Spire in Yosemite (see piton).

natural gear—Removable, non-invasive protection equipment (in addition to sharing the broad definition of "gear," natural gear also can mean placement of a sling around a tree or horn of rock or use of a rock as a chockstone, etc.).

nuts—Removable, non-invasive protection equipment (a.k.a. wedges, stoppers, chocks, etc.)

off-hands—Cracks typically 2 to 3.5 inches wide.

on-sight—Style of climbing where leader attempts to climb route from the bottom up without prior knowledge (see flash).

off-width (OW)—Cracks typically 3.5 to 8 inches wide.

pitch—Rope-length of climbing.

piton—Specially designed metal spike made to drive into cracks as a point of protection or an anchor; removable and invasive.

prow—Projection or portion of a cliff or mountain face that protrudes.

quick draw—Short loop of nylon webbing (see runner) with two carabiners attached for quick attachment to protection equipment.

rack—Assortment of protective hardware (see gear) needed for a climb.

rappel anchor—Secure attachment to the rock for rappelling (bolts and slings, bolts and chains, slings around rock horns or trees, welded cold shuts, pitons, nuts, etc.).

rappel/rap—Method of descending from a mountainside or cliff by means of a rope.

redpoint—To free climb a route/pitch without falls, hangs, or rests on equipment, but with prior knowledge or rehearsal of route.

roof—Severely overhanging rock formation.

RP (Roland Pauligk)—Specific type of protection wedge/nut originally designed in Australia and made of brass, equipped with a short loop of cable; removable, non-invasive.

runner—Tubular webbing tied or sewn into loops of various lengths and used as protection and anchor attachments.

runout—Section of climbing where protection is far apart.

RURP (Realized Ultimate Reality Piton)—Specific type of small, thin piton for extreme aid climbing (about the size of a postage stamp and about as useful for holding a lead fall; see piton).

sandbag—Underrated difficulty (most locals are "sandbaggers").

sling—See runners.

solo climbing—Climbing alone with or without a rope or protective hardware.

smear—Climbing technique using friction to stick to the rock surface (shoe rubber works better than skin).

thin crack—Crack up to 1.25 inches wide; typically small enough to accommodate portions of the fingers.

thin face—Holds that typically are narrow and small (see face).

thin hands/rattly fingers—Cracks (0.75 to 1.5 inches wide) typically too small to insert the entire hand but too large to get a good grip/jam with finger knuckles.

toprope—Technique of practice climbing where rope is anchored above the climber.

Tri-Cam—Specific type of passive cam device that has sewn slings attached to the cam; removable and non-invasive.

TCU (Three Cam Unit)—Specific type of small spring-loaded cam device; removable and non-invasive.

webbing—Nylon strapping made in a tube shape ("tubular" webbing) and specially designed for climbing applications.

wired stopper/wires—Wedge made of metal alloy and equipped with a short loop of cable; removable, non-invasive.

yo-yo—Type of free climbing style where the lead climber lowers to the ground if a fall occurs or for a rest and then ascends back to the previous high point and beyond without weighting the rope or any of the protection equipment.

INDEX